# Tank Battles of
# the Cold War
# 1948–1991

# Tank Battles of the Cold War 1948–1991

Anthony Tucker-Jones

Pen & Sword
**MILITARY**

AN IMPRINT OF PEN & SWORD BOOKS LTD
YORKSHIRE – PHILADELPHIA

First published in Great Britain in 2021 by
**PEN & SWORD MILITARY**
An imprint of Pen & Sword Books Ltd
Yorkshire – Philadelphia

Copyright © Anthony Tucker-Jones, 2021

ISBN 978-1-52677-801-7

Typeset by Concept, Huddersfield, West Yorkshire, HD4 5JL
Printed and bound by CPI Group (UK) Ltd, Croydon, CR0 4YY

Pen & Sword Books Ltd incorporates the Imprints of Aviation, Atlas, Family
History, Fiction, Maritime, Military, Discovery, Politics, History, Archaeology,
Select, Wharncliffe Local History, Wharncliffe True Crime, Military Classics,
Wharncliffe Transport, Leo Cooper, The Praetorian Press, Remember When,
White Owl, Seaforth Publishing and Frontline Publishing.

For a complete list of Pen & Sword titles please contact
PEN & SWORD BOOKS LTD
47 Church Street, Barnsley, South Yorkshire, S70 2AS, England
E-mail: enquiries@pen-and-sword.co.uk
Website: www.pen-and-sword.co.uk
or
PEN & SWORD BOOKS
1950 Lawrence Rd, Havertown, PA 19083, USA
E-mail: uspen-and-sword@casematepublishers.com
Website: www.penandswordbooks.com

# Contents

# List of Plates

American troops examining a knocked-out North Vietnamese Army PT-76 amphibious light tank.

An Israeli M48 Magach taking on ammunition somewhere in Sinai in 1973.

A column of Israeli M48 Magachs moving towards the Suez Canal during the Yom Kippur War.

Israeli Centurions supported by armoured infantry firing on Syrian tanks on the Golan Heights, 1973.

Syrian T-54s knocked out on the Golan Heights.

More Syrian T-54/55 tanks destroyed whilst fighting the Israelis.

The business end of an Israeli Centurion.

South Vietnamese soldiers with a damaged North Vietnamese Type 59 captured in 1972 south of Dong Ha during the North's Easter Offensive.

The Ethiopian Army captured this Somali T-54 tank during the Ogaden War.

This T-54/55 came a-cropper in Ethiopia during the long and brutal civil war.

Mujahideen with a burnt-out T-34/85.

A Mujahideen tank hunter.

A resistance anti-tank team ambush a Soviet armoured vehicle with their RPG-7.

The British Chieftain tank.

Dug-in Iraqi T-55s.

Israeli Zelda M113 armoured personnel carriers in Lebanon.

An Angolan T-54.

### Plate Section III (between pages 180 and 181)

A British Challenger with the Royal Scots Dragoon Guards in Iraq in 1991.

France's AMX-30 armed with a 120mm gun, used by the French, Saudis and Qataris during operations in 1991.

An M1A1 Abrams of the 3rd Brigade, US 1st Armored Division, races across the desert in northern Kuwait during Operation Desert Sabre.

# Acknowledgements

My thanks to the marvellous team at Pen & Sword, Rupert Harding, Sarah Cook, Ron Wilkinson and Tara Moran. Also very belated thanks to Professors Ron Barston and Christopher Clapham who first awakened my interest in international conflicts and in particular the Cold War.

# Introduction

The Cold War was not spared the brutality of armoured warfare. The fate of tank crews around the world hung in the balance, as it always had since the First World War. A British reporter who visited the Ethiopian battlefield of Afabet in 1988 wrote with amazement:

> The Eritrean fighters were lazing around in the sun, laughing. A motley looking bunch in khaki shirts, denim jeans and rubber sandals, they had just overwhelmed Ethiopian armour, artillery and infantry and taken Afabet. It was one of the biggest battles in the history of the war with Ethiopia.

An entire Ethiopian mechanized brigade had been destroyed and many crew perished with their tanks. A British cameraman at Afabet also witnessed the scene:

> Burnt-out tanks stretched as far as the eye could see; guns and bodies so badly burned they barely resembled corpses littered the roadside; the remains of Ethiopian truck drivers could be seen hanging out of windows, burnt to death as they attempted to flee. It was a place of horror and slaughter from which the world could be told about the war by television.

Before tank school, many of the Ethiopian crews had been simple farmers or herdsmen. At best they were familiar with a tractor or a truck. They had died in steel coffins far from their farmlands. Three entire Ethiopian infantry divisions also vanished from the face of the earth, such was the scale of the Eritrean victory.

There is a general perception that the supremacy of the tank ended with the Second World War. It did not. The subsequent Arab-Israeli conflicts witnessed some of the biggest tank battles in history. Armoured warfare was conducted on a lesser scale in Afghanistan, Korea and Vietnam. The tank also played a role during the many guerrilla wars that plagued the post-war period.

What is not generally appreciated is that sizeable tank battles were fought in Africa, most notably at Afabet and at Mavinga in Angola, using Soviet tactics intended for central Europe. 'Had the battle of Afabet taken place anywhere with a large media congregation,' wrote Glenys Kinnock with the charity War on Want, 'the loss of life and the scale of the fighting would have inspired worldwide interest and demands for action to stop the war.' Instead Ethiopia tried to pass it off as 'a little skirmish'.

The great irony of the Cold War was that it was only ever cold in Europe. It became very hot around the world when the two opposing superpowers, the United States of America and the Soviet Union, backed their various warring proxies. The US, with its policy of containment, chose to fight Communism wherever it took hold, while the Soviet Union sought to support it. These regional conflicts proved ideal testing grounds, where equipment and tactics could be tried out. This was especially the case in Africa, the Middle East and Southeast Asia. For a long time after the Second World War the tank retained its pre-eminence on the battlefield. This did not really change until the mid-1960s, when man-portable anti-tank weapons became ever deadlier and the dedicated mechanized infantry fighting vehicle emerged. The latter was designed to both transport infantry and fight tanks. The Cold War, however, was undoubtedly the heyday of the tank.

The five Arab-Israeli wars were particularly important testing grounds for a variety of equipment, including American, British and Soviet tanks. The Arabs and the Israelis became guinea pigs for the much-feared Third World War between NATO and the Warsaw Pact, which fortunately never came to pass. Just three years after the Second World War ended, the state of Israel came into being. The newly-formed Israeli armed forces had to create their armoured forces from scratch, but these quickly helped them gain victory in 1948 over their hostile Arab neighbours. The creation of the elite Israeli Defence Forces' famed armoured corps is literally a tale of an Englishman, an Irishman and a Scotsman, who begged, stole and borrowed armoured vehicles to help defend the fledgeling Jewish state. These early experiences stood them in good stead for the subsequent Arab-Israeli wars, during which the Israelis had to rely on quality to counter the Arabs' vast quantities of Soviet-supplied tanks and other weaponry.

Shortly after the first Arab-Israeli War, the Communist North Koreans, equipped with surplus Soviet T-34 tanks, almost overran South Korea in 1950. Following the invasion, the North Korean People's Army's tanks swiftly dominated the battlefield. The South had no tanks and few effective anti-tank weapons. The outcome was predictable and the South Korean Army was sent reeling. The South Korean and American forces had to conduct a rapid build-up and a major amphibious assault at Inchon to turn the tide. Initially, the American light tanks rushed into South Korea proved no match for the T-34s. Field guns firing over open sights and Second World War-vintage bazookas were about all they had to stop the North's marauding tanks. Once the US Sherman, Pershing and Patton tanks began to arrive in numbers, supported by dominant air power, the T-34's reign came to an end. However, there were few full-scale tank battles, and tanks on both sides soon found themselves relegated to their original role of providing infantry support or acting as mobile artillery and pill-boxes.

Just as the conflict in Korea ended in armed stalemate, so the Middle East once more spiralled into war. Britain, France and Israel attacked Egypt in 1956 to reclaim the newly nationalized Suez Canal. Operation Kadesh saw Israeli tanks successfully overrun Egyptian defences in the Sinai desert. This operation convinced the Israelis that they needed to form divisional-sized armoured units. Alarmed at the enormous military build-up by its Arab neighbours, Israel in 1967 launched a remarkable pre-emptive war and its armoured forces ended up fighting simultaneously on three fronts in the Egyptian Sinai, the Jordanian West Bank and the Syrian Golan Heights north of the Sea of Galilee. These presented very different combat conditions for Israel's armour. Quite miraculously, however, within just six days the Israelis had won a resounding victory. As well as geography, technology proved a key factor in the tank battles of the Arab-Israeli wars. In 1967, in a historic confrontation, the British Centurion and Soviet T-54/55 went head-to-head for the very first time. The Arabs' T-54/55s could cross soft ground, which the Israelis Centurions could not, but the latter could kill armour beyond the range of the Soviet tanks and carried more ammunition. In a stand-off fight it would win hands down. This helped neutralize the Arabs' superior numbers.

In 1973 Egypt, Jordan and Syria tried to overwhelm Israel using enormous tanks forces, resulting in some of the biggest tank engagements ever seen. In the Sinai the Egyptians relied on sheer weight of fire and their superiority in armour, artillery and new Soviet-supplied anti-tank guided weapons to overcome the Israelis' superior training and tactics. Likewise, on the Golan Heights the Syrians tried to wield an iron fist made up almost entirely of tanks. The deadly struggle hung in the balance as the Israelis were almost swamped on two decisive fronts. However, the Egyptians, after successfully crossing the Suez Canal, moved beyond the umbrella of their air defences and were eventually surrounded and trapped in the Sinai. The Israelis also clung on in the Golan Heights after repulsing the massive Syrian tank assault.

For a moment the world held its breath for fear that the US and the Soviet Union would go to war over their respective Middle Eastern allies. Instead, the Americans poured thousands of tons of ammunition into Israel just as the Israeli Defence Forces were at the point of running out; similarly, the Soviets sent 1,300 replacement tanks to the Arabs, which helped stave off complete collapse in the closing days of the war. Such generosity was possible only because of the vast strategic reserves already amassed by the superpowers in preparation for the Third World War.

Vietnam, with its highlands and jungles, was not considered tank country, and this led to the development of the armoured cavalry concept, whereby armoured personnel carriers became versatile infantry fighting vehicles. Although not known for tank warfare, Vietnam gave rise to the mechanized infantry combat vehicle thanks to the M113. The Soviets were to adopt this concept with their tracked BMP-1, the turret of which made it look like a tank. When North Vietnam tried using conventional tactics against South Vietnam in 1968 it failed because of devastating American firepower. Four years later the outcome was the same. It tried again, after the Americans had pulled out, in 1975 and this time the North Vietnamese tanks successfully steamrollered through the demoralized South Vietnamese Army and took Saigon.

The Soviet Union invaded Afghanistan in 1980 using tanks and tactics intended for the open plains of central Europe. In the mountains of Afghanistan Soviet armour soon suffered at the hands of the Mujahideen. Just as the Americans had discovered in Vietnam, the Soviets soon learned that all-arms battle groups supported by helicopters were the way ahead. Just two years later Israeli armoured columns successfully stormed into Lebanon to drive the Palestinian Liberation Organisation from Beirut. In the process they bumped into Syria's armoured divisions and fought major tank battles in the Bekaa Valley.

Tank warfare dramatically made itself felt in Africa during the Somali-Ethiopian Ogaden War in 1977. Somalia tried to replicate the success of the North Koreans by invading eastern Ethiopia using T-34 tanks. It scored one notable victory, defeating Ethiopian tanks at Jijiga, but it was then that the Soviet Union firmly allied itself with the emergent Marxist governments in Angola, Ethiopia and Mozambique. For these countries it was a bonanza time for Soviet weapons supplies. As a result, Somalia was swiftly defeated. Throughout the 1980s the Angolan and Ethiopian militaries persisted, thanks to their Soviet and Cuban advisers, in conducting inflexible large-scale armoured operations against highly mobile guerrilla armies. In the case of Mavinga, it became a graveyard for Angolan tanks. The presence of Cuban armoured forces in Angola almost sparked a conventional war with South Africa, which could have dragged in the superpowers. In the same year as Afabet, Colonel Edgar O'Ballance warned that '[Angolan] Government forces mustered at Cuito Cuanavale included the Cuban 50th Mechanized Division, and several brigades, some armoured and some mechanized, and during the late summer and autumn, the [rebel] UNITA conventional army awaited a main offensive against it'.

The American-built M1 Abrams main battle tank finally fought the Soviet-built T-72 not in Europe, as anticipated, but in the Middle East in the closing days of the Cold War. President Saddam Hussein of Iraq overplayed his hand by invading Kuwait and was thrown out by an international coalition in 1991. This saw his Republican Guard armoured divisions fighting fierce tank battles against the Americans and British. Saddam's defeat graphically showed just how dated much of the Arab armies' Soviet weaponry had become. The irony was that at that point the Soviet Union, with its economy already in tatters from decades of defence spending, imploded, finally bringing an end to the Cold War. A new era was ushered in, an era dominated by the war on terror that had little need for tanks.

# Chapter 1

# Tanks in Indo-China
## The First Indo-China War, 1946–1954

The French deployed at least half a dozen tank regiments in Indo-China during the early 1950s. France, with a long history of fighting colonial wars, saw Indo-China as just another inconvenient colonial revolt that needed to be suppressed in the usual manner. (This approach was a mistake, but once the Korean War broke out was perhaps more understandable. There the Communists had very much gone straight for the conventional warfare phase.) The result was that the French assumed they could bludgeon the Communist Viet Minh into submission through the use of superior strength and firepower. What they did not take into account was the strength of the Viet Minh's ideology. In addition, they were fighting for their country, whereas the French were not.

The spearhead force for France in reclaiming her colonies was the Foreign Legion. It had a proud and colourful history and during its formative years had fought all around the world, including Indo-China. In 1883–84 Legionnaires took part in the storming of the forts at Son Tay and Bac Ninh that were held by Chinese irregulars. When the fighting finally came to an end a decade later, the Legion's battalions formed the Régiment de Marche d'Africa au Tonkin, which helped to keep the peace largely undisturbed until 1941.

This tough force fought with distinction during the Second World War and afterwards there was no shortage of foreign volunteers trying to escape or forget their troubled pasts. The Legion was happy to turn a blind eye to criminals or those who had committed war crimes. During the Indo-China war the Legion would reach 30,000 men. In May 1945 their training and administrative base at Sidi-bel-Abbès, 100 kilometres south of Oran in northwest Algeria, started the creation of a régiment de marche to be sent to reoccupy Indo-China. Most of the Legion contingent in Indo-China, numbering 20,000 men, had been deployed in Tonkin during the second half of the war. Inevitably they were to play a key role in the fighting at Dien Bien Phu.

Although the French sought to regain control of Saigon and southern Vietnam in the summer of 1945, it was not until the following February that the French Expeditionary Force was able to enter northern Vietnam. In the meantime, in October 1945 General Leclerc arrived in Saigon with elements of the French 2nd Armoured Division and the 3rd and 9th Colonial Infantry Divisions. They were reinforced by the 2nd Foreign Legion Infantry Regiment (REI) that landed in February 1946, followed by the 13th Foreign Legion Demi Brigade in March and the 3rd Foreign Legion Infantry Regiment between April and June. A 3,000-strong naval brigade was also deployed to patrol Indo-China's numerous waterways.

Over the next few years the French parachute units who were to become famous in Indo-China began to arrive, including the 1st, 2nd and 5th Colonial Commando Parachute Battalions (BCCP) and the 1st Chasseurs Parachute Regiment. By the end of 1948 French paras had made forty combat jumps, three of which had involved over 1,000 paratroops. The 1st Foreign Legion Parachute Battalion (BEP) arrived late that year and the 1st Indo-Chinese Parachute Company was formed. By mid-1949 the French Union Forces in Vietnam totalled almost 150,000. Most of the fighting, though, was conducted by some 5,700 French paratroops. The most important arrivals that year were the 3rd and 6th BCCP, the 2nd BEP and the 5th REI.

France's colonial forces were always regarded as the poorer cousins of the metropolitan French Army. In Indo-China this meant that the local commander-in-chief had no autonomy and was answerable to his military superiors in Paris and his political masters in Paris and Hanoi. Even when the roles of commander-in-chief and high commissioner were combined in 1950 under General Jean de Lattre de Tassigny, political interference continued unabated. In France the politicians played to the gallery with a war that was very unpopular with the electorate. This often led to extraordinarily foolhardy decisions. For example, in 1950, just as the Viet Minh were capturing the Cao Bang Ridge defences, the government cut the size of the forces in Indo-China by 9,000 men. Also to curry favour with the French public, conscripts could only serve in France, Algeria (considered part of France) and French-occupied Germany. The result of this was that all French citizens sent to Indo-China had to be volunteers. Inevitably this greatly restricted the French military contingent and meant they never accounted for more than half of the total of the French Expeditionary Force – the average was about 52,000, or slightly over a third. The bulk of the ethnic French units bore the brunt of the fighting, and they also made up most of the mobile reserve. In the mobile infantry role, French soldiers travelled in half-tracks with the support of American-supplied M4 Sherman and M24 Chaffee tanks, as well as armoured cars. The paratroop units which formed the cutting-edge of most operations were largely self-contained, though they relied on the French Air Force for transport. Initially, transport aircraft were always in short supply and it was not until the early 1950s that American-supplied C-47 Dakotas (or Skytrains) and C-119 Flying Boxcars were available to replace the last of the French-built Junkers Ju-52s (a hangover from the Second World War). By 1954 the first American-supplied H-19B helicopters also became available. The French Air Force's main role, in addition to supplying the ground forces, was to provide direct support, especially for troops in contact. Principal aircraft included American B-26 Marauder bombers and F8F Bearcat fighters, along with Canadian-built Beaver and French Morane 500 Cricket reconnaissance aircraft. The French Navy provided coastal fire support and river patrols, along with Privateer maritime bombers and F4U Corsair fighters.

The paucity of French regulars in Indo-China meant colonial troops from other parts of the French Union had to be deployed. Throughout the conflict Algerian, Moroccan, Tunisian and Senegalese troops served in Indo-China. They were commanded by French officers and were organized and equipped the same as French regulars. One exception to this rule was the Algerian units, which were allowed native officers as Algeria was considered part of metropolitan France (although Algerian losses were lumped in with the 15,000 North Africans killed in Indo-China, indicating they were not truly considered 'French'). At the close of 1952 there were around 175,000 troops in Indo-China comprising 54,000 French, 30,000 North Africans, 18,000 Africans, 20,000 Legionnaires and 53,000 Indo-Chinese. The French Air Force deployed 10,000 personnel and the Navy 5,000. Local national forces were also quite sizeable. At Dien Bien Phu nearly half the members of the 2nd Battalion, 1st Parachute Light Infantry, were Vietnamese.

The French employed Second World War-vintage tanks and armoured fighting vehicles. The standard tank of the French Expeditionary Force was the American M5A1 light tank; although it had been superseded by the Chaffee from 1944 onwards under the US Military Aid Program, it remained in service throughout the war. The Chaffees were dubbed 'Bisons' by the French troops and the Viet Minh knew them as 'Oxen'. The French also deployed the ubiquitous American Sherman, the M36B2 tank destroyer and M8 self-propelled howitzers. Tank units included the 1st Foreign Cavalry, 1st Light Horse, 5th Cuirassiers, 6th Moroccan Spahi and the Far Eastern Colonial Armoured Regiments. Motorized infantry were transported in M3 half-tracks. The M8 variant of the latter, mounting a 75mm gun, was also used in Indo-China. The tank destroyers were initially deployed in case the Chinese committed armour to the fighting in Tonkin, but instead they ended up acting in a fire support role.

To facilitate amphibious operations in Indo-China's flooded paddy-fields, vast river deltas and swamps, the Expeditionary Force operated American M29C Weasel amphibian cargo carriers (known to the French as 'Crabs') and tracked landing vehicles known as Alligators. Both these types were likewise veterans of the Second World War. The LVT(A)4, armed with a 75mm howitzer, packed a particular punch. The Crabes, although only armed with a machine gun, were eventually formed into effective amphibious fighting units by the Foreign Legion, which likewise deployed the LVTs.

At the start of the fighting the tanks were parcelled out in penny packets to protect vulnerable convoys and static outposts. This made them difficult to maintain and reduced their effectiveness. Only after General de Lattre de Tassigny took charge in 1951 were the armoured units reorganized with their own supporting infantry. This led to the creation of the *sousgroupements blindées*, comprising a squadron of tanks and two mechanized infantry companies, and *groupements mobile*, with up to three battalions of infantry, an artillery battery and up to a squadron of tanks.

France attempted to tap into the huge manpower reservoir in Indo-China, but the French commanders were wary of training a fifth column and local units were never fully trusted. It did not help that the Vietnamese and Cambodians were traditional enemies, while the Vietnamese viewed the Chinese in much the same manner. General de Lattre in 1951 instructed each French unit in Vietnam to form a locally recruited second battalion. He also opened an officer cadet school, followed by two more for reserve officers. A small Vietnamese National Army was formed under French command, along with anti-guerrilla units raised particularly amongst the mountain tribes. By 1952 the Vietnamese National Army numbered 50,000 men, the Laotian Army 15,000 and the Cambodian Army another 10,000.

Although the full potential of these Indo-Chinese forces was never realized, some 27,000 Indo-Chinese died fighting for the French.

French training efforts for local Vietnamese units were concentrated in the north. In late 1948 they established the Vietnamese National Military Academy in the city of Hue. This was designed to train infantry platoon leaders with a nine-month officers' course. It moved to Dalat two years later, where the weather was better. Dalat had been home to the armour school, but this moved to Thu Duc, along with the engineer school. By the end of 1951 there were 800 Vietnamese officers serving with the French Army. The French also set up the national non-commissioned officers academy in Quang Yen Province, Tonkin, in 1951. The following year this was followed by a staff college in Hanoi. This was as a result of the French Expeditionary Force setting up a tactical instruction centre designed to train mobile group, battalion and company commanders. Notably, intelligence and logistics schools were not established until the late 1950s. This was to prove to be a serious omission on the part of the French.

French forces in Indo-China included a postscript from Korea. The French Bataillon de Corée (Korea Battalion), which was raised from volunteers from all branches of the French Army – metropolitan, colonial and Foreign Legion – to serve in Korea, arrived in Indo-China in October 1953 and formed the cadre of the two battalion-strong Régiment de Corée. This was practically destroyed in the central Highlands around An Khe and Pleiku while operating with Groupe Mobile 100 in June–July 1954.

The French logistical supply chain, stretching all the way back to Algeria and France, proved to be the Expeditionary Force's Achilles' heel. In Paris the war was not a priority and many either did not support it or simply saw it as an overblown police operation. Shipping or flying ammunition and weapons to Indo-China was a lengthy and expensive process and again was unpopular for this reason. Once in-country, the high command in Hanoi struggled to distribute supplies to the troops. In the immediate Red River delta area around Hanoi, and indeed in the south, it was not such a problem, but getting supplies to the outlying garrisons and to large-scale operations was another matter.

The French were reliant on two methods of supporting their soldiers. The first was land-based, using roads and rivers. Whilst this was relatively easy to do, both forms of movement were always vulnerable to ambush. Viet Minh attacks on supply barges on the Black river trying to reach the garrison at Hao Binh contributed to General Salan's decision to abandon the town. The second method was by air, but French air lift capabilities were simply insufficient for the task. Initially they had to rely on old Ju-52s but even with the arrival of newer C-47s and C-119s they could never muster more than 100 transport planes. These were required to run supply flights, move reinforcements and drop paratroops. By the time of Dien Bien Phu they were stretched to the limit.

Under General Leblanc the French gathered some 10,000 men for Operation Camargue, a combined ground, airborne and amphibious operation that was intended to trap the Viet Minh. The 3rd Amphibious Group deployed 160 tracked Crabs and Alligators to get their men ashore and into the dunes. Camargue commenced on 27 July 1953 with the landings unopposed. The first resistance was met at Dong Que when the 6th Moroccan Spahis with their M24 tanks, supported by the 1st Battalion Moroccan Rifles and the 69th African Artillery Regiment, were ambushed. The Moroccan Spahi cavalry regiments had been equipped by the French as light armoured reconnaissance units during the Second World War to support the Moroccan infantry divisions. The Moroccans managed to destroy almost an entire Viet Minh company, but the delay enabled the rest of the 95th Viet Minh Regiment to retreat into the southern portion of the developing pocket.

At 1045 hours the 2nd Battalion, 1st Parachute Light Infantry Regiment, were dropped near Dai Loc to block the Viet Minh's retreat, and began to push towards the mouth of the Van Trinh Canal to close the pocket. Despite hazardous drop conditions caused by 48km/h winds, the 3rd Vietnamese Parachute Battalion dropped near Lang Bao. This helped seal the southern escape routes. However, during the night of 28/29 July most of the Viet Minh managed to slip the net. The ambitious operation was ended on 4 August having achieved modest success.

At Dien Bien Phu, despite any reservations he may have had, General Navarre, having made his decision to fight, poured men and equipment into the valley to ensure that it would be the rock upon which the Viet Minh tide was finally broken. During December 1953 and January 1954 infantry, armour and artillery units streamed into Dien Bien Phu by air. The garrison at this stage numbered around 10,800 men, backed up by two groups of artillery with 75mm, 105mm and 155mm guns, ten Chaffee light tanks and nine Bearcat fighter bombers stationed on the main airfield. The French showed great ingenuity in getting some of their heavier equipment to the base. When base commander Colonel de Castries requested a squadron of tanks this posed a particular problem as they were simply too heavy to be air-dropped. The 18-ton Chaffee tanks had to be dismantled and flown into Dien Bien Phu. Each was broken down into 180 parts that took six C-47 sorties and two by British Bristol air freighters requisitioned from a commercial Indo-Chinese airline to deliver. The latter were the only aircraft capable of taking the tanks' hulls. Foreign Legion mechanics reassembled the Chaffees beside the main runway, completing one every two days. Similarly, each 155mm howitzer needed two C-47s and one Bristol flight, plus another seventeen C-47 flights for the gun crews and ammunition. The tanks served with the 1st Light Horse Regiment. They were too few to prevent Dien Bien Phu being overrun on 7 May 1954. The last remaining operational Chaffee supported a final futile French counterattack that day. When the Viet Minh occupied Isabelle, the last French strongpoint, on 8 May they found the garrison had blown up their tank rather than let it be captured. After this catastrophic French defeat, the Viet Minh were left in control of northern Vietnam, sowing the seeds for the Vietnam War in the 1960s.

*Chapter 2*

# Beg, Steal or Borrow

## The First Arab-Israeli War, 1948

During all the Arab-Israeli clashes, armoured vehicles played a very promi-
nent and usually decisive role. An extraordinary range of Second World
War and post-war tanks, armoured cars and armoured personnel carriers
were deployed by all sides; to counter the Israeli Shermans, Pattons,
Centurions and AMX-13s, the Arabs fielded the Russian T–34s, SU-100s,
T–54/55s, T–62s and T–72s.

Israel came into existence on 14 May 1948 and immediately found itself
under attack by hostile Arab neighbours. The Israelis literally stole the
armour to form the basis of their very first armoured brigade, attempting to
take four Cromwell tanks from under the very noses of the British Army
before their withdrawal from Haifa Airport, but only got away with two
of them. The Israeli forces – now renamed Zvah Haganah Le Israel (Zahal)
or Israeli Defence Forces (IDF) – set about completing two armoured
units, the 7th Mechanized and 8th Armoured Brigades. The latter's order
of battle consisted of a Daimler armoured car, an Otter reconnaissance
vehicle, the two Cromwell tanks and a solitary Sherman. These formed the
'English Company' of the 82nd Tank Battalion, and ten newly arrived
French Hotchkiss tanks formed the 'Russian company'. Syrian tanks were
rebuffed at Degania Kibbutz, but Egyptian armour fared better at Yad
Mordechai and Nitzanin kibbutzim.

When fighting broke out, the Israelis began to buy old German guns
from Czechoslovakia, with 4,400 rifles and machine guns arriving in two
shipments. As a result, towards the end of the conflict the Israeli forces
were better equipped, although still outnumbered. The army had Czechoslovak and French weapons and the air force had British-built Spitfires
and Czech-built Messerschmitts. Ironically, a ship carrying much-needed
armoured vehicles and other weapons imported by the Israeli terrorist
group Irgun was sunk by the Israeli government for fear of an armed revolt

by dissidents. Just as important as the hardware were Czech-Jewish volunteers who were allowed to emigrate to Israel; these included tank crews and pilots.

On the outbreak of the war in 1948 the Egyptians were able to muster about 200 assorted British hand-me-downs, including a few Matilda, Valentine and Sherman tanks, as well as Humber, Marmon-Herrington and Staghound armoured cars. The Syrians and Lebanese were equipped with second-hand French light tanks. Officially subject to an arms embargo, the Israelis initially managed to get hold of a few M3 half-tracks and French light tanks, all of which were Second World War veterans.

In mid-1948, during the third stage of the War of Independence, Israel was invaded by the armies of five Arab countries: Egypt, Iraq, Lebanon, Syria and Transjordan. Field Marshal Montgomery estimated that the Israelis would not be able to withstand the Arabs' heavy weaponry and they would be crushed within two weeks. However, the Israelis launched a ten-day counter-offensive on 9 July 1948, with their tanks spearheading the attack on the vital Lydda Airport. Yitzhak Sadeh's 8th Armoured Brigade drove southwest from near Tel Aviv and took a number of Arab villages and Lydda, north of the city. However, they became bogged down in fighting with the armoured cars of the Arab Legion near Beit Nabala. The Arab Legion from Transjordan (modern-day Jordan) was eventually driven back, as were the Egyptians and Syrians. By the time of the truce, Israel held the initiative. The 8th Armoured Brigade was bolstered with half-tracks mounting 20mm, 2-pounder and 6-pounder guns to provide a much-needed self-propelled anti-tank capability. When the fighting renewed three months later, the Egyptians were pushed back once more.

By October 1948 the Egyptians were deployed mainly in defensive strips running along the main roads in the Negev. These defences, some 3 to 8 kilometres deep, were held by 15,000 men from two regular infantry brigades, nine volunteer battalions, a reinforced brigade, two regiments of artillery and an armoured battalion. Starting on 4 October, the Egyptians counter-attacked six times, throwing away their entire armoured battalion, equipped with Bren gun carriers and armoured cars.

These attacks convinced the Israelis that they needed to conduct an all-out attack on the Negev. The Israeli High Command decided to commit the Givati, Negev and Yiftach Infantry Brigades, supported by a battalion from the 8th Armoured Brigade, some 15,000 men in total. On 15 October the Israeli tanks, including four ex-French Hotchkiss tanks and the two old

British Cromwells, struck at Iraq el-Manshya. In one of the Cromwells was Sergeant Major Desmond Rutledge, a deserter from the British Army, and in the other were Sergeants Michael Flanagan and Harry MacDonald. The tanks and infantry soon came under Egyptian artillery fire. Flanagan and MacDonald's tank suffered gearbox failure and Flanagan was wounded through the driver's port but still broke through the Egyptian barbed wire. Finding themselves on their own, Flanagan and MacDonald withdrew, and managed to take Rutledge's tank under tow. One of the Hotchkiss tanks ended up in an anti-tank ditch.

On 9 November 1948 the Israeli tanks were thrown into battle again, making a successful attack on Iraq es-Suweidan following a heavy artillery bombardment. The following month, on 27 December, the tanks, half-tracks and armoured troop carriers of the 8th Armoured Brigade, after much hardship, stormed El Auja. Rutledge recalled, 'What a Christmas this was! Stuck in the desert, freezing, miserable, and waiting for a road to be built under the enemy's nose!' Just before the cease-fire the brigade launched one last attack in the midst of a sandstorm south of Rafah, suffering heavy casualties. After the war Rutledge and Flanagan settled in kibbutz settlements with their families.

While the Lebanese invasion was half-hearted, the fighting against the Syrians was much more threatening. A Syrian Army column supported by tanks gathered south of the Sea of Galilee with the aim of breaking through toward Tiberias and Nazareth. To block the Syrian armour, the men of Kibbutz Degania had to rely on petrol bombs. As the tanks broke through the defences they were set alight with Molotov cocktails and shelled by two ancient artillery pieces in the nearby hills. The Syrians switched their efforts to the north and took Mishmar Hayarden. In the aftermath of the 1948 Arab-Israeli War discontented young officers in Syria booted out the politicians and there followed twenty years of military government.

The city of Jerusalem found itself partitioned, with the Israelis holding the western half and the Jordanians the eastern half. Jordan annexed East Jerusalem in 1950 and three years later declared it Jordan's second capital. Inevitably, this sowed the seeds for yet more conflict. The presence of Jordanian troops in Jerusalem and on the West Bank of the river Jordan was to have serious ramifications for the Six Day War in 1967.

What makes the Israeli Defence Forces particularly fascinating is that few armies have gained combat experience with such a wide variety of armour. Over the years the Israelis deployed the American M4 Sherman,

M48 and M60 Patton, the British Centurion, the French AMX-13 and the Soviet T-54 and T-62, as well as a plethora of modified hybrids such as the Super Sherman/Isherman, the Sho't, the Magach and the Sabra, as well as the home-grown Merkava.

Tactics and technology played a key part in repeated Israeli victories. While the Arabs' Soviet-supplied armour was designed for a massed armoured charge, Israeli tanks were more versatile and accurate, which gave them a much better kill ratio. They also had better ammunition. In part this was as a result of the British and Americans drawing on their experiences in North Africa during the Second World War. This meant their tanks were better able to cope with desert warfare than the Soviet tanks that were designed to fight on the Steppes and the central European plain.

Sho't ('Whip' in Hebrew) was the Israeli designation for the 105mm L7-armed British-built Centurion. The Magach 1, 2, 3 and 5 were based on the American M48, while the Magach 6 and 7 utilized the American M60, while the Sabra tank was in turn an upgrade of the Magach 7C. During the 1990s the Magachs were placed in reserve, having been succeeded by the Merkava. The Sho't came in a number of versions, but principally consisted of the Meteor, which had the original Rolls-Royce Meteor engine, and the Kal Alef, Bet, Gimel and Dalet models that were modernized Centurions with diesel engines. The Centurion was also converted into the Puma, a heavily armoured combat engineering vehicle. In the wake of the 1967 war the Israelis sought to upgrade their M48s to M48A3 standard, which led to the Magach 3. The most notable improvement was replacing the original 90mm gun with the British 105mm L7 and the replacement of the combustible and underpowered gasoline engine with a 750hp diesel version.

Soviet tanks were designed to present the minimum-sized target out in the open. The T-55, for example, has a much lower profile than the American M48 or British Centurion. The problem with this immediately becomes apparent: because of its low turret a Soviet tank gun has very limited depression. Israeli tanks had the distinct advantage that they could point their guns down 10 degrees below the horizontal, while the guns of the T-54 and T-62 could only depress 4 degrees. When fighting in sand dunes or on rocky ridges, the Soviet tanks would have to expose themselves in order to engage the enemy, and in many instances Soviet tanks were unable to fight from a 'hull-down' position, rendering them vulnerable to enemy fire.

T-54 gunners had to estimate range by eye (the 'Eyeball Mark I'), whereas the M48 and M60s had accurate optical-prism range-finding systems that allowed gunners to zero in on targets within seconds, while the Centurion gunners used machine-gun tracer bullets to correct the main gun targeting. Ammunition gave the Israelis another advantage. The T-54 and T-55 had ordinary armour-piercing shot, which consisted of solid, full calibre shot of steel, which dissipated much of its energy before reaching the target and thus gave limited penetration at long range, while the Israelis had armour-piercing discarding-sabot (APDS) rounds and high-explosive anti-tank (HEAT) ammunition that provided kills at greater range.

The T-62's 115mm gun could match the Israeli guns but were in short supply in 1973. They were armed with armour-piercing fin-stabilized discarding-sabot (APFSDS) ammunition. The sabot – the packing around the shell – was stripped off by air resistance to reveal an arrow of metal that offered far greater penetration. HEAT rounds, by contrast, used a blast of molten copper to burn their way through to the interior of a tank.

Following Israel's remarkable victory in 1948, one of its two armoured brigades was disbanded but the 7th Mechanized was reorganized and strengthened with 50 Sherman tanks, which included both cast and welded hull variants. France sold the Israelis another 60 Shermans, plus 100 AMX-13 light tanks, 60 self-propelled 105mm howitzers on the AMX chassis and 150 M3 half-tracks. This brought the Israeli tank strength to around 200 vehicles and resulted in the creation of the 27th and 37th Reserve Armoured Brigades. This set a trend that the Arab armies could not match.

By the mid-1950s the transformation of the Israeli Defence Forces from a Second World War era force to a more modern one had become a matter of some urgency, as Egypt received vast quantities of Eastern bloc tanks, jets and other equipment. When fully mobilized, Israel could muster about 100,000 regulars and reservists, but of these fewer than half were available for deployment against Egypt; the rest had to face Jordan, Lebanon and Syria. These forces were again tested in 1956 when Israel invaded Sinai and in 1967 when Israel launched a pre-emptive attack on the growing military might of its neighbours.

The Yom Kippur War in 1973 was a clash of armoured Titans that resulted in some of the largest tank battles since the Second World War. The Arab states committed some 3,000 tanks, and during the fighting the Soviet Union shipped in another 1,300 tanks to Egypt and Syria. Israel had about 1,700 tanks at the start of the war; about half of them were Centurions and the rest were mostly M48s, but also some M60s. They also deployed about 150 Super Shermans, which they had up-gunned with a French 105mm gun, and some modified T-54/55s. The Israeli Defence Forces should have been overwhelmed, especially as Sagger, the Soviet wire-guided suitcase missile, greatly embarrassed the Israeli tanks. But luckily for the Israelis, the T-54/55 was already obsolete and they had superior stand-off capabilities and tactics.

The Israeli invasion of southern Lebanon in 1982 involved 78,000 men supported by 1,240 tanks, including the brand-new indigenous Merkava Mk II and Mk III. The Merkava ('Chariot') tank evolved from Israel's unique operational requirements and exemplified the power of the Israeli Armoured Corps, or Heil HaShirion in Hebrew. The Israelis developed the Merkava based on their long combat experience against Soviet-designed armour, especially on the Golan Heights, which are far from ideal tank country. The first prototype appeared a year after the Yom Kippur War, but it was not issued to the Israeli Defence Forces until 1978 and first saw combat four years later in Lebanon. The performance of the Merkava was particularly impressive, particularly in terms of its agility and the protection it afforded the crew. Its two key features were that the engine was in the front and not the back, to enhance crew protection, and the turret was very small. Israel's small population has always meant that it can afford to trade equipment but not manpower in its conflicts with its stronger neighbours.

The Syrian Army knocked out a number of Merkavas during the 1982 Lebanon War, but no crew were lost. It performed well against the then modern and state-of-the-art T-72, of which the Syrians had 200. Moscow was not pleased that the very first T-72 had fallen into Western hands. Likewise, the Merkava outperformed the Syrians' large fleet of T-62s and also proved to be resistant to the anti-tank weapons of the day, notably the ubiquitous RPG-7 and the AT-3 Sagger. As a result, it was viewed as a major improvement on the British-supplied Centurions, which, in much upgraded form, had previously served as the Israelis' highly effective main battle tank. The Merkava Mk IV saw action in the Gaza strip in 2009, where it proved highly versatile even in an asymmetrical warfare environment.

The Israeli armoured corps evolved into the 36th Armoured Division, comprising the 7th and 188th Armoured Brigades, the 162nd Armoured

Division, consisting of the 401st Armoured Brigade, and the 366th Armoured Division, made up of the 460th Armoured Brigade (which is a training unit). The Israelis also have a number of reserve units. The most famous formation is undoubtedly the 7th Armoured Brigade, dubbed Sa'ar ('Storm'), which has served in all of Israel's wars. The Israeli Combat Engineering Corps also utilizes tanks and armoured personnel carriers.

*Chapter 3*

# Dangerous War Surplus
## The Korean War, 1950–1953

For the invasion of South Korea seven North Korean People's Army divisions were gathered under General Kim Chaek. These were grouped into the 1st Army, consisting of the 1st, 3rd, 4th and 6th Divisions as well as the 105th Armoured Brigade, and the weaker 2nd Army with the 2nd, 5th and 7th Divisions. The 1st Army was given the job of overrunning the Ongjin peninsula and the South Korean capital, Seoul. It was the NKPA's tanks that provided their key striking force: 'The enemy, after penetrating the defences with his armour,' noted General Matthew B. Ridgway, who commanded the US 8th Army in Korea, 'would envelop both flanks with infantry, surround artillery units, and roll on rearward.'

Crucially, the NKPA opened the war with about 150 T-34/85 tanks armed with the 85mm gun, which was superior to anything else in theatre at the time. The United Nations forces were to dub them 'Caviar Cans'. While 120 tanks were deployed with the 105th Armoured Brigade, the NKPA infantry divisions' self-propelled gun battalions fielded a total of 120 Soviet-supplied SU-76 assault guns. In addition to the tanks of the armoured brigade, personnel from the tank training unit at Sadong with a further thirty tanks were assigned to the 7th Division. They deployed on the east-central front for the attack on Inje. For whatever reason, Stalin did not see fit to supply the NKPA with armour equipped with heavier guns, such as the SU-100, ISU-122/152 or the IS-2. All of these would have presented the United Nations forces with major problems and posed a real threat to the Pershing and Patton. But the North Koreans' grasp of mech-anized warfare was rudimentary at best and the T-34 was largely fool-proof. Indeed, it would continue to see combat around the world after the Korean War, especially in Africa and the Middle East.

In the early stages of the fighting the North Koreans also used their tanks in built-up areas to some considerable effect, neutralizing the United

Nations defenders. During the assault on Taejon they moved in pairs or singly carrying supporting infantry. Afterwards, though, they used their armour much more circumspectly because of improving American counter-measures. After the capture of the South Korean capital the 105th Armoured Brigade became the 105th 'Seoul' Armoured Division and was strengthened with the 308th Self-propelled Battalion. The 3rd and 4th Divisions which were also involved were likewise given the honorary title 'Seoul Division'. By 1953 the NKPA had seven tank regiments (104–107th, 109th, 206th and 208th).

During the battles for the Pusan pocket the NKPA received reinforcements including another eighty T-34/85s, which equipped two new tank units, the 16th and 17th Armoured Regiments. Some were also sent to the 105th Armoured Brigade, but the United Nations' air supremacy meant that many were destroyed before they could reach the front. UN estimates at the end of September 1950 were that the entire NKPA T-34 force (then believed to stand at 239) had been destroyed, whereas UN forces had only lost sixty tanks.

China committed six armies, each of three divisions, in support of the North Koreans in November 1950. Significantly, they had no tanks, vehicles or artillery, allowing these units to slip into North Korea largely undetected. The Chinese armies also lacked air support. To compensate for the lack of anti-tank weapons, each platoon was issued with satchel charges sufficient to take the track off a tank. It was not until the summer of 1951 that the Chinese began to deploy artillery and mortars. While the Chinese Nationalist forces had created a mechanized division, equipped initially with Soviet- and then American-supplied tanks, the Chinese Communists had never taken to armour and simply relied on manpower alone. Soviet assistance to the Nationalists stopped once Moscow had signed a non-aggression pact with Tokyo. The Chinese People's Liberation Army (PLA) produced a copy of the Soviet T-34/85 in the 1950s known as the Type 58, but few, if any, saw combat in Korea. It is likely that most of the Soviet T-34s supplied to the PLA were passed on to the North Koreans.

Reports of Chinese tanks in Korea are non-existent, although on 26 October 1950, when the 26th Division of the Army of the Republic of Korea (RoK) came up against the Chinese 124th Division, General Ridgway reported, 'When the Marines came up to relieve the RoKs a few days later they met and destroyed Chinese tanks (the only ones the X Corps was to encounter) and picked up prisoners from a fresh Chinese division, the 126th.' One can only assume that Ridgway was mistaken and these were supporting NKPA tanks, though it is not impossible that the Chinese brought a few with them.

In north-western Korea the PLA assembled the Chinese 9th Army Group under Lieutenant General Song Shilun. This was a new command, consisting of 120,000 men, which was tasked with taking on the US Marines around the Changjin reservoir. Two of Shilun's three field armies, the 20th and 26th, had been detached from the forces once earmarked to attack the Nationalist-held island of Taiwan; the 27th Field Army came from Shandong. Each of the three was supplemented by one division from the 30th Field Army.

Facing the US 8th Army was the PLA's 13th Army Group, totalling 180,000 men, commanded by General Li Tianyu. His forces initially saw action at Unsan, along the Chungchon river and in the area of the Changjin reservoir. Tianyu's original three field armies, the 38th, 40th and 42nd, were rapidly reinforced with the 39th, 50th and 66th Field Armies. Notably, the 50th Field Army consisted of former Nationalist troops who had surrendered in Manchuria in 1948. Their commander, Lieutenant General Zeng Zesheng, had spent most of his career fighting the Communists. Three years earlier he had worked with David Barr, the American adviser to the Nationalist forces, who now commanded the US 7th Infantry Division fighting on the other side. Zesheng's former Nationalist Corps was almost wiped out in the final battle for Seoul.

As well as armour, artillery and fighter aircraft, the PLA lacked even the most rudimentary logistical support. Soldiers were expected to carry what food and ammunition they needed to live and fight. Only 800 trucks belonging to the 5th and 42nd Truck Regiments were assigned to support the Chinese troops in Korea, and only 50 per cent were expected to remain operational. In addition, more than half a million coolies were recruited to carry supplies across the Yalu river, but they created their own logistical headache as they had to be fed and housed over considerable distances. Many Chinese commanders considered them an unwanted distraction and a drain on resources.

During the Japanese occupation of Korea, many Koreans were conscripted into the Imperial Japanese Army, while others fought for the Soviets and the Chinese. After the Japanese military surrendered to the Americans south of the 38th Parallel (the dividing line between the North and South), former Japanese Army veterans were used to form a 15,000-strong Korean Constabulary. In 1948 they became the South's army, which was expanded to 60,000 to counter North Korean border raids and internal subversion.

Disastrously, South Korea – or more correctly the Republic of Korea – had no tanks or effective anti-tank weapons at the start of the Korean War. (To be fair the South Korean security forces had little need for tanks as their main role was countering ill-equipped Communist insurgents who caused a headache for the authorities throughout the late 1940s.) Due to these inadequate defences, the NKPA's armour understandably had a demoralizing effect on RoK troops. When the invasion began, the NKPA's tanks simply drove down the roads in column. They sliced straight through the South Korean positions, whilst the NKPA's infantry surrounded them and finished the job. On the large Korean island of Cheju, which lies to the southwest of the Korean peninsula, much of the interior was taken over by the 4,000-strong Communist forces. The fighting that followed to stamp them out resulted in around 20,000 islanders being killed in the late 1940s.

Two RoK regiments numbering 2,000 troops destined for Cheju rebelled in the southern port city of Yosu. Although the rebellion was stamped out by late 1948, the mainland was suffering from organized guerrilla warfare being conducted by up to 6,000 fighters. It was believed that the hand of North Korea was behind all this unrest, though there was little evidence of Soviet or North Korean support for the southern guerrillas. Most of them had Japanese or American weapons, though some Soviet ones were found near the 38th Parallel.

Before leaving in 1949, the US military had trained the RoK Army; however, it was little more than a paramilitary police force and in June 1950 only numbered about 98,000 men. Just three of its seven infantry divisions were up to full strength and these were guarding the 38th Parallel. The only armour the RoK Army possessed consisted of twenty-seven M8 armoured cars belonging to the Capital Division in Seoul. Other than these armoured cars, Major General Chae Pyongdok's forces had no medium artillery, heavy mortars, air support or armour. His men were equipped only with rifles, carbines, light mortars and 2.36-inch bazookas (which were ineffective against the T-34 tank) and 140 light 37mm anti-tank guns. The entire RoK Army had just ninety-one American-supplied M3 105mm howitzers organized into three artillery battalions supporting the 7th and 8th Divisions and the elite 17th Independent Regiment. Under US organisation there should have been 432 divisional artillery pieces supported by other independent artillery battalions. This lack of firepower was to cost the RoK Army dearly.

Of RoK's eight divisions only the 1st, 6th and 7th Infantry Divisions and the Capital Division were at full strength, fielding about 11,000 men each; these, along with the 8th Division, were the best units. However, the 6th Division was one of the few units that were actually combat ready before the invasion, having just undergone a bout of intensive training. The outcome of any initial clash between the RoK Army and the heavily armed NKPA when it invaded was inevitable. Although the soldiers of the RoK Army fought hard, there was little they could do against the North's heavy weaponry. Both the 6th and the 1st Divisions made gallant efforts to try to stem the tide of NKPA troops. After the fall of Seoul, the 1st, 2nd, 3rd, 5th, 7th and Capital Divisions retreated southwards, while the 6th and 8th headed east. Almost half the army, some 44,000 men, were trapped north of the Han river after the bridges were blown too early.

After fighting at Taejon alongside the Americans, the RoK forces withdrew into the 160-mile Pusan perimeter. The remains of five RoK divisions numbering 45,000 men defended the northern side, while 30,000 troops of the US 1st Cavalry and 24th Infantry Divisions defended the western side. During the summer the US 2nd Infantry Division, 1st Provincial Marine Brigade and the British 27th Infantry Brigade arrived as reinforcements. Inside the Pusan perimeter the RoK Army's 8th and Capital Divisions formed I Corps, while the 1st and 6th Divisions formed II Corps and the 3rd was assigned to Army Headquarters. The rest were disbanded. In October III Corps, comprising the 5th and newly formed 11th Divisions, was formed for security duties.

Following the UN's successful Inchon landings, by late November 1950 the Capital Division was within 100 kilometres of the Soviet border. The Chinese, though, were able to take advantage of the poor firepower of the RoK divisions. Once they had forced the US 8th Army to withdraw, the exposed Capital and 3rd Divisions fell back on Songjin and Hungnam respectively and had to be evacuated to South Korea. The US Navy successfully rescued 105,000 troops, 91,000 Korean refugees, 17,000 vehicles and several hundred tons of supplies from Hungnam.

It was not until April 1951 that a South Korean armoured force was finally formed as part of the infantry school near Kwangju. Equipped with American M24 Chaffee light tanks and M36B2 tank destroyers, it first went into action in October 1951 on the east-central front. By mid-1952 the RoK Army had eight tank companies (51st–53rd and 55th–59th) giving it far greater punch. Nonetheless, the vast bulk of tanks deployed in Korea belonged to the American armed forces.

By the end of the Second World War in 1945 America had sixteen active armoured divisions. (In reality, American tank strength during the Second World War was such that, including units serving with the infantry divisions, it had enough tank battalions to form thirty-six armoured divisions.) When the war ended, most of the US Army had been demobilized and sent home, and the armoured units were disbanded and their equipment mothballed, redistributed or sold off. By the outbreak of the Korean War the US Army had only ten combat divisions, including a single armoured division, and the American presence in South Korea consisted of a mere 500 advisers who were busy training the RoK Army and advising on counter-insurgency operations. Although never deployed in large numbers, US armour was eventually to be instrumental in providing infantry support and fire support and for static defence.

General Douglas MacArthur's US forces stationed in nearby Japan were equipped only with M24 Chaffee light tanks, as it was feared anything heavier would damage Japanese roads and bridges. In the face of the North Korean invasion, Lieutenant General Walton H. Walker's US 8th Army, which was on occupation duties in Japan, was put on alert. Four light tank battalions supported his infantry divisions – the 71st, 77th, 78th and 79th – but each was only of company strength. In response to the T-34 tank's success in Korea, the 8072nd Medium Tank Battalion (later redesignated the 89th) was hurriedly activated in Japan with fifty-four rebuilt M4A3 Sherman HVSS (Horizontal Volute Spring Suspension) armed with a 76mm tank gun. The Americans quickly rushed this armour over to support their forces in South Korea in late July 1950.

In the meantime, Task Force Smith from the US 24th Infantry Division was rushed to the front on 1 July 1950 and held up the NKPA's advance on Osan. This unit numbered just 500 men, consisting of two rifle companies, two platoons of 4.2 mortars, a single 75mm recoilless rifle crew and six 2.36-in bazooka teams. None of these weapons was capable of knocking out the NKPA's T-34s. For several days they were the only American fighting force on the ground and they had to contend with massed enemy troops, tanks and artillery. The North's armour first came up against the Americans on 5 July 1950. Some thirty-three T-34/85s of the 107th Tank

Regiment took part in the attack, advancing in groups of four with all guns blazing. The Americans were able to stop two tanks using high explosive anti-tank (HEAT) rounds, but only four more were immobilized and after seven hours of fighting the Americans were forced to withdraw with their tails between their legs.

'At 8am on 5 July, the enemy attacked near Osan with 30 tanks and a strong force of infantry,' General Ridgway later wrote. 'Task Force Smith soon had to choose between retreat and annihilation. Having held their positions until their ammunition was gone, they withdrew in some disorder, receiving heavy casualties.' At Taejon the 24th Infantry Division gained valuable time for the arrival of the 25th Infantry and 1st Cavalry Divisions from Japan, as well as the 29th Regimental Combat Team from Okinawa.

Five days later three of the Americans' completely inadequate M24 light tanks came up against the T-34/85s at Chonui for the first time. They fared little better, losing two of the tanks, though they did manage to destroy a single T-34. On 10 July 1950 the US Government put three tank battalions in America on alert: the 6th, equipped with the M46 Patton, belonging to the 2nd Armoured Division, the 70th, with the M26 Pershing and M4A3 Sherman, and the 73rd, also with the M26 Pershing; the latter two were school troop battalions from the Armour School at Fort Knox and the Infantry School at Fort Benning. They were the only armoured units in America that were combat ready and they arrived at Pusan on 7 August 1950.

It was not until late July 1950 that an effective infantry anti-tank weapon was supplied in the shape of the 3.5-in 'Bazooka' rocket launcher. The NKPA's attack on the city of Taejon on 20 July saw no fewer than ten tanks lost to this weapon the very first time it was deployed. However, in one case it took three rockets before the crew were killed and the tank immobilized, and the victor was none other than Major General William Dean, Commander of the 24th Infantry Division, who was to later boast 'I got me a tank.'

Three refurbished M26 Pershings (the only medium tanks in the whole of Korea) crewed by men from the 77th Tank Battalion engaged the enemy at Chinju on 31 July. A blown-up bridge cut off their retreat and the tanks had to be abandoned – another humiliation for the Americans. On 2 August the newly arrived M4A3 HVSS Shermans went into action for the first time, with better results. After the loss of Taejon, the UN forces fell back to the Pusan perimeter. There US Marine M26s were used both in a defensive role and in the battle of the Naktong Bulge, in which the 1st Marine Provisional Brigade, under the 24th Infantry Division, tried to destroy the NKPA 4th Division bridgehead over the river. The tide was about to turn against the T-34.

On 12 July Company A, 1st Marine Tank Battalion, which employed the M4A3 but was issued with the Pershing, as well as units of the 1st Marine Amphibian Tractor Battalion sailed from America. They were committed first to the Sachon counter-offensive, and then, during the fighting between Observation Hill and Hill 125, a Pershing came face to face with a T-34 from the 107th Armoured Regiment; the Pershing came out on top, destroying both this T-34 and a second one with a combination of its 90mm gun, plus Bazooka and recoilless rifle fire. By the end of August the Americans had more than 500 medium tanks in Korea, including M4A3 Shermans, M26 Pershings and M46 Pattons. More than 400 of them were in the Pusan pocket, outnumbering the enemy by at least four to one. Although the NKPA received about 100 T-34 replacements, many of them were knocked out by air-strikes before they could even reach the battlefield.

The North Koreans were in a race against time in trying to unify the two Koreas, and they had anticipated completing this process in about two weeks. Once the Pusan perimeter was formed, they soon found themselves heavily outnumbered. By the time of the Inchon landings there were about 83,000 US troops and another 57,000 Korean and British soldiers facing the NKPA. Although North Korea raised the number of its forces along the front to 98,000, more than a third of them were raw recruits. This meant that they were unable to withstand the two-pronged attack on Inchon and from Pusan when the time came.

During August other UN forces began to arrive, including the 27th British Commonwealth Infantry Brigade, which was later joined by the 29th Independent Infantry Brigade (plus the 28th very briefly). The 29th Brigade had three infantry battalions as well as tank, artillery and engineer units. The 8th King's Royal Irish Hussars, 1st, 5th and 7th Royal Tank Regiments and 5th Royal Inniskilling Dragoon Guards at various times served with the brigade. Three tank squadrons of Lord Strathcona's Horse, of the Royal Canadian 2nd Armoured Regiment, deployed with the 25th Canadian Infantry Brigade.

British forces were equipped with the Churchill Mk VII infantry support tank, the Cromwell Mk VII cruiser tank (both veterans of the Second

World War) and the Centurion Mk III main battle tank. Churchills of C Squadron, 7th Royal Tank Regiment, were the first British tanks to arrive in Korea. Originally they were configured as Crocodile flame-throwers, but their trailers were discarded and they were used as standard gun-tanks despite being terribly slow. When Lord Strathcona's Horse arrived they were initially equipped with M10s but these were exchanged for American M4A3E8 Shermans (the prototype for the M4A3 76mm HVSS).

Along with the Churchills, Cromwell tanks of Cooper Force fought a rearguard action at Chunghung Dong to cover the withdrawal of the 29th Brigade to Seoul. The Centurion was the heaviest tank of the war and sported the thickest armour. Although also the slowest, it had a creditable power-to-weight ratio and better range than the American tanks. Unfortunately, it was never used in great numbers. The Dingo Mk II Scout Car was used by British forces in Korea, including seeing action on the Imjin river with the 8th King's Royal Irish Hussars. Most Commonwealth forces in Korea used some variant of the Universal or Bren Gun Carrier (such as the Canadian version, the Ford Windsor, the Ford Carrier, the Universal No. 3 Mk II and the American T16 Carrier). However, for load-carrying they were only suitable for use on roads. The later Oxford Carrier was more successful across country but it was not deployed in any great numbers.

When the Korean War broke out, the 8th Hussars under Lieutenant Colonel William Lowther converted to the Centurion and then sailed from Southampton as part of the British 29th Independent Brigade, arriving at Pusan on 14 November 1950. After reaching the front north of Pyongyang, they were pushed back to the Han river. Early the following year they lost twenty-three men killed or missing during fighting in the 'Compo Valley'. Captain Donal Astley-Cooper, commanding the Recce troop, put together Cooper Force with Cromwell tanks borrowed from the 7th Battalion, Royal Tank Regiment, which went to the assistance of the Royal Ulster Rifles. The Hussars found themselves caught up in the Battle of the Imjin River. Unfortunately, A and B Squadrons had sailed to Japan, leaving C Squadron, initially commanded by Captain Ormrod and then by Major Henry Huth, to hold the Hussars' position on its own. The tankers fought bravely to help the Glosters, the Northumberland Fusiliers and the Royal Ulster Rifles.

The UN's subsequent pursuit into North Korea and Chinese intervention in support of the North brought the war to a stalemate. On 22 April 1951 three Chinese Armies attacked the UN forces. Directly in their path lay the British 29th Independent Brigade, holding the Imjin river from Choksong on the left to the junction of the Imjin and Hantan on the right. In support were Centurion tanks of C Squadron, 8th King's Royal Irish Hussars, and the 25-pounders of the 45th Field Regiment, Royal Artillery. In the ensuing battle the 1st Battalion, Gloucestershire Regiment, was cut off, and some of the Centurions and three Filipino M24s attempted to reach the trapped men. However, the light tanks were knocked out by mines and blocked the road, and the Centurions were forced back. Attempts to rescue other units of the 29th Brigade were more successful, but for the Glorious Glosters there was to be no withdrawal.

Peter Ormrod was one of the heroes of the Battle of the Imjin River, just as he had been in the battle for Normandy in 1944. He first saw serious action in Korea with C Squadron, 8th Hussars, in February 1951, when they were supporting the 1st Battalion, Gloucestershire Regiment, as the Glosters were moving onto Hill 327 overlooking the Han river east of Seoul. In his role as squadron second-in-command, Ormrod moved forward with the Glosters on foot so that he could direct tank fire onto Chinese-held bunkers. During the Battle of the Imjin River he found himself in temporary command of C Squadron. His tanks were soon under threat after the Chinese infiltrated British positions and stuck explosives on their side armour and tracks. Following the loss of several tanks, Ormrod withdrew to form a more effective defensive perimeter. As Chinese troops tried to encircle Ormrod's tanks, he led half the squadron forward to clear a gap. The crew of the following tank had to machine-gun Ormrod's tank to prevent Chinese soldiers attempting to climb aboard. He was wounded just as the enemy were driven off and his squadron leader arrived with the reserve tank troop. On one occasion they could see around 2,000 Chinese troops swarming down the western hillsides, and their Centurion tanks simply ran over the enemy. For his actions Ormrod was awarded the Military Cross.

Ten countries outside the Commonwealth sent armed units to Korea and four sent medical teams. Of the 344,000 UN troops committed to the war, 300,000 were American. In particular, the Philippines provided a medium tank company, and its forces were equipped with light tanks and self-propelled artillery. Filipino M24 Chaffees unsuccessfully tried to relieve the British on the Imjin river. Turkish troops were considered the best of the smaller UN forces, fighting with distinction at Sinnimini and Osan, though they provided only an infantry brigade.

The daring amphibious assault at Inchon, west of Seoul, was to prove the turning point in the war. General MacArthur conceived of the landings as a way of breaking the Communist stranglehold on the South. This 'left hook' would distract the NKPA by turning their flank and permit the UN forces trapped in the Pusan bridgehead to break out. Both US Army and Marine Corps armour was to play its part. About 70,000 troops were transported from Pusan and Japan to Inchon. The armada of 260 ships comprised vessels from the US, France, Britain, Canada, New Zealand and the Netherlands. On 15 September 1950 the Americans launched the assault, which was intended to envelop the over-extended enemy from the rear and liberate Seoul. Codenamed Operation Chromite, the first objective was the capture of the island of Wolmi-do, at the entrance to the port of Inchon. Once this was secured, large numbers of troops could be brought forward, and the island would then act as a springboard for the invasion.

Spearheading the attack was the US 1st Marine Division; its 1st Tank Battalion consisted of a headquarters and service company, as well as three tank companies with fifteen Pershings. The 1st Amphibian Tractor Battalion was equipped with Landing Vehicle Tracked (LVT), known as Amtracs. The US 7th Infantry Division also included tank and engineer combat battalions, plus a reconnaissance battalion. The tank companies of the 73rd Tank Battalion had twenty Pershings, while the reconnaissance units had Chaffees and M8 and M20 armoured cars. The Marines deployed both the LVT3(C) and the LVT(A)5 (Modified). The former was a post-war modification of the LVT3 (of which 2,962 were built), with a machine-gun turret and aluminium hatches over the troop compartment (hence the C). The latter was a post-war modification of the LVT(A)5 with an improved bow, the hull machine gun removed, access doors added in the hull sides and the addition of a fully enclosed turret with a 75mm howitzer. America built 269 LVT(A)5s, but too late to see action during the Second World War. Both vehicle types were involved in the Inchon landings with the US Marine Corps.

The Communist defences so far behind their main front lines were fairly weak. The key armoured units – the 42nd and 43rd Tank Regiments equipped with T–34/85s – were in the Seoul area. Most of the artillery defending Inchon comprised Soviet-supplied 76.2mm M1942 field guns, which could also be used in an anti-tank role so were a threat to the Pershings. The North Korean 226th Marine Regiment, consisting of around 2,000 men, manned the defences at the port. Further inland to the northeast Kimpo airfield was held by the 2,500 troops of the 107th Security Regiment. At Yongdungp'o were elements of two rifle divisions, the 9th and 18th, numbering about 10,000 men. Units from the 31st and 42nd Divisions plus the 25th Rifle Brigade, totalling at most 10,000 men, held Seoul itself.

During the assault US fighters flew 2,533 sorties, with eleven aircraft lost to enemy ground fire. Communist air cover was negligible, and would not become threatening until the introduction of the MiG-15. At that time they had a number of Soviet-supplied Yakolev and Lavochkin prop-driven fighters, but no jet fighters or bombers. The US Marine Air Wing alone dropped 5,328 bombs and 50,420 pounds of napalm during the operation. In the face of this onslaught, the North Korean Air Force had severely limited air defence capabilities.

The 1st Marine Tank Battalion stormed ashore with its M26s, M4A3 flamethrowers and M4A3 tank-dozers. Inland, six T-34s of the NKPA's 42nd Tank Regiment heading for Inchon lost three of their number to Marine Corsair fighter-bombers at Kanson-Ni and the rest to the advancing M26 Pershings. On 17 September the Pershings surprised another six tanks and killed up to 250 NKPA infantry for the cost of only one man wounded. The US 1st Marine Division was credited with knocking out a total of forty-four enemy tanks during the fighting, but it did not lose a single tank to enemy armour during the operations, though several fell victim to enemy infantry attacks and mines.

To the south, one of the largest tank actions occurred on 16 September during the UN's breakout from Pusan, designed to link up with the landings. The US 70th Tank Battalion, supporting the US 1st Cavalry Division of Task Force Lynch, claimed only one T-34 for the loss of two Shermans. The NKPA, though, lost an additional five T-34s to American Bazooka teams. It took three days to gain a bridgehead on the far side of the Naktong river and begin the drive on Seoul. By 26 September Task Force Lynch had destroyed thirteen enemy tanks for the loss of two Shermans.

MacArthur was proved wrong when he predicted that Seoul would fall in five days; in fact it took fourteen as the North Koreans had turned the city into a fortress. It was finally recaptured on 27 September. The NKPA lost fifty T-34s during the Inchon campaign. The North's armour was no longer having everything its own way. The US 7th Infantry Division then took part in a second amphibious assault, this time on the east coast, landing at Wonsan on 26 October and Iwon three days later.

Following the hugely successful amphibious assault at Inchon by the US 10th Corps, the US 8th Army pushed north along the western coast of Korea, while the RoK Army's 1st Corps and the US 10th Corps advanced north via the eastern coast. In October 1950 the Chinese Army secretly crossed into North Korea to prop up the Communists. After the landing at Wonsan, the US 1st Marine Division, part of 10th Corps, engaged the Chinese 124th Division in early November and inflicted heavy casualties.

On 21 November the US 17th Infantry Regiment reached the banks of the Yalu river, one of the northernmost advances of the UN forces during the course of the war. The Chinese then withdrew, luring the UN forces into a trap at the Chosin reservoir. By 24 November the Marines had taken up positions on both sides of the reservoir, and during the retreat from Chosin the 7th Infantry Division lost 2,657 men killed and 354 wounded. The terrible ratio of dead to wounded shows the ferocity of the fighting. By April 1951 the entire US 8th Army was advancing north on a line stretching across the Korean peninsula, reaching the 38th Parallel the following month. The US 7th Infantry Division, assigned to 9th Corps, fought a fierce three-day battle culminating in the recapture of terrain that had been lost near the Hwachon reservoir just over the 38th Parallel in North Korea. After taking the town bordering on the reservoir they cut off thousands of enemy troops. After this, thanks to the presence of the Chinese, the war bogged down into a bloody stalemate that dragged on until 1953. Armour acted as little more than artillery during this stage of the conflict.

# Chapter 4

# Jungle Cavalry

## The Vietnam War, 1955–1968

After the French experiences in Indo-China, it was hard to imagine armoured warfare being conducted in the jungles and highlands of Southeast Asia again, but that is exactly what happened during the Vietnam War. Following the French withdrawal, North and South Vietnam remained in an armed stand-off. As a result of the increased US military presence in South Vietnam, the US Military Assistance Command Vietnam (MACV) came into being on 8 February 1962. It was initially tasked with assisting the US Military Assistance Advisory Group (MAAG) Vietnam, controlling every advisory and assistance effort in Vietnam. As this task expanded, on 15 May 1964 MACV's role was extended and it absorbed MAAG Vietnam when combat unit deployment became too large for advisory group control. MACV continued directing US military operations in Vietnam until 29 March 1973, when the Paris Peace accords agreed to the withdrawal of all foreign troops.

Initially MACV felt that because of the terrain armour had little role to play in fighting the Communists. General William Westmoreland, commanding US forces in Vietnam, stated that 'except for a few coastal areas ... Vietnam is no place for either tank or mechanized infantry units'. General Harold K. Johnson, Chief of Staff of the US Army, supported this, noting that 'The presence of tank formations tends to create a psychological atmosphere of conventional combat, as well as recall[ing] the image of French tactics in the same area in 1953 and 1954.' America was keen to avoid the same mistakes. This meant that when the first US Army divisions arrived in 1965 they had no tanks or armoured personnel carriers. In contrast, supporting the first US Marine Corps (USMC) landings at Da Nang on 8 March 1965 were the 3rd Tank Battalion, the 3rd Anti-Tank Battalion and the 1st Amphibious Tractor Battalion. The next year they were followed by the 1st Tank Battalion, the 1st Anti-Tank Battalion, the

3rd Amphibious Tractor Battalion and the 1st Armored Amphibian Company.

These battalions were equipped respectively with the M48A3 Patton tank, the M50A1 Ontos anti-tank vehicle and the LVPT-5A1 amphibian tractor (Amtrac). These constituted the three main armoured fighting vehicles deployed by the Marines during the Vietnam War. However, they also fielded the M67A2 flamethrower tank and the M51 Heavy Recovery Vehicle. The primary role of the USMC's tanks was in direct support of Marine infantry operations, with five tanks per infantry battalion. The Ontos, peculiar to the American Marines, was a lightly armoured, air-portable tracked vehicle mounting six 106mm recoilless rifles. Designed as a tank killer, it was mainly used for perimeter defence or bunker-busting. The Amtracs acted as troop and cargo carriers on land and at sea.

The Marines were followed by the US 1st and 25th Infantry Divisions, then the 4th Infantry Division, the 1st Mechanized Brigade, the 5th Infantry Division and the 9th Infantry Division. Once the Viet Cong guerrillas and the North Vietnamese Army became more sophisticated, armoured vehicle protection from small arms, rocket-propelled grenades and anti-personnel mines became increasingly desirable, not to mention their mobility and firepower. In 1966 the US 11th Armored Cavalry Regiment and the 25th Infantry Division arrived in South Vietnam complete with their armoured complement. The 25th's armoured support comprised the 3rd Squadron, 4th Cavalry; the 1st Battalion, 5th Infantry (Mechanized); and the 1st Battalion, 69th Armored Regiment. General Frederick C. Weyand, commander of the 25th Infantry Division, insisted on taking his tank battalion regardless of objections from staff planners in Vietnam and the US Department of the Army. These initial US Marine Corps and US Army tank units were obliged to make up tactics and techniques as they went along. Notably, the Armor Officer Advanced Course of 1964–1965 did not formally address Vietnam, even though American troops were being deployed there.

The most important armoured fighting vehicle of the war was undoubtedly the ubiquitous tracked M113 armoured personnel carrier. Most mechanized units in Vietnam employed it and it became known as the ACAV or Armored Cavalry Assault Vehicle. Doctrine for mechanized infantry recognized that the APC's most important role was for transporting infantry safely to the battlefield, but it had a much wider role than this. Armoured cavalry also excelled as combat manoeuvre battalions rather than reconnaissance. Whilst the Patton and M113 were the mainstays of American armoured fighting vehicles during the Vietnam War, there were a host of others with specialized roles. These included the M551 Sheridan air mobile tank, the M107 175mm and M109 155mm self-propelled artillery, the M42A1 'Dusters' and the M55 Quad 50s of the Air Defence Artillery battalions, and the V-100 Commando armoured car. The Sheridan was deployed by the 11th Armored Cavalry Regiment and from 1969 replaced some of the Pattons and ACAVs in the other armored cavalry regiments. Company D of the 16th Armored Regiment, with the 173rd Airborne Brigade, was the only unit to use the Scorpion 90mm self-propelled anti-tank (SPAT) gun. Ironically, the US, believing that missiles had super-seded anti-aircraft artillery, had to retrieve its self-propelled guns from the Reserve and National Guard. As the North's air power was little threat, these weapons were used in a ground support role to devastating effect, firing 14 million 40/50mm rounds during the war.

An Australian task force arrived in 1965 with an armoured personnel carrier troop. The Philippines also despatched a security force consisting of seventeen armoured personnel carriers and two M41 Walker Bulldog light tanks. The following year Royal Thai Army forces deployed an M113 platoon and a cavalry reconnaissance troop. South Korea also offered to supply a tank battalion, but this was turned down, though their forces were to deploy ACAVs in Vietnam.

Marine Corps tank units took part in their first major tank battle in Operation Starlite. This was conducted in August 1965 when three Marine battalions, each supported by a platoon of tanks, pre-empted the 1st Viet Cong Regiment's attack on Chu Lai airfield to the southeast of Da Nang. In two days of fire-fights seven tanks were damaged, one of which was a write-off. However, the Marine tank crews destroyed numerous enemy fortifications, captured twenty-nine weapons and killed sixty-eight Viet Cong.

A pivotal tank action took place in April 1966, which demonstrated the utility of US armour in jungle warfare. The US 1st Cavalry Division west of Plei Me requested self-propelled howitzer support. Nine M48A3 and seventeen M113s formed the escort for the guns and the column successfully ploughed its way through the jungle. Then, whilst the guns spent two days on firing missions, the tanks searched the local hills for Viet Cong. The whole operation went off without mishap, convincing planners of the usefulness of armour in Vietnam.

Within three weeks of their arrival, the three armoured units of the 25th Infantry Division took part in their first multi-battalion mission with Operation Circle Pines. This was designed to drive the Viet Cong from the jungle and rubber plantations to the north of Saigon. Although the ground was marshy, the vegetation did not really impede the tanks or the armoured personnel carriers. After eight days it had been shown that a large armoured force could successfully drive the Viet Cong from their jungle strongholds.

As a result, more armoured formations were deployed to Vietnam. The infantry divisions were now each supported by a squadron of Pattons. For example, the 3rd Squadron, 5th Cavalry, was assigned to the 9th Infantry Division. The 11th Armored Cavalry Regiment was involved in Junction City, the largest operation to that point in the war, which commenced on 22 February 1967. This resulted in 2,728 enemy casualties. The regiment was also involved in operations in Cambodia and was not sent home until 1971. Amongst its ranks were three recipients of the Medal of Honor. The Marines' 3rd Tank Battalion and 1st Amphibious Tractor Battalion were not sent home until 1969.

Apart from American-built tanks, the only others to be used in support of the South were the British-made Centurions of the 1st Australian Tank Force. In 1968 Australia sent twenty-six tanks and an additional cavalry platoon. Four squadrons served in Vietnam on a rotating basis from February 1968 to September 1971. They mainly operated in Phuoc Tuy Province east of Saigon, near Vung Tau.

The Army of South Vietnam consisted of a collection of former French colonial units. With American help it slowly improved, gaining some counter-insurgency capabilities, but political upheaval undermined it. The newly elected American president, John F. Kennedy, agreed to MAAG's requests for increases in the Army of the Republic of Vietnam's (ARVN) troop levels and the US military commitment in both equipment and men. In response, Kennedy provided $28.4 million in funding for the ARVN, and overall military aid increased from $50 million per year to $144 million in 1961.

Despite the American dollars, by 1968 the general condition of the South Vietnamese Armed Forces (SVAF) can only have encouraged the Communists. In 1954–55 the SVAF numbered 279,000, by 1968 they had almost tripled to 820,000; ARVN had grown from 170,000 to 380,000. However, in 1967 ARVN was relegated to a secondary role, with pacification and security operations. The large-scale US military intervention precluded equipment modernisation for the ARVN until after 1968. This was to have far-reaching ramifications for the US. Furthermore, absenteeism and desertion from the ARVN were major problems and large numbers of men were missing at the start of Tet. Desertions for the whole of 1968 totalled 139,670 and were the largest single cause of manpower loss in South Vietnam.

Furthermore, ARVN was weak in armour. It established its first armoured units in 1956, equipped with Chaffees, M8 armoured cars and M3 half-tracks abandoned by the French. Six years later two mechanized companies were formed using the M113 APC, which saw service for the first time on 11 June 1962 in the Mekong Delta. The ARVN was soon to learn that the M113 was not just an armoured bus, but also an effective armoured fighting vehicle in its own right. The ARVN's old Chaffees were replaced by the M41A3 Walker Bulldog light tank in 1965 and its forces expanded to eight armoured cavalry regiments, equipped with the M41A3, the M113, the M8 and the M106 (self-propelled 4.2-inch mortar). During the Tet Offensive ten ARVN armoured cavalry regiments fought to contain the Communist insurgents.

Although a North Vietnamese Army (NVA) armoured force had been created as early as 1959, equipped with Soviet-supplied T-54 and Chinese Type 59 main battle tanks and Soviet PT-76 light tanks, they did not make use of their armour until the closing years of the war. Up until 1972 NVA armour only appeared on or near the battlefields of South Vietnam on four recorded occasions. Before the NVA's conventional invasion of the South, their only notable use of armour was at the Lang Vei special forces camp near Khe Sanh on 6–7 February 1968, involving just thirteen PT-76 amphibious light tanks.

The NVA launched their attack at Lang Vei at 2230 hours on 6 February 1968, using elements of the 304th Division. Their plan was to occupy the base and ambush any relieving force. They quickly breached the wire and took up positions in the forward trenches. From the observer tower on top of the camp's Tactical Operation Centre (TOC), two PT-76s were spotted, and five more were also seen approaching another position. Calls to Khe Sanh and Da Nang that enemy tanks were in the wire were met with initial disbelief. The defenders disabled three or four tanks, and one was knocked out by an American aircraft (the first recorded tank kill by a helicopter did not occur until 1973 at An Loc), but the defenders were still overwhelmed at the perimeter and forced to flee the base. PT-76 tanks of the 202nd Armoured Regiment also tried to overrun the special forces camp at Ben Het in March 1969. Two years later the NVA used them against ARVN troops in Laos and then in their 1972 offensive.

The North Vietnamese did not deploy their T-54 tanks until late in the Vietnam War, although deliveries of T-54A, T-54B and Type 59 tanks began in the 1960s. They also obtained some 200 Type 62 light tanks (but these were difficult to tell apart from the Type 59s) and 150 Type 63 light amphibious tanks. Their tanks first went into combat in neighbouring Laos in early 1971 when seven were lost resisting South Vietnamese tanks near Hill 31.

*Chapter 5*

# Operation Kadesh
## The Suez Crisis, 1956

During 1955 and 1956 Israeli civilians were subjected to escalating Arab terrorist attacks conducted from Gaza and the Sinai. When Egypt then sealed off the Israeli port of Eilat by blockading the Gulf of Aqaba, Israel considered this an act of war. Operation Kadesh, the Israeli invasion of Sinai in 1956, proved the lasting value of the tank on the battlefield to the Israeli Defence Forces, and demonstrated that Second World War weaponry was still more than serviceable. Despite the vast quantities of Soviet-supplied military hardware deployed by the Egyptian Army, the relatively ill-equipped Israelis were able to drive up them from their well-prepared and well-fortified positions in the space of just three or four days.

In the summer of 1956 roughly a third of Egypt's 150,000-strong army was deployed to the Sinai, the vast peninsula bordered by the Gulf of Suez to the west and the Gulf of Aqaba to the east. Most of them were infantry, with the bulk of the armour protecting northern Egypt. Troops were also positioned in the Canal Zone and along the Mediterranean, especially in the Nile Delta, to counter any attacks by the British or French. The Egyptians had 150 MiG jet fighters but just thirty fully trained pilots to fly them. Ironically, Egyptian intelligence concluded that the danger of an Israeli pre-emptive war had passed. Crucially, an infantry division and two armoured brigades were withdrawn from Sinai, leaving one Egyptian division and the Palestinian division holding Gaza, plus a battalion of scout cars in the south and a reinforced infantry battalion in Sharm el-Sheikh.

The defence of northern Sinai relied on a series of fixed defences, which included the heights at Rafah near the coast and Abu Aghelia, where a defensive system covered the road to Ismailia. Once the Israeli paratroops landed, Cairo sent in reinforcements consisting of an infantry brigade followed by the 4th Armoured Division. Under Operation Beisan, the Jordanian and Syrian armies were to counter-attack Israel, but this never got off the ground and, like the Egyptians, the Syrians did not really know how to use their Soviet-supplied hardware.

By October 1956 Israel had 100 French-supplied AMX-13s and several hundred Shermans and Super Shermans. Just two days before D-Day, France supplied 200 6 × 6 trucks with front wheel drive. Half were assigned to the paratroop brigade and half to the 9th Brigade, which was to trundle to Sharm el-Sheikh in southern Sinai. They had three objectives: to take control of the Straits of Tiran, which the Egyptians had closed to Israeli shipping, thereby blockading the port of Eilat at the head of the Gulf of Aqaba; to secure the approaches to the Suez Canal; and finally to destroy the Egyptian forces in Sinai.

For the invasion of Sinai, each of the IDF task forces was allocated two infantry brigades and a mechanized brigade. In the case of the Northern Task Force, it was backed by the 27th Mechanized Brigade, consisting of one motorized infantry battalion, three squadrons of Shermans and one squadron of AMX-13s. The Southern Task Force was allocated the 37th Mechanized Brigade, this time with two battalions of motorized infantry, a battalion of Shermans and one squadron of AMX-13s. The Command Reserve comprised the 7th Armoured Brigade with the Shermans of the 82nd Tank Battalion and the AMX-13s of the 79th Tank Battalion.

On 26 October 1956 some 395 Israeli paratroops from the 202nd Parachute Brigade dropped on Mitla Pass about 50 kilometres from the Canal, while more drove on Kuntilla in central Sinai, Kusseima and Nakhl. Only half the contingent of supporting AMX-13 tanks survived the journey to Sinai, for the brigade had been acting as a decoy on the Jordanian frontier. To the south the 9th Infantry Brigade attacked Ras an-Naqb on the Gulf of Aqaba, while to the north the 7th Armoured and 4th Infantry Brigades pushed on to al-Qusamah.

The Israeli 7th Armoured Brigade soon found itself tangling with the Egyptian 1st and 2nd Armoured Brigades. In the meantime, unfortunately, the Israeli Air Force attacked friend and foe alike. The Egyptian-Israeli air war during the 1956 Suez crisis was fairly limited, with only fourteen recorded engagements. The Israelis lost two aircraft in air-to-air combat and the Arabs seven. However, the Egyptian T-34s and SU-100s were driven back towards al-Ismailiyah. To the south of Abu Uwayulah the Egyptians had positioned ten elderly British-built Archer self-propelled anti-tank guns, supported by artillery and anti-aircraft guns. Although the

Israelis lost all their tanks in the assault, they took Ruafa. The 37th Mechanized and 10th Infantry Brigades then attacked Umm Qataf.

At Rafah the Israelis attacked the Egyptians, employing the 27th Mechanized Brigade equipped with AMX-13s and Super Shermans. This cut Gaza off from the Sinai and left the Israelis free to advance on al-Arish, Sinai's most important city. This then led to a major battle at Jeradi Pass, but AMX-13s, supported by the Israeli Air Force, hooked left and stormed the summit of the pass. Unfortunately, on 2 November the Israeli 37th Mechanized Brigade ran into an ambush set by the 7th Armoured Brigade, leading to a number of friendly fire casualties.

The British Foreign Secretary, Selwyn Lloyd, recalled:

We had no knowledge of the Israeli campaign plans but it was clear that they were carrying all before them ... While this was going on, our invasion fleet was sailing towards Port Said. Its speed was limited by the fact that the tank landing craft could only do 5 knots an hour.

On 6 November 1956 the lead units of 1,000 Royal Marines from 40 and 42 Commando attacked Port Said using Buffalo tracked landing vehicles at Sierra Red and Sierra Green assault beaches. The lack of LSTs meant that subsequent waves had to come in via landing craft. They were supported by Centurion tanks of C Squadron, 6th Royal Tank Regiment. These were used to good effect against the defenders of the Customs House, but it took air-strikes to force the Egyptians from the Navy House.

Once the port facilities were secured, A and B Squadrons, plus the regimental HQ, of the 6th Royal Tank Regiment were able to land. These provided invaluable covering fire and mobile defence for the Marines. They were also used to move towards al-Qantarah, setting up defensive positions at al-Cap with 2nd Para. Selwyn Lloyd in his book *Suez 1956* wrote 'it is interesting to speculate as to what would have happened if we had succeeded in establishing an international regime for the canal. I doubt whether the Six Day War in June 1967, or the Yom Kippur War in 1973, would have taken place.'

Meanwhile, for the loss of thirty tanks and half-tracks, the Israelis destroyed or captured in excess of 200 Egyptian armoured vehicles. This victory convinced Israel of the need for large mobile armoured formations and led to the grouping of units to create *Ugdas* or divisional strength task forces. These comprised a mixture of armoured brigades supported by mechanized or infantry brigades. In the aftermath of Operation Kadesh, Brigadier Israel Tal was instrumental in transforming Israel's armoured corps into a truly formidable weapon. A former veteran of the British Army, he had fought in North Africa and Italy during the Second World War. Subsequently he joined Haganah, the Jewish underground movement fighting to oust the British from Palestine. He used skirmishes along the Syrian border as a training opportunity and got his tank gunners so proficient that they could hit targets up to 11 kilometres away.

In terms of training, effectiveness, equipment and firepower, by 1967 Israel easily had the best armed forces in the Middle East. Combined, the Arab armies had more weapons than the Israelis, but they were incapable of deploying them in a decisive manner. Egypt and Israel had roughly the same numbers of artillery, tanks, armoured personnel carriers and self-propelled guns, but with Jordan and Syria the Arabs had an advantage of two-to-one. Likewise, the Israelis and Egyptians had about the same number of jet fighters, though the Egyptians had four times as many bombers. But again, the Israeli pilots were far superior and were capable of launching highly effective pre-emptive strikes. In addition, the IDF was able to mobilize much faster than the Arab armies. It could muster its full twenty-six brigades, including four armoured and four mechanized, in the space of 48 hours. By contrast, the Egyptians could only muster ten brigades in the same timeframe, while Jordan could manage eight and Syria six. The Arabs had another five brigades that they could call on, but Israel's intention was that the fighting would be over before the reinforcements ever reached the battlefield. In the case of the Egyptian Army, many of the reservists called up were badly trained. For example, some had served with the artillery, only to be sent to the armoured forces.

In response to Moscow supplying Egypt with T-54 main battle tanks, Israel purchased Centurion Mk IIIs and Vs from Britain. These were up-gunned with the new L7 105mm gun replacing the older 20-pounder. Initially, the Israeli tank crews were far from keen on the Centurion, but by 1967 they had 250 of them and they had been modified into a war-winning weapon. America also supplied 200 M48 Patton tanks via West Germany during the early 1960s.

In addition, with the assistance of the French, the Israelis also up-gunned 200 Shermans, replacing the 75/76mm guns with 105mm guns in an effort to counter ever-growing numbers of Egyptian T-54s. The up-gunned tanks were dubbed the M51HV or Isherman (i.e. Israeli Sherman).

The Israelis also began to up–arm their M48s with the 105mm gun. In 1967 the Isherman was one of the fastest tanks in Israeli service and, despite the age of the basic design, it proved quite effective. To give the Israeli tank battalions close support, Zahal Ordnance developed the M9 half-track mounting a 120mm mortar. Somewhat surprisingly, these were to prove effective against Jordanian Patton tanks during the Six Day War. Israel became convinced that it needed to neutralize the growing military might of its neighbours. In a pre-emptive strike Israel sought to take out the Egyptian garrison in Sinai and then turn on Syrian forces on the Golan Heights; Jordan also found itself dragged into the hostilities. All this new armoured kit would be put to the test in 1967 with the Six Day War.

*Chapter 6*

# Six Days to Victory

## The Arab-Israeli War, 1967

### Sinai

Lieutenant Yaël Dayan (daughter of General Moshe Dayan, the newly appointed Israeli Defence Minister) recalled on 3 June 1967, just two days before the Six Day War broke out:

> We flew [in a helicopter] very low above our lines – an armoured brigade composed of three battalions; one Centurion battalion commanded by Natke; the others, Sherman tanks and armoured infantry, headed by Sason and Herzel; a specially combined reconnaissance force with AMX light tanks and half-tracks and jeeps commanded by Arie.

Brigadier General Israel Tal noted the Egyptians were:

> blocking all the main lines of advance through the desert with massive troop concentrations and strongly fortified positions, some of which had been prepared over the last 20 years. The only line of advance westwards from Israel's southern border that was not blocked was the one taken by General Yoffe and his armoured brigade across the dunes – the Egyptians evidently believed them impassable.

The Israelis struck on 5 June 1967, with their air force swiftly gaining almost complete air supremacy in a series of highly coordinated raids on Arab air bases just before the tanks rolled forward. The Israeli Air Force's timing and coordination were superb, particularly in catching the Egyptian Air Force as the early morning mists lifted on the Nile Delta. Multiple targets were bombed not only in the Sinai but also west of the Suez Canal.

The preliminary Israeli air-strikes hit eight Egyptian airfields in Sinai, on the Canal and in the Cairo area, and the attacks then broadened to encompass a further nine airfields.

The Egyptians lost a staggering 304 aircraft in a single day. The blow was decisive; Egypt's Air Force could not now support its ground forces in the Sinai, giving the Israelis a free hand. After securing air superiority over Egypt, the outcome was never in doubt, and the Israelis then turned their attentions on their other Arab neighbours, claiming another ninety-nine aircraft. The Israelis destroyed the Jordanian Air Force, damaged the Iraqi Air Force and inflicted such losses on the Syrian Air Force that it took no further part in the fighting. Israel's losses on 5 June 1967 were just nineteen aircraft. In the whole of the conflict Israel claimed 452 Arab aircraft destroyed for the loss of forty-six.

Defending the Sinai, the Egyptians had about 100,000 troops, 950 tanks, 1,100 armoured personnel carriers and over 1,000 artillery pieces. They were organized into one mechanized, two armoured and four infantry divisions supported by four independent brigades. While the Egyptian infantry divisions were supported by T-34/85s, the 4th Armoured was equipped with the newer T-54/55 tanks and PT-76 amphibious light tanks; the 6th Mechanized was also equipped with Soviet T-54/55s and some ancient Joseph Stalin heavy tanks. Crucially, some of the units in Sinai were 40 per cent under strength and some armoured units had only half their allotted number of tanks. When the Israelis attacked, General Salah Mushin and his deputy were absent from the Egyptian field army head-quarters in Sinai as they were attempting to attend a conference with Field Marshal Abd al-Hakim Amer at Bri Tamada airfield. The following day the Egyptian commander-in-chief gave the order to fall back on the Suez Canal. The Egyptian Army collapsed, though a rearguard action at Jebel Libni brought the fleeing troops some time.

The Israelis had three Ugdas facing Egypt and a fourth opposite Jordan. Against the Egyptians the Israelis had 70,000 men, comprising eleven brigades, two of which were independent while the rest were divided amongst the three divisional task forces. Four of the brigades were armoured, equipped with Centurion and Patton tanks; two were mechanized, each with a battalion of Shermans and two battalions of infantry transported in half-tracks.

Despite their shortcomings, the Egyptian forces in Sinai were well supported by tanks. Their defences were heavily influenced by Soviet doctrine.

They comprised a series of infantry strongpoints, which included dug-in T-34s and IS-3 tanks. Behind these lay the two armoured divisions with 450 T-54s and T-55s. The first defence line, with the Egyptian 7th Infantry Division holding Gaza and Rafah, was backed by approximately seventy T-34 and IS-3 tanks; in addition, the 20th Palestinian Division in the El Arish and Bir Lahfan sector was supported by about fifty Shermans. The Shazli Force in the Kuntilla area was made up of a mechanized task force with 120 T-54/55 tanks and the 6th Mechanized Division with ninety T-54/55s and some IS-3s. The second line of defence was the responsibility of the Egyptian 3rd Infantry Division holding the Jebel Libni, Bir Hassana and Jebel Harim sector with about ninety tanks. The 4th Armoured Division with some 200 T-54/55 tanks was in the Bir Gafgafa and Bir Thamad sector.

The Israeli armour rolled forward, supported by the Israeli Air Force, and made short work of Egypt's tanks. Lieutenant Dayan was with General Arik Sharon's division, whose main target was Abu Agheila, defended by 16,000 men of the Egyptian 2nd Division holding Um-Katef ridge with ninety tanks. Israeli gunners laid 6,000 shells on the Egyptian defences at Um Katef. On the opening day Lieutenant Dayan observed:

> The Centurions met the first 'danger' or defence fire from one of the outposts and we moved to a higher point from which we could see our forces moving. For a while I felt as though I were watching a game. Tanks dispersed in the area, shells heard and seen, the wireless set like a background running commentary – there was something unreal about it all.

The Centurions came under heavy artillery fire and became stuck in a minefield until air support enabled them to push back or destroy the defending Egyptian T-34s. Sason's Shermans made a feint frontal attack on the Egyptians to draw their fire for the Israeli artillery spotters. In the meantime Natke's Centurions took Hill 181. Six of his tanks got into the enemy's defensive positions where they put about fifteen T-34s to flight after knocking out five of them.

Yaël Dayan recalled in her diary:

> Perplexed, wandering, indecisive enemy tanks were roaming on the road, along the road, on the sides, in opposite directions. About

twenty of them were destroyed, one point blank from ten yards, after he was trodding [plodding] along for five miles in our own column, either pretending he was Israeli or not knowing he wasn't amongst his own Egyptian tanks.

Once inside the Um-Katef defences the Israeli tanks had to do battle with the Egyptian armour in order to open the Ntzana–Abu-Agheila road. This fight took place on the Egyptians' second line of defences at Sinai-Bir-Hassana and Gebel-Libni. The Israelis lost nineteen tanks but claimed sixty Egyptian tanks in return. This battle had special resonance for the Israelis, for in 1956 both the 37th Mechanized and the 10th Infantry Brigades had been mauled fighting for the very same ground.

The bulk of the Egyptian armour deployed in central Sinai, comprising the 7th Armoured Division and a couple of armoured brigades totalling over 500 tanks, remained largely untouched. Had one of the Egyptians' armoured brigades acted quickly, it could have counter-attacked the Israeli Centurions that had struggled through the supposedly impassable sand dunes to the north of Um Katef. Instead they stayed put, ensuring an Israeli victory at Abu Agheila.

Egyptian tank losses continued to mount, and about 150 wrecked tanks were counted on the road from Temed to Nahel, an area that was described as the 'Valley of Death of the Egyptian Army'. At Gaza the Israeli 7th Armoured Brigade, part of Brigadier General Israel Tal's division, headed west over the border with Gaza and into Khan Younis. His second armoured brigade, the 60th, struck south into the sand dunes to outflank the minefields screening Rafah. The 7th Armoured ran into the Egyptian 7th Infantry Division and a battalion of Palestinians supported by heavy Joseph Stalin tanks, with predictably bloody results.

In the early hours the Egyptian 4th Armoured Division was ordered to strike Tal's left flank at B'ir Lahfan. However, it came off second best against the Israelis' superior gunnery, losing nine tanks for the loss of just one Israeli tank. When the sun came up Israeli gunnery and the air force drove the battered 4th Armoured back towards Bir Gifgafah, the Egyptians losing anything between thirty and eighty tanks. The Israeli Air Force pounded the retreating Egyptian Army all the way back to the Mitla Pass and beyond.

The Israeli 7th Armoured Brigade sought to trap the Egyptian 4th Armoured Division at Bir Gifgafah, but only caught a brigade that became

ollowing the first Arab-Israeli War in 1948, Israel built up its armoured corps into a formidable rce. It began this process by buying up surplus Second World War M4 Sherman tanks.

1950 the North Koreans spearheaded their assault on the South with Soviet-supplied T-34/85s. ne South Koreans and Americans had to rely on air strikes to stop them.

An American M4 Sherman serving in Korea. Like the T-34, it was a veteran of the Second World War.

An M26 Pershing tank engaging a North Korean target.

An American M46 Patton deployed as a self-propelled gun in Korea.

The US and South Korean armies employed the American-built M24 Chaffee light tank in the Korean War.

The French Expeditionary Force used the Chaffee in Indo-China.

M113 armoured personnel carriers in the jungle. Initially the American high command deemed Vietnam unsuitable for armoured warfare.

A mixed convoy of 48 Patton tanks and M113 armoured personnel carriers in Vietnam.

A Pakistani Sherman destroyed during the 1965 Indo-Pakistan War.

Israeli M51 Shermans in the Negev desert in southern Israel prior to the Six Day War.

Egyptian T-34/85s on the move in the El Aris area in late May 1967.

This wrecked Egyptian T-34/85 was destroyed during the fighting at Rafah in the Gaza Strip during the Six Day War in June 1967.

The buckled remains of an M48; such tanks equipped the Jordanian 60th Armoured Brigade in 1967.

The fate of all the Arab armies in 1967: total destruction.

The RG-7 came into service in the 1960s and served as the standard Soviet infantry anti-tank weapon throughout the Cold War.

The bulky AT-3 Sagger anti-tank missile first made its mark in the Yom Kippur War, giving the Israeli tanke a nasty surprise.

The man-portable version of the Sagger, as deployed by the Egyptians, consisted of the missile, launch rail, joystick control unit, sighting mechanism and carrying case.

embroiled in a tank battle with their Shermans. Two battalions of Egyptian T-54s, which had come across the Canal, ran into a single battalion of Israeli AMX-13s, but luckily for the Israelis a company of Centurions arrived just at the right moment to save the day. By midday on 9 June the three Ugdas had all linked up. The Israelis lost 122 tanks fighting their way across the Sinai; the Egyptians, though, had just 115 remaining from a force of 935.

The British defence attaché, a veteran of the Second World War, was flown over the Mitla Pass and reported the Israeli attack was:

> devastating over a four to five mile stretch of road running through the defile. All vehicles were nose to tail and in places double and treble banked. There was considerably more destruction than I had seen after the Axis retreat from Alamein. So far as can be ascertained, this destruction was the result of continuous air attack.

The Israeli Air Force continued to pound the fleeing Egyptian armour mercilessly. Uri Gil, an Israeli pilot, recalled:

> It was the greatest vehicle cemetery I ever saw. I was not happy about the situation. They looked like humans, like victims, I blew up a fuel tanker at close range. There was no fire from the ground. It was slaughter. I didn't think that it was necessary. The war against Egypt was finished.

The stubborn Egyptian rearguards fared no better. Elements of the 3rd Infantry Division holding the defences at Jebel Lini were surrounded and obliterated. At Bir Gifgafah approximately forty T-54s of the 4th Armoured Division brushed aside the Israeli AMX light tanks blocking the way. Nonetheless, an entire Egyptian brigade was surrounded and wiped out. Subsequently, only about a third of the division escaped back over the Suez Canal.

In the face of the relentless bombing and shelling, many terrified Egyptian tank crew simply abandoned their vehicles. After first light on 8 June Sharon's division discovered an entire brigade of Egyptian Stalin tanks and self-propelled guns. When the unit's commander was captured, he feebly explained that he had left them where they were because he did not have orders to destroy them and if he had done so, it would have alerted the Israelis to their presence.

The Israelis also came across Soviet-supplied PT–76 light tanks. Yaël Dayan recalled:

> Well camouflaged and dug in was a brand-new amphibious Russian tank, large and yellow and unused. While we were trying to open a screw on it, Sason, the Shermans' commander, showed up with a few tankists. In five minutes they were in it, traversing its gun. Seconds later the engine was started, and, grinning, Sason drove it out, manoeuvring it towards his battalion in a cloud of happy dust, saluting Arik [Sharon] on the way.

Sharon's division then ambushed a column of Egyptian armour, knocking out 60 tanks, more than 300 other vehicles and 100 guns. Although some 5,000 Egyptian troops escaped into the desert, many perished from heatstroke and thirst. On reaching the Suez Canal on 8 June Tal's division had knocked out fifty Egyptian tanks for the loss of just five. That day Egypt reluctantly accepted the terms of the cease-fire resolution passed by the UN Security Council on 7 June. Staggeringly, 80 per cent of the Egyptian Army's equipment had been smashed or seized by the Israelis. They lost 700 tanks, 50 self-propelled guns, 400 field guns, 30 155mm guns and 10,000 trucks, and much of this haul was pressed back into service by the triumphant Israelis.

## The West Bank

While the Israelis confronted the build-up of Egyptian forces on their western border, to the east the Jordanians also had considerable tank forces on the West Bank that posed a potentially direct threat to Israeli-held West Jerusalem. Following their surprise offensive into the Sinai, the Israelis switched their attentions from Egypt and launched pre-emptive attacks on both Jordan and Syria. Israeli jets were swift to silence the Jordanian 25-pounders and 155mm guns on the West Bank, which had started to lob shells over the border to hit Tel Aviv and Kfar Saba.

The Jordanian Army in June 1967 consisted of the Western Command responsible for the West Bank, the Nablus and Jerusalem-Hebron sectors, and the Eastern Command responsible for the Jordan Valley. The Western Command's key armoured units were the 40th Armoured Brigade in the Damiya area and the 60th Armoured Brigade in the Ain Qilt-Jericho area. In the northern area of the West Bank Jordanian forces in the Jenin-Nablus area were supported by the 12th Armoured Regiment equipped with M47 Patton tanks. However, there were only two battalions from the Princess Alia Brigade covering the border between Qalqiliya and Tulkarem some 25 kilometres away. These were supported by just 200 men from the local Palestinian National Guard, though the Jordanians were very reluctant to arm the Palestinians. It was south of Jerusalem that the Israeli 10th Mechanized Brigade and Ugda Peled (consisting of the Bar Kochva and Uri Ram Armoured Brigades and an infantry brigade) faced the Jordanian 40th and 60th Armoured Brigades' M48 Pattons and M113 armoured personnel carriers. In addition, the 10th Armoured Regiment with Centurions was also in the Hebron sector.

Initially, the Jordanians had planned Operation Tariq as a pincer attack to cut off the Jewish half of the contested city of Jerusalem. In reality, Jordan's small army (comprising nine infantry brigades and two independent armoured brigades) was simply not strong enough to hold the armistice line with Israel, let alone seize West Jerusalem. Holding the latter as a bargaining chip was a sound strategy but the Jordanian armed forces were simply not up to the task of capturing it. As a compromise, the 60th Armoured Brigade was deployed south to Hebron and the 40th moved from the northern area of the West Bank to the Jericho area. This was based on the assumption that a Syrian armoured brigade would move in behind the 40th and that an Egyptian division would attack Beersheba via the Negev desert, but in the event neither happened.

In the face of Israeli attacks, Jordanian troops were driven from Latrun but at Jenin they set up three coordinated defence lines supported by anti-tank guns. Also in the third line was a battalion of Jordanian Patton tanks that were dug in and could not be outflanked. Initially their defences held but the Israelis lured out the Pattons, which ran into the heavily gunned Super Shermans. South of Jenin Brigadier General Rakan al-Jazi arrived with his 40th Armoured Brigade, having been on a wild goose chase to Jericho. He successfully caught the Israelis by surprise, hitting Brigadier General Elad Peled's armoured brigade. Up to sixty Jordanian Pattons opened fire and destroyed seventeen Super Shermans. When the Jordanians tried to follow-up, they were driven back by concentrated Israeli artillery and air-strikes. Israeli tanks finally scattered the 40th Armoured at the Qabatiya crossroads. Some of the Jordanian tanks managed to reach the Damiya bridge and escaped to the east bank of the river Jordan. Again the Israelis reaped a cruel harvest as they bombed and strafed the Jordanian troops retreating down from the mountains of the West Bank into the Jordan Valley.

Prince Sharif Zaid Ben Shaker, commanding the 60th Armoured Brigade, lost half of his eighty tanks, largely to air attacks. He himself had a near miss, recalling:

> When you're strafed you have to jump out of your vehicle – I was in a Land Rover – and throw yourself in a ditch. They hit the wireless car behind me. They used a lot of napalm. A napalm bomb ricocheted on the asphalt near me, went about 200 yards and exploded. God was on my side.

All in all, it was a disaster for the Jordanian armoured forces. By the evening of 7 June 1967 the Israelis' job was done: they had captured East Jerusalem and the entire West Bank. The war against Jordan was over, but it had been a tough and bloody battle. The Jordanian Army suffered 700 dead and 2,500 wounded. The fighting cost the Israelis 550 killed and 2,400 wounded. While the Jordanians lost 179 tanks, they gave a very good account of themselves, knocking out 112 Israeli tanks.

King Hussein of Jordan went on the radio to acknowledge the performance of his armed forces and said, 'Our soldiers have defended every inch of our earth with their precious blood. It is not yet dry, but our country honours the stain . . . If in the end you were not rewarded with glory, it was not because you lacked courage but because it was the will of God.' The truth was that his men had simply been outmatched by the Israeli tankers who had got the better of the Jordanian Centurions and Pattons.

## The Golan Heights

To the north Israel is bordered by Lebanon and Syria. During the period 1948–1967 the Syrians constructed a 'Maginot Line' along their mutual border formed by the Golan Heights, building numerous bunkers, tank pits and gun emplacements along the ridge that runs northwards from the Sea of Galilee and dominates the low-lying plains of Israel to the west. These defences were more than 16 kilometres deep and were protected by 265 guns. As in the case of Egypt and Jordan, the Israelis saw the Syrian military presence as a threat.

At the time of the Six Day War the Syrians had on the frontier 65,000 men supported by 350 tanks, 300 artillery pieces and 200 anti-aircraft guns.

The plan was that should the Israelis ever get through the Syrian defensive shield and threaten Damascus, then the armoured reserves would counter-attack and throw them back. As usual, things were not as simple as they first appeared, for the Syrian Army, which included two armoured brigades, was greatly weakened by an ongoing purge following a failed coup.

In response to the Israelis' surprise attacks on its air force, the Syrians bombarded the Israeli settlements of Shear Yusuv and Tel Dan, then launched an attack on 6 June with a dozen T–34s supported by several hundred infantry. Three days later Colonel Albert Mendler's armoured brigade pushed into Syria, tasked with tackling the Syrian 14th and 44th Armoured Brigades holding the strategically important Golan Heights. The Syrians also had several additional battalions of ancient Panzer Mk IVs, T–34/85s and newer T–54s attached to the infantry formations in the region, plus some SU-100 tank destroyer companies. Mendler's command was equipped with one battalion of Centurions and one with a mix of M50 and M51 Shermans.

The mountain slopes from Kfar Szold were a serious natural obstacle that the Syrians fortified with minefields and anti-tank gun positions. This was the route that Mendler's armoured brigade, followed by the Golani Brigade, would have to take. Eight unarmoured bulldozers were used to clear a path for the Israeli tanks up a 1,500ft-high ridge. Despite their assis-tance, the Israeli tanks soon lost purchase and their tracks became clogged by boulders. To support Mendler's attack two more armoured brigades were brought up from the West Bank, and five infantry brigades were assigned to take part.

The Syrian bunkers were well protected and, with Egypt and Jordan knocked out of the war, the Syrian soldiers knew they would be next in the firing line. In theory, the Israeli frontal attack – in broad daylight, up a steep slope towards well-prepared defensive positions – should have been suicidal. The Syrian troops poured heavy fire into the advancing Israelis, knocking out three of the bulldozers; some Israeli tanks were also swiftly destroyed and their officers killed. However, the Israelis enjoyed unchal-lenged air power which enabled them to force their way up the slopes and they did not stop, despite the mounting loses.

Fortunately for the Israelis, the Syrians foolishly kept the bulk of their armoured forces in reserve at a safe distance. Their defences were relatively light, with limited numbers of dug-in tanks and supporting anti-tank guns. Once the fighting started, the Syrians had no way of getting reinforcements up the escarpment without attracting air attack. Israeli fighter-bombers flew 1,077 ground attack sorties against Syrian targets, more than against Egypt and Jordan.

The Syrians fought desperately to hold their positions at Tel Azaziyat, Tel Faq'r and Bourj Bravil. At Tel Faq'r the officers and their men stood firm and shot down the first wave of Israeli infantry and only a few men of the second wave reached the wire and the minefield. The third wave, though, carried the Israelis into the Syrian trenches, where for three hours both sides fought desperate hand-to-hand combat. Elsewhere the Syrians simply fled, especially once the Syrian Government had prematurely announced the fall of Kuneitra, the 'capital' of the Golan Heights.

On the whole the Syrian troops, steeped in Soviet doctrine, lacked the flexibility and initiative required for fast-moving mechanized combat. Often the officers abandoned their men and in two instances when the Israelis overran Syrian gun emplacements they found the unfortunate crews chained to their guns to prevent desertion. Despite the bitter hand-to-hand fighting in the Syrian trenches, their defences were pierced and by evening the Israelis were outside Kuneitra, some 25 kilometres inside Syria and just 65 kilometres short of Damascus. The Syrian Army withdrew, abandoning much of its equipment in the process.

One Israeli commander reported on 10 June 1967, 'We arrived almost without hindrance at the gates of Kuneitra ... All around us there were huge quantities of booty. Everything was in working order. Tanks with their engines still running, communication equipment still in operation had been abandoned. We captured Kuneitra without a fight.' Another senior Israeli officer complained, 'It was very difficult to make contact with the retreating enemy. Whenever we arrived, they had withdrawn their forces and we could not make contact. We fired on a number of tanks only to discover that they had been deserted. Their crews had abandoned them.'

By this stage the Syrian General Staff knew that it was pointless to try to fight off the Israeli advance any further. They requested a cease-fire, which took effect that evening. Although the Israelis were left in possession of the Golan Heights, their tank losses amounted to 160, whereas the Syrians only lost seventy-three. Such was Syrian resistance that by the time the road junction at Kala had been captured, the Sherman battalion was down to its last three tanks. Another victory had been secured, but at considerable sacrifice by the Israeli tank corps.

# Chapter 7

# Doc Lap Palace

## The Vietnam War, 1968–1975

Within just five days of North Vietnam's large-scale Tet offensive commencing in 1968, most of the South's provincial capitals had fallen. Despite
the widespread attacks, two areas emerged as major objectives: the cities
of Saigon, the South's capital, and Hue. These were the only places where
the fighting was particularly protracted. The Communists' most significant
success was at Hue, where the North Vietnamese Army's 4th and 6th
Regiments and six Viet Cong battalions, under General Tran Do, captured
most of the city and held it for a month. As with all the Communist assaults
across South Vietnam, the seizure of Hue was a race against time before the
Army of the Republic of Vietnam and its US allies could muster enough
forces to mount determined counter-attacks.

While General Tran Do gathered around 10,000 men for the attack on
Hue, General Truong, the commander of the weak 1st Division of the
Army of the Republic of Vietnam (ARVN), was able to call on forces from
outside the city. These included infantry, armoured and airborne units,
while to the southeast were three US Marine Corps battalions protecting
the Phu Bai air base, Highway One and all the western approaches to the
city. To keep the Marines occupied, the Communist forces had to attack
the air base and the Truoi river and Phu Loc areas. Key amongst the
ARVN reinforcements were the 1st Airborne Task Force, located 17 kilometres north of Hue, and two battalions of the 3rd Regiment with the 7th
Armored Cavalry Squadron (equipped with Chaffees) based to the southwest. Communist blocking forces would have to fight to prevent these units
getting into the city.

The assault on Hue started in the early hours of 31 January 1968. The
North Vietnamese Army's 6th Regiment attacked the western bank of the
Citadel with the aim of seizing the Mang Ca compound, the Tay Loc
airfield and the imperial palace. The NVA's 4th Regiment assaulted the

American Military Assistance Command Vietnam compound situated in the southern part of the city. The Western Gate was seized and the NVA's 800th and 802nd Battalions drove north. At Tay Loc the 800th was stopped by the ARVN Hac Bao ('Black Panthers') Strike Company and the 802nd was thwarted at Mang Ca by an ad hoc force of 200 South Vietnamese troops.

South of the city the troops of the ARVN's 7th Armoured Cavalry Squadron attempted to fight their way into the outskirts. Although they got over the An Cuu bridge and reached the New City, the column was forced to retreat after its commander, Lieutenant Phan Hu Chi, was killed. To the southeast the US Marines at Phu Bai also found themselves under attack, but the 1st Battalion, 1st Marines, was despatched to Hue with its tanks and fought its way to the MACV compound. Marine M48 and ARVN Chaffee tanks were then sent to secure the bridge over the Perfume river. They soon found that Hue beyond the river had fallen to the enemy, who had dug in.

The attack on Hue was launched on the same day as the assault on Saigon and by nightfall the Communist forces had raised their flag over the ancient Citadel. During the day US/ARVN forces pushed into the city to rescue some American advisers and then promptly withdrew. Only in Hue did the attackers receive any measure of local support, principally from the pro-Communist student population. The commitment of US/ARVN troops to the defence of Khe Sanh and other locations in the northern provinces had the desired effect, causing a critical delay in gathering sufficient reinforcements to regain control of Hue.

The Marines were ready by early February, after Lieutenant General Cushman, the commander of the 1st Corps Marines, and Lieutenant General Lam, the Vietnamese force commander, had rounded up enough men. Three US Marine and eleven ARVN battalions had to fight a bloody three-week battle for Hue. The Communist forces refused to withdraw or surrender. They hoped that the longer they held out, the more likely it was that they would spark a general rising.

One problem that arose in Hue, but which was not an issue in Saigon, was that the city was full of sacred religious and historical buildings. Initially, the attackers showed restraint in using artillery and air power, but it rapidly became apparent that the only way to force the enemy out of the city would be to destroy it building by building. When the Marines approached the Citadel, the NVA/VC defenders blew up the main bridge over the Perfume river. For four days the Marines were held on the far banks in the full knowledge that they would have to storm the ancient fortifications and clear it inch by inch. Eventually they forced a crossing and surrounded the Citadel.

During the period 11–15 February the South Vietnamese forces, with American support, fought to clear the rest of the city. The street fighting was bitter and even after massive bombardment the surviving NVA/VC converted the rubble into strongpoints. The assault on the Citadel did not commence until 20 February, but within two days the Communist forces held only the southwestern corner and on the following day even that position was finally eliminated. On 25 February the whole city was described as 'secure'.

At 0300 hours on 31 January 1968 some 5,000 NVA/VC troops under General Tran Van Tra successfully infiltrated Saigon and launched their surprise attack. Over 700 men assaulted Tan Son Nhut outside the city and the neighbouring MACV compound in order to eliminate the command post of the US 7th Air Force. Because it was Tet (the Vietnamese New Year), the sound of firecrackers exploding masked any gunfire, giving an element of surprise to the Communists. In fact, the surprise was so complete that the entire force slipped into Tan Son Nhut without the alarm being raised. The NVA/VC forces got to within 1,000 yards of their objective before being challenged. It was then that the shooting started.

For a while chaos reigned across the city as enemy guerrilla units popped up everywhere. It took until 5 February to stabilize the situation and confine enemy resistance to the suburb of Cholon. It soon became apparent that this area had been the original staging post for the assault on Saigon. While the ground troops struggled to regain control, American B-52 heavy bombers attacked suspected enemy troop concentrations 16 kilometres from the capital. This was the closest the big bombers came to the city and although they hit their targets, subsequent intelligence confirmed only forty-two kills, none of whom could be positively identified as Communist troops.

The Americans and the ARVN, supported by tanks, artillery, helicopters and ground-attack aircraft, fought to drive 1,600 Communists from their stronghold in Cholon. However, NVA/VC forces launched a counter-attack from Cholon and other parts of the city on 18 February. Tan Son Nhut was attacked once more but the NVA/VC got no further than the outer perimeter as the defenders were on their guard this time. Reports estimated that up to three NVA divisions were outside the city, but they failed to get in and Cholon was pacified three days later. Although skirmishing continued on the outskirts of the city, the Tet Offensive in Saigon was over.

The leadership in South Vietnam was traumatized by the whole affair and realized, a little too late, that the ARVN was not up to the job of protecting the country from the combined efforts of the NVA and Viet Cong. As a result, the government moved to mobilize 200,000 extra troops – previous attempts to do so had been thwarted by political opposition. The average South Vietnamese rallied behind their government as they were appalled by the North's actions over Tet and the widespread guerrilla attacks that had targeted their homes.

Peace talks commenced in Paris in May 1968 and the following year America began to reduce its military presence. After Tet there was a general mobilization in South Vietnam, heralding the policy of 'Vietnamization', and the period 1968–1972 saw a major expansion of South Vietnam's armed forces. The North was biding its time, infiltrating 115,000 men into the South to make good its losses. The bulk of the American, Australian, New Zealand, South Korean and Thai troops pulled out in the early 1970s.

After the US had begun to withdraw its forces from South Vietnam, the NVA had become ever bolder in its use of tanks. The first major tank-vs-tank engagement took place in 1971 when the ARVN forces deployed during Operation Lam Son 719 (designed to cut the Ho Chi Minh Trail in Laos) found their M41A3 tanks up against NVA PT-76s and T-54s near Hill 31. For the loss of just four tanks they destroyed seven T-54s and sixteen PT-76s. In the NVA's Easter offensive the following year they used large numbers of tanks to spearhead their attacks on three separate fronts. These units were the most heavily armed ever to enter South Vietnam; the attacking forces were equipped with T-34, T-54 and PT-76 tanks, along with SA-2 and SA-7 missiles and 130mm guns. The offensive, launched from North Vietnam, Laos and Cambodia, was fought as a conventional battle and the North's tank crews, lacking infantry and artillery support, suffered at the hands of the better-trained South Vietnamese.

The main attack, which began on 30 March 1972, across the northern demilitarized zone employed a total of 100 tanks. To fend them off, the South Vietnamese deployed their 20th Tank Regiment. This had been formed only the previous year, equipped with M48A3 tanks and supported by an armoured rifle company. In practice, the latter were to ride on the tanks to provide close protection from anti-tank weapons. The regiment came under the 1st Armored Brigade, which also took control of four armoured cavalry regiments.

The 20th Tank Regiment, with forty-four operational tanks, went into action along the Mieu Giang river at Dong Ha in April 1972. There it engaged North Vietnamese PT-76s and T-54s on 9 April and successfully destroyed sixteen T-54s and captured a Type 59, suffering little more than superficial damage in return. However, on 23 April the North Vietnamese began to use the Soviet AT-3 Sagger wire-guided anti-tank missile for the very first time. By the end of the month the much-depleted regiment had only eighteen operational tanks. In danger of being surrounded, the 1st Armored Brigade withdrew and in the process the 20th Tank Regiment and the 4th, 11th, 17th and 18th Armored Cavalry Regiments lost all their tanks. The brigade had been deployed mainly in a static defensive role, but its sacrifice helped slow the enemy long enough for reinforcements to be brought up to halt the offensive.

Elsewhere, the South's 2nd Armored Brigade, with elements of the 14th and 19th Armored Cavalry Regiments, was lost defending the Tan Canh area. Two North Vietnamese divisions, supported by the 203rd Tank Regiment, reached Kontum City but failed to take it. Kontum was relieved by the 3rd Armored Cavalry Regiment on 19 June 1972. Those Communist tanks used for attacks on Kontum and Binh Long provinces, without adequate artillery or infantry support, fell prey to ARVN anti-tank weapons. US air power again played a decisive role and the North Vietnamese Army lost 250 armoured vehicles. In one engagement ARVN M48s destroyed eleven NVA tanks and from that point onwards conventional tank warfare became commonplace. Despite the peace treaty of 1973, the North kept up the military pressure.

By 1975 the North had amassed approximately 600 Soviet T-54 and Chinese Type 59 medium tanks. The NVA had learned their lesson from three years earlier and had trained for combined arms operations. This time there was no stopping the NVA, employing sudden assault and deep, advance tactics. By this stage the ARVN armoured units had been greatly weakened due to shortages of spares and ammunition. Under such conditions they were unable to halt the enemy armour. The ARVN was exhausted and without American air support it was unable to prevent the NVA rolling south into Saigon.

Advancing 50 kilometres a day, within two months the NVA were in striking distance of Saigon. Four NVA armoured columns converged on the city on 30 April 1975. The last of the ARVN's M41s were knocked out by T-54s belonging to the 203rd Armoured Regiment on Hong Tap Tu Street. This was the final tank-vs-tank engagement. Shortly afterwards, Communist tanks entered the grounds of the Doc Lap Palace, thereby bringing the Vietnam War to an end. A tank bearing the turret number '844' symbolically crashed through the gates. South Vietnamese officers trapped in the palace surrendered under the watchful eye of a North Vietnamese light tank. It was one of the high points in the T-54's career and an iconic episode in the wider Cold War. It was also a humiliating moment for American foreign policy in Southeast Asia. The image of triumphant North Vietnamese tanks outside Doc Lap Palace flashed around the world.

It was not long before China fell out with its former ally. Several hundred tanks, including Type 59s, were involved in China's invasion of northern Vietnam in 1979 in response to Vietnamese actions in Cambodia. This region was not suitable for tank warfare and tough Vietnamese resistance persuaded the Chinese to withdraw after they suffered an estimated 26,000 dead and 37,000 wounded. Notably, the Chinese lost tanks at Cao Bang. The Vietnamese claimed rather fancifully to have destroyed 280 tanks during the fighting, which is probably more than were committed to the invasion.

Even if exaggerated, the Chinese casualties and the swift end to the war highlighted the embarrassing shortcomings of the People's Liberation Army. Although the Type 59 upgrade was under way in the shape of the Type 69, it was not available in 1979. When the latter first appeared military experts considered it a formidable weapon, bearing little resemblance to the obsolete T-54 from which it was derived. Nonetheless, it was a prime example of China's continued policy of modernizing its armed forces by improving old obsolete Soviet designs and utilizing existing factories rather than designing or importing brand-new weapons.

*Chapter 8*

# Confusing Enemies
## The Indo-Pakistan War, 1971

The partition of the Indian sub-continent into independent Hindu India and Muslim East and West Pakistan in 1947 was far from satisfactory, leaving simmering resentment between all three areas. The two halves of Pakistan were separated by 1,600 kilometres of Indian territory, making effective centralized government impossible. Almost immediately India and West Pakistan went to war over the future alignment of Kashmir. When the fighting ended, Pakistan had suffered the heaviest casualties and India was left in control of two-thirds of the state. From that point on, both sides began to build up their armed forces.

Pakistan's close relationship with America and Britain changed when they aided India after the 1962 Indo-China Border War. The Indian 4th Corps lost more than 7,000 men killed, wounded or captured in just twenty days, having failed to stop Chinese incursions into disputed territory. Having made their point, the Chinese withdrew and returned all the Indians' captured weapons. This embarrassing defeat led to a major reform of the Indian armed forces. The fighting, though, had taken place along India's northeastern frontier in the Himalayas, so did not witness any armoured warfare.

Three years later India and Pakistan went to war again. On 5 August 1965 Pakistani forces attacked the Indian-held eastern part of partitioned Kashmir and the fighting spread to encompass the northern Punjab. The Pakistanis countered the Indians in the Chhamb area with a major armoured attack. In response, the Indian Army conducted Operation Grand Slam, which was a three-pronged armoured assault along the axis from Amritsar towards Lahore on 6 September 1965. Their intention was to draw out Pakistan's tanks from the Chhamb sector and then overwhelm them in battle. Both sides fought each other to a stalemate. Shortly after they agreed to a cease-fire, with each side having lost about 200 tanks.

The arms embargo after the 1965 Indo–Pakistan War forced Pakistan into the arms of China and the Soviet Union. India was supplied with Soviet T-54s in the late 1960s, while Pakistan obtained both T-54/55s and Chinese-built Type 59s. Confusingly, they subsequently used these against each other during the 1971 Indo–Pakistan War. In this conflict India was able to muster about 450 T-54/55s, while Pakistan had 250 T-55s and Type 59s. These represented a third of the Indian tank force and a quarter of the Pakistanis'. Inevitably, using the same tanks caused unwelcome recognition problems. The Indians fitted a large dummy fume extractor two-thirds of the way up the gun barrel of their T-54s, making the gun look like an L7 105mm, which armed their Centurions. Also, a drum was installed on the rear of the turret to alter the tank's silhouette in the hope of avoiding friendly fire. Examples of this ad hoc conversion were later photographed on the outskirts of Dacca and at Chamba. The Indians had 200 Centurions and 250 Shermans, while the Pakistanis had 200 M-47 and M-48 Pattons. In addition, the Indians were able to field some 300 Vijayanta (British Vickers-designed battle tanks manufactured in India under licence).

East Pakistan greatly resented being dominated by West Pakistan and on 26 March 1971 declared itself the independent state of Bangladesh. To try to prevent this, the Pakistani military went on the rampage in Bangladesh, though some 70,000 troops defected. Massacres followed and 6 million Bangladeshis fled into India. In response, the Indian government refused to allow Pakistani aircraft to fly over India, obliging them to go via Sri Lanka. The Indians decided that supporting the separatists would be a good thing and began to plan the defeat of the Pakistani Army in Bangladesh. In the meantime, India began to train the Mukti Bahini – Bangladeshi guerrillas.

When war broke out, the Pakistani forces operating in West and East Pakistan had the problem of fighting a two-front war against their much larger neighbour. The Pakistani high command decided the best way to help its surrounded forces in Bangladesh was to launch armoured attacks from West Pakistan in order to distract as much of the Indian Army's strength as possible. First, they attempted to neutralize the Indian Air Force. In the opening stages of the war the Pakistani Air Force tried to catch India's jets on the ground, but failed to do so. As a result, the Indians were able to launch air attacks on the massing Pakistani divisions from 4 to 6 December 1971.

The key tank units in West Pakistan were the 1st and 6th Armoured Divisions allocated to the 1st and 2nd Corps respectively. To the north the

Pakistanis deployed their 12th and 23rd Infantry Divisions in the mountainous Kashmir region. Either side of Lahore was held by the 2nd Corps, with the 8th, 15th and 17th Infantry and 6th Armoured Divisions, and 4th Corps, with the 10th and 11th Infantry Divisions. Further south was the 1st Corps, with the 7th and 33rd Infantry and 1st Armoured Divisions, holding the Multan to Ramgarh sector. In the most southerly region of the Sind, the 18th Infantry Division was responsible for Hyderabad and Nayor Chor.

In Kashmir the Pakistani attack towards Poonch made little progress and instead the Indians penetrated the Pakistani defences in front of Kahuta. At Chamba the Indians were forced back over the Munawar Tawi on 7 December. However, the Pakistani 2nd Corps was prevented from crossing the river and the Indians pinched out the Pakistani salient over the Munawar below Chamba at Akhnur. A tank battle engagement took place around Zafarwal and Pathankot on 15 and 16 December 1971, south of the Chamba salient, involving the 6th Armoured Division.

In the Punjab the largest tank battle of the war occurred around the Shakargarh salient. Here the British-supplied Centurion tanks of the Indian Army's Poona Horse Regiment fought the Pakistani's American-supplied Pattons serving with the 6th Armoured Division. This division also contained elements of Hodson's Horse and Skinner's Horse. Ironically all three regiments had once been part of the British Indian Army. The Poona Auxiliary Horse was first raised way back in 1817, while Skinner's Horse was formed by James Skinner even earlier, in 1803, to serve with the Bengal Army. By the Second World War it was known as Skinner's Horse (1st Duke of York's Own). William Hodson created three Bengal irregular cavalry regiments during the Indian Mutiny in the late 1850s. One regiment was disbanded but the other two became the 9th and 10th Bengal Cavalry Regiments. They eventually became Hodson's Horse (4th Duke of Cambridge's Own Lancers). After independence the Indians and Pakistanis maintained these regiments.

The fighting did not go well for the Pakistani tankers. The Indians claimed they knocked out forty-five Pattons and also made gains around Khem Karan south of Amritsar. As a result, the Indian Army gained control of 1000 square kilometres of Pakistani territory in the Punjab. Way to the south the Pakistani 1st Armoured Division came to grief in the soft sands at Ramgarh. The Indian Air Force pounced on the division and claimed thirty-four tanks and around a hundred other vehicles. In the Sind the Pakistanis lost even more territory. Indian tanks attempted to take Naya Chor and this forced the Pakistanis to redeploy their armour from the centre and the north. The Indians struggled to make progress across the open desert and Naya Chor was saved by the cease-fire. Nonetheless, by the end of the war the Indians were in control of more than 2,500 square kilometres of West Pakistan.

Meanwhile, the Indian attack on Bangladesh opened on 4 December 1971 with a successful assault on Akhaura to the east of Dacca. They also took Feni, which cut the road south to Chittagong. Three days after the war broke out India recognized Bangladeshi independence. Western Bangladesh was one of the few places suitable for armoured warfare and it was here that the Indians deployed substantial armour. On Bangladesh's western frontier the Indian forces seized Darsana and Jessore.

The Pakistani Army was reliant on its infantry divisions, which, under attack from three sides, had an impossible task trying to defend the country. However, most of Bangladesh is bisected by rivers and marshes, so the Indians deployed their Soviet-supplied PT-76 light amphibious tanks. During the river crossings the Indians discovered that these tanks overheated after 30 minutes in the water. In consequence many of the tanks had to be towed and the Indians relied on helicopter assaults to secure their initial bridgeheads. Once they had reached Tangail north of Dacca the city was surrounded. By 14 December 1971, despite numerous river obstacles, the Indian Army had taken most of Bangladesh and the local Pakistani forces surrendered two days later.

The British *Sunday Times* was suitably impressed and reported on 19 December 1971, 'It took only twelve days for the Indian Army to smash its way to Dacca, an achievement reminiscent of the German Blitzkrieg across France in 1940. The strategy was the same: speed, ferocity and flexibility.' The war was a humiliating defeat for Pakistan, which lost control of Bangladesh's resources. The Pakistanis also lost a considerable number of tanks before the Indian Prime Minister announced the cease-fire. Because India was a much bigger customer and a counterweight to China, the Soviet Union stepped up its arms supplies to Delhi. By the end of the decade the Indian Army could field some 900 T-54/55s. Even by the mid-1990s, when it was equipped with the newer T-72, it still had 500.

While the Chinese Type 59 delivered to Pakistan reportedly had 'a good degree of finish', their rate of fire was hampered because the main gun lacked a stabilizer and the turret had no power traverse. The armour was also poor, with just 100mm on the turret and 85mm on the hull. The Soviets were perhaps understandably dismissive of the Type 59, with Colonel K. Borisov noting that it does 'not fully meet requirements, since [it] possess inadequate manoeuvrability'.

Nonetheless, Pakistan desperately needed more tanks to defend itself against India and with Chinese assistance set up a tank rebuild factory at Taxila in the late 1970s. This was equipped to overhaul tank engines as well as repair and manufacture parts needed for the rebuild programme. Colonel Borisov may have had political motives for criticizing the Type 59, but China's willingness to open the Taxila plant not only signalled Pakistan's commitment to the tank but also that there was an underlying problem with it. By the mid-1990s Pakistan had amassed a mighty tank fleet some 2,000 strong that included 1,200 Type 59s, 200 Type 69s and around 50 T-54/55s. The Bangladeshi Army created after the war was also equipped with T-54/55 and Type 59/69 tanks.

# Chapter 9

# Clash of the Titans

## The Yom Kippur War, 1973

### Sinai

Despite Israel's victories, the threats to its very existence continued. The Arabs neither forgot nor forgave the humiliation they had suffered during the Six Day War, and they planned retribution. At 1400 hours on 6 October 1973 the Arabs launched a surprise two-front assault under the codename Operation Badr. Egyptian and Syrian armour swept all before them and the state of Israel teetered on the very brink of collapse. It was Yom Kippur or the Day of Atonement, the Jewish fast day, when the Israelis were least prepared for war. The Israeli Defence Forces suffered staggering losses and struggled desperately to stem the tide – and then a miracle happened: the Arab Blitzkrieg was stopped in its tracks.

The Yom Kippur War was a clash of armoured titans. The Arab states committed 3,000 tanks: the Egyptians had around 1,650 T-54/55s, plus about 100 more modern T-62s; the Syrians had around 1,100 T54/55s and an unknown number of T-62s; and between them they also had about 300 T-34s. As the battle progressed, Iraq committed up to 250 T-54/55s and Jordan about 100 Centurions. During the fighting the Soviet Union shipped in another 1,200 tanks to Egypt and Syria as battlefield replacements.

Israel deployed about 1,700 tanks at the start of the war; about half were Centurions, and the rest were mostly M48s, but also some newer M60s. They also deployed about 150 Super Shermans, which they had up-gunned with a French 105mm gun, and some modified T-54/55s. The IDF should have been overwhelmed, especially as Sagger, the Soviet wire-guided suit-case missile, greatly compromised the Israeli tanks. But luckily for the Israelis, the T-54/55 was obsolete and their forces had superior stand-off capabilities and tactics.

Following the Six Day War Israel had been left in control of the Egyptian Sinai desert, the Palestinian Gaza Strip, the Syrian Golan Heights and the Jordanian West Bank and East Jerusalem. The result was that for the first time Israel had some good natural defensive barriers to protect its borders. Six years later Egypt and Syria and their neighbours were determined to recapture this lost territory. By 1973 the Arab armies were armed to the teeth, thanks to the Soviet Union, which had equipped them with thousands of tanks, jet fighters, missiles and artillery. Holding the Egyptian, Jordanian and Syrian frontiers was the IDF 'Zahal', consisting of just 75,000 regulars and reservists.

The Israeli triumph during the Six Day War and the key role played in it by their armoured corps ensured a central role for the armoured forces in post-war planning. After 1967 Israel upgraded its M48s to produce the Magach 3 and 5, followed by the M60 upgrade known as the Magach 6 and 7. The Israelis captured several hundred repairable T-54s and T-55s and these were modified and reissued for Israeli use as the Ti-67 or Tiran. Similarly, captured T-62s were reissued as the T-62I. The French-supplied AMX-13 proved to be wholly inadequate when it came up against the Egyptian T-54s and was relegated to a reconnaissance role. Likewise, the Israeli M3 half-tracks, which had been in service since 1948, were now too vulnerable and were replaced by the American M113 tracked armoured personnel carrier, which the Israelis called the Zelda.

Israel's 252nd Armoured Division, with around 280 tanks in three brigades, was deployed along the Suez Canal, supported by three reserve armoured divisions. Across the Canal massing for the attack were ten Egyptian divisions supported by 1,600 tanks, organized into two armies. The key Egyptian armoured formations were the 4th and 21st Armoured Divisions and the 3rd, 6th and 23rd Mechanized Divisions. They were supported by various foreign allied contingents that included Algerian and Libyan armoured brigades. General Gonen was in charge of Israel's Southern Command, which included the 143rd, 162nd and 252nd Armoured Divisions; in all these mustered some nine armoured brigades. Once the Syrian front had been stabilized, these forces were later reinforced by elements of the 146th and 440th Composite Divisions.

The armoured forces supporting the Egyptian 2nd Army comprised the 21st Armoured Division (with two tank brigades and one mechanized brigade) and the 23rd Mechanized Division (with two mechanized brigades and one tank brigade). The armoured spearhead of the 3rd Army was made up of the 4th Armoured and 6th Mechanized Divisions, while the Egyptian GHQ had the 3rd Mechanized Division plus an independent tank brigade held in reserve. The Egyptian offensive was to take them over the Canal between Kantara and Ismailia and to the south of the Great Bitter and Little Bitter Lakes in the Suez City area. These two separate crossings by the Egyptian 2nd and 3rd Armies respectively, divided by the two lakes, immediately betrayed a fatal flaw that the Israelis would later capitalize on.

The Egyptian assault opened with 2,000 guns firing a deluge of 100,500 shells onto the Israeli defences known as the Bar-Lev Line. Then 150 MiG fighters attacked Israel's air bases, command posts and communications centres. When the Israeli Air Force tried to intervene, it was met by a barrage of Soviet-supplied surface-to-air missiles (SAMs). The Israeli Air Force lost a huge number of planes, though only fifteen were actually downed in air-to-air combat.

The Egyptians' phased attack was designed to cross the Canal, neutralize the Israeli defences on the eastern bank, establish divisional bridgeheads to meet the inevitable Israeli counter-attacks and then link up the bridge-heads. Using powerful hosepipes, the Egyptians breached the Israeli sand berm protecting the eastern bank and threw a series of pontoon bridges over the Suez Canal. Getting across was a considerable feat and its success depended on several factors: firstly, the choice of date – Yom Kippur was one of the holiest Jewish days and many troops were on leave; second, meticulous planning; and third, the Egyptians' impressive air defence system, which was much more sophisticated than it had been in 1967, and for a while at least kept the Israeli Air Force at bay.

During the early 1970s the Egyptians and Syrians, with Soviet assis-tance, constructed surface-to-air missile networks that were even more formidable than those used by North Vietnam. The Arabs also deployed the SA-6 Gainful SAM system for the first time and it was this that posed the greatest threat to the Israeli Air Force. Being fully mobile, and with unknown target acquisition radar frequencies, the Israelis were reduced to the expedient of dropping Second World War-style 'chaff' to blind it. Crucially, the Israelis greatly benefited from America's experiences in the Vietnam War. The SA-2 and SA-3 missile systems also used by the Egyptians were relatively immobile and most of their codes had been broken. Nor did the SA-6 threat last long either.

During the crossing of the Suez Canal the Soviets were able for the first time to operationally test their PMP bridge, which had been developed to tackle Europe's wide rivers. The bridge consisted of box-shaped pontoons carried on tracked vehicles; hydraulic arms deployed the first pontoon, then a vehicle would drive onto the pontoon and deliver a second section, and so on. The PMP system was able to lay the pontoons at a rate of about 15 feet a minute, so the Egyptian engineers were able to get over the canal in just under half an hour. (Using old Second World War-style pontoon bridging would have taken the Egyptians at least two hours.) The net result was that Egypt's tanks were soon rumbling over the canal at a faster rate than had been anticipated by Israeli intelligence. Within ten hours the Egyptians had successfully deployed 500 tanks and their protective air defence system on the eastern bank. However, this was to be the high point of the Egyptian military achievements.

Over the next two days the Egyptian 2nd and 3rd Armies successfully swarmed across the Canal and fought off twenty-three desperate Israeli counter-attacks. During Operation Badr the Egyptians took about 1,000 tanks over the Suez Canal, leaving behind some 330 as an operational reserve on the west bank, while there was also a strategic reserve of another 250 tanks (though 120 of the latter were from the Presidential Guard and would only be released in the direst of emergencies). Egyptian tank-hunter squads also came over the Canal, lugging their RPGs and Sagger wire-guided anti-tank missiles. These proved deadly to the Israeli armour. One Egyptian unit knocked out eight M60s defending the Bar Lev line within the space of just ten minutes. Sergeant Ibrahim Abdel Monein el Masri was the most successful tank killer, accounting for twenty-six Israeli tanks, which gained him the Star of Sinai, Egypt's highest bravery award.

To protect the tank-hunter teams from air attack, the Egyptians were equipped with the man-portable surface-to-air missile launcher known as the SA-7 Grail. This 5ft-long shoulder-fired weapon provided low-altitude air defence. The Israelis, though, were already familiar with the SA-7, as the Egyptians had employed it extensively against Israeli jets during the War of Attrition following the Six Day War, and Israeli counter-measures greatly hampered its already poor kill ratio. Nonetheless, combined with the Egyptian Army's other air defence missiles, for a while the SA-7 helped stop the Israeli Air Force pressing home its attacks on the advancing Egyptian armoured columns.

The first Israeli counter-attacks by General Mendler's 252nd Armoured Ugda (consisting of the 14th, 401st Reserve and 460th Reserve Armoured Brigades) were easily beaten off with heavy losses thanks to the roaming Egyptian tank-hunters. It was also in part due to a lack of mechanized infantry support that left the Israeli armour vulnerable. By the afternoon of

7 October 1973 the 252nd had lost some 200 of its 300 tanks. Counter-attacks on 8 October were also repulsed with further heavy losses suffered by the 167th Armoured Division near Kantara, the Chinese Farm and Fridan. The division's three brigades were left with just 120 tanks that night. General Sharon's 143rd Armoured Division then suffered smaller losses attacking the Chinese Farm defences on the 9th.

The Israelis moved a reserve armoured division into Sinai on 8 October, tasking the 190th Brigade to counter-attack towards the Egyptian pontoon bridges over the Canal. They ran into determined Egyptian resistance using the latest anti-tank weapons, including Sagger anti-tank missiles and RPG-7s. The brigade was cut to pieces. In the meantime, the Israelis had defeated the Syrians by 9 October and easily fended off the supporting Iraqi and Jordanian tanks. This left the IDF free to redeploy its armour against the Egyptians.

By 10 October the Egyptians had 75,000 men, supported by 800 tanks, deployed in the Sinai. In light of the Syrian defeat on the Golan Heights, both sides now prepared to go on the offensive. The Israelis decided to allow the Egyptians to move forward first, beyond the cover of their air defences. The Egyptians duly struck on 14 October, but this was tank warfare and the Israelis excelled at it; their gunners pinned down the Egyptian attacks, while other forces struck them in the flanks. By the end of the day the Egyptians had lost up to 300 tanks and the survivors were soon in full retreat. The following day the Israelis counter-attacked, crossed the Canal in the Deversoir area of Great Bitter Lake and then drove back the Egyptian 2nd Army along the eastern bank of the lake.

General Sharon, commanding three armoured and two parachute brigades, located a gap between the Egyptian 2nd and 3rd Armies to the east of the Great Bitter Lake on 15 October. He launched an armoured brigade in a diversionary attack against the Egyptian 2nd Army in front of Ismailia. He then sent a second one in southward loop to outflank them with the aim of crossing the Canal just north of Great Bitter Lake. This was achieved, though initially Sharon could only get forces across by pontoon ferry until bridges had been built the following day.

Disastrously for the Egyptians, they had no contingency plans for the Israelis crossing the Canal. At most they had anticipated that the IDF might try to clear the east bank with encircling operations, but there was no thought that they might cross the Canal. It took the Egyptians 24 hours to launch both their 2nd and 3rd Corps into a counter-attack against the neck of the Israeli penetration just northeast of the Great Bitter Lake, resulting in what became known as the 'Battle of Chinese Farm'. The fighting raged throughout the night of 16/17 October with heavy losses on both sides. By the middle of the 17th Israeli armour was pouring over the Canal, sealing the fate of those Egyptian forces on the eastern bank.

By the time of the first cease-fire, the IDF had secured a foothold on the far bank of Great Bitter and Little Bitter Lakes, west of the Suez Canal. At the same time the Egyptian 2nd Army held a swathe of territory east of the Suez Canal between Port Said to the north and Ismailia to the south. South of the lower Bitter Lake and beyond Suez City the Egyptian 3rd Army held another strip. Despite the cease-fire, both sides sought to improve their positions. Crucially, the IDF not only enlarged its bridgehead west of the lakes, but also drove south to Suez City and beyond to Adabiya on the Gulf of Suez. Despite Egyptian counter-attacks, this move trapped 20,000 men of the 3rd Army, cutting them off from drinking water, food and ammunition supplies. In the area west of the Canal the Egyptians had dug in many of their elderly T–34s hull-down in the sand, and in the space of half a mile eighteen of them were destroyed by Israeli jets. Having caught the Egyptian 3rd Army, Israel finally agreed to a cease-fire on 24 October. This left the Israelis occupying 1550 square kilometres of Egyptian soil west of the Canal, encircling the 3rd Army and holding 9,000 prisoners.

## The Golan Heights

Israeli Defence Minister Moshe Dayan was not blind to the Arabs' military build-up both in the Sinai and on the Golan Heights during the early 1970s. He inspected the IDF forces on the Golan Heights on 26 September 1973 and warned them, 'Stationed along the Syrian border are hundreds of Syrian tanks and cannon within effective range, as well as an anti-aircraft system of a density similar to that of the Egyptians' along the Suez Canal.' While Dayan put a brave face on things, he also put the army on alert and quietly reinforced the single under-strength armoured brigade in the area by redeploying the 7th Armoured Brigade, which had been drawn back to armoured headquarters at Beersheba.

It has been estimated that the first wave of the Syrian assault involved up to 700 tanks, with 300 striking towards Kuneitra in the middle of the Golan and the other 400 striking up the road from Sheikh Miskin to Rafid to the south of Kuneitra, all supported by infantry divisions. The intention was that the northern attack would cut the IDF's Golan defences in half by thrusting down the main Kuneitra–Naffak road. The southern attack would then link up at Naffak as well, as pushing south to El Al. In principle, it was a very sound plan.

The Golan was the fulcrum on which Israel's fate rested: if the IDF could not achieve victory there, then it would not have the resources to redeploy for a counter-attack against the Egyptians in the Sinai. While the latter offered strategic depth of 200 kilometres in which the IDF could conduct a fighting withdrawal, if ousted from the Golan the IDF faced defeat. From the front line of the IDF's forward defensive positions, facing east to the cliffs overlooking northern Israel, the Heights are just 27 kilometres deep. The IDF had no option but to stand and fight where it stood. The only advantage the IDF had on the Golan was that they were masters of tank warfare and expert gunners. The question was whether the Israelis would be able to knock out the Syrian tanks fast enough to prevent their positions being overrun.

Sitting on the Golan were two Israeli tank brigades, one of them only at three-quarters strength. To the north, defending the narrowest sector, was the 7th Armoured Brigade with about 100 tanks. The central and southern sectors from Kuneitra to Benot Jacov Bridge was held by the Shoam Brigade with around seventy-five tanks. The latter were outnumbered by five to one, and in some places even as much as twelve to one.

After the 1967 war, Israel had occupied and improved the Syrians' existing triple defence lines that it had overrun, and behind these lay sixteen fortified Jewish settlements. It would take at least 30 hours to mobilize reserves and get them up the road from Rosh Pina southwest of the Benot Jacov Bridge over the river Jordan and up the ascent to the Golan. It is not good tank country, as visibility is poor. Mount Hermon is the only place that gives a clear view of the Golan and all the way to Damascus. From there, the Israelis were able to watch the Syrian tanks marshalling on the plain below. Mount Hermon itself would soon fall to a Syrian helicopter commando assault. Meanwhile, the Syrian tanks were dug in to convince the IDF that they were adopting a purely defensive posture.

West of the Golan Heights Israel's Northern Command under General Hofi was made up of the 146th Armoured Division (the 9th, 19th, 20th and 70th Armoured Brigades) and the 240th Armoured Division (the 79th and 17th Armoured Brigades), plus the 36th Mechanized Division (the 7th and 188th Armoured Brigades). The Syrian and allied armoured forces facing the Golan Heights in October 1973 were quite formidable, on paper at least. They consisted of the Syrian 1st and 3rd Armoured Divisions, each comprising two tank brigades and a mechanized brigade. In addition, the 68th, 47th and 46th Tank Brigades supported the three Syrian infantry divisions allocated to the attack.

Arab allied units consisted of the Iraqi 3rd Armoured Division (the 6th and 12th Tank Brigades and the 8th Mechanized Brigade), along with the Jordanian 3rd Armoured Division; the latter fielded the 40th Armoured Brigade (the 2nd and 4th Armoured Regiments, the 1st Mechanized Battalion and the 7th Self-propelled Artillery Regiment) and the 92nd Armoured Brigade (the 12th and 13th Armoured Regiments, the 3rd Mechanized Battalion and the 17th Self-propelled Artillery Regiment). Morocco also provided a mechanized brigade and Saudi Arabia a mechanized regiment.

At the same time as Egypt launched its assault across Suez, Syria threw its five divisions, equipped with 1,200 tanks, into an operation that was expected to drive the Israelis from the Golan Heights in two days. In their path lay the two Israeli brigades with just 175 tanks. These units bought precious time while Israeli reinforcements were rushed to the front. What followed was a brutal slugging match as both sides attacked head-on. Quite remarkably, two damaged Israeli Centurions managed to hold off about 150 Syrian tanks, and during a 30-hour engagement knocked out more than 60. During the fighting in 'the Valley of Tears' the destruction was terrible. The Syrian 7th Division and the Assad Republican Guard lost 260 tanks, along with well over 200 tracked armoured personnel carriers, light armoured cars and bridge-layers. Of the Israelis' 100 'runners' from the 7th Armoured Brigade, they had just seven operational tanks left. Although the Syrians broke through, they lost 867 tanks to superior Israeli tactics and the timely arrival of reinforcements.

By 9 October the Israelis had triumphed against the Syrians. The Iraqi and Jordanian armour did not intervene until the second week of fighting; the Israelis broke up a counter-attack by the Iraqi 3rd Armoured Division on 13 October. It performed fairly poorly, losing 140 tanks to the Israelis. Three days later the 40th Armoured Brigade from the Jordanian 3rd Armoured Division ran into the Israelis and lost twenty tanks in two days; after this, it took no further part in the battle. When the fighting on the Golan Heights finally came to an end, it had cost the Syrians and their allies a total of 1,200 tanks.

\*   \*   \*

Altogether, the Egyptian and Syrian forces suffered 19,000 men killed and 51,000 wounded. The Israelis lost 606 officers and 6,900 men. Although Yom Kippur ended in a resounding Israeli victory, the 'Great Crossing', as the Egyptians dubbed it, was a major psychological victory for the Arabs. It had shown them that they could take on the hitherto invincible IDF and win. For the Syrians there was no such compensation. In addition, Egypt's Soviet-supplied wire-guided anti-tank missiles had shown how vulnerable tanks could be to tank-hunter groups.

The men of the Israeli armoured corps had paid a heavy price for their victory. In total, 1,450 tank crew were killed in the Sinai campaign, with another 3,143 wounded in action. The Israelis lost approximately 400 tanks, although many were later repaired. This led the Israelis to develop the Blazer reactive armour system (explosive blocks fitted to the outside of their tanks) and composite armour to protect them against the Arabs' new anti-tank weapons.

The Israeli armoured corps lost almost 40 per cent of its southern armoured groups in the first two days of the war, which highlighted the vital need for infantry support and ultimately led to the Merkava main battle tank being fitted with a rear troop bay. One of the most glaring deficiencies of the Israeli armour was their lack of night-vision equipment. The Egyptian and Syrian tanks had infra-red, including the British-made Xenon infra-red projector, giving them a serious advantage over the Israelis during the many night encounters. After 1973 the IDF began acquiring image-intensification and thermal-imaging night-vision systems with some urgency.

On the eve of the Yom Kippur War the Israelis fielded 540 M48A3s (with the upgraded 105mm gun) and M60A1s. By the end of the fighting they only had around 200 still operational. This was largely because of a severe vulnerability caused by the flammable hydraulic fluid at the front of the turret, which proved a major problem in fighting the Egyptians in the Sinai. If hit, the rapid turret traverse system tended to spray the fluid into the tank and onto the crew.

During the bitter and desperate fighting America airlifted vital military supplies to the Israelis through Operation Nickle Grass. Key amongst the supplies they brought in were artillery rounds and anti-tank missiles. According to the US Defence Intelligence Agency, the latter accounted for most of the Israeli tank kills. Fighter replacements totalling seventy-six aircraft were especially welcome after the heavy losses to the Egyptian air defences. It was this resupply that emboldened the Israelis to break through the Egyptian defences on the west side of the Canal. In contrast, American tank replacements were in insufficient numbers to have any real bearing on the fighting. The airlift delivered just twenty-nine tanks, but only four arrived before the cease-fire came into effect on 22 October 1973.

*Chapter 10*

# Armour in the Horn

## The Ethiopian Civil War, 1974–1991

It is hard to imagine the African bush witnessing armoured warfare, but that is exactly what happened across the vast continent. Fierce battles were fought involving large numbers of Soviet-built tanks. Like most Soviet weaponry the T-54/55 tank was a simple design, and this meant it was very easy for Third World armies to use, especially in Africa. The changing dynamics of the Cold War meant that allegiances constantly changed as countries sought willing arms suppliers. The T-54/55 became the most common tank to be found in Africa, where it saw widespread combat. It was employed in the wars fought in Angola, Ethiopia, Mozambique, Somalia and Sudan from the 1960s to the 1990s.

T-54/55 tanks from the Soviet Union were first supplied to Sudan in the late 1960s, by which time the country was blighted by civil war between the north and the south. By the late 1970s the Sudanese Army still had about 130 T-54/55s. When the Portuguese left Angola and Mozambique in 1975, both countries spiralled into bitter civil war. Moscow willingly supplied their newly installed Marxist governments with copious quantities of weapons, including tanks, to fight the rebels. In the mid- and late 1980s the Angolan Army deployed some of its 200 T-54/55s against the rebel UNITA (Union for the Total Independence of Angola) guerrillas during offensives towards the rebel strongholds at Mavinga and Jamba. Cuban troops, including a mechanized division supporting the Angolan Army, also operated the T-54/55 in Angola. The fighting involved the South Africans, who supported UNITA as part of their policy to contain the spread of Communism. Likewise, the Mozambican government had around 100 T-54/55s which it used against the Renamo rebel group.

In North Africa both Algeria and Morocco took delivery of T-54s. About fifty were supplied by the Soviet Union to the Algerians, while the Moroccans received twenty, plus another eighty built in Czechoslovakia during the mid-1960s. The Algerian-backed Polisario guerrillas employed them against the Moroccans during the war for Spanish Morocco in 1976–1991. Colonel Gaddafi's Libyan Army deployed the T-55 to Chad during the 1981–1987 war. Angola and Ethiopia in particular experienced prolonged and bitter fighting involving tanks.

The Ethiopian Revolutionary Army learned the value of tanks during the brief Ogaden War. At the start it was largely equipped with American-supplied armour, though some Soviet bloc equipment was just beginning to arrive. In early 1977 Somali guerrillas, numbering about 6,000 fighters, invaded eastern Ethiopia with the aim of incorporating it into a Greater Somalia. The invasion was a disaster for Ethiopia, as its military was already stretched thin by conflict in the northern provinces of Eritrea and Tigray. Morale was not good either. The Somali guerrillas soon claimed to have destroyed six Ethiopian battalions and eleven tanks. In the summer they cut the vital railway from Addis Ababa, the Ethiopian capital, to Djibouti. This crippled the country's foreign trade. The fighting then escalated dramatically.

The Somalis launched a full-scale armoured invasion on 12 July 1977, with their regular forces attacking north of the mountains towards Dire Dawa and south of them towards Harar. These forces numbered about 50,000 men supported by several hundred T-34 and T-54/55 tanks, as well as BTR armoured personnel carriers. They were backed by artillery and fighter jets. Just before the invasion, Somalia paraded its T-34s through the streets of Mogadishu in a blatant show of strength. At Gode the Ethiopian 5th Brigade, part of their 4th Division, collapsed, leaving large stocks of ammunition and weapons for the Somalis.

The Somalis reached Dire Dawa in mid-August with their 16th Armoured Battalion and two brigades, including the 15th Motorized Brigade. These forces consisted of thirty-two tanks and at least 2,500 soldiers. There they were met by the weak Ethiopian 2nd Division, supported by two additional infantry battalions and a tank platoon with just two tanks. Under covering artillery and rocket fire the Somalis surged forward. It seemed as if nothing could stop them. However, it soon became very apparent that the Somali tank crews were inexperienced. Two Somali T-54/55 tanks trying to overrun the airport ended up overturned in a dry river bed. Another four were stopped on the road outside the city. Surprised by the level of resistance, many of the Somali crews attempted to flee and in some instances quickly abandoned their vehicles. The Somali attack completely collapsed after two days of fighting. They lost twenty-one tanks, half of which were captured intact, along with 700 dead. The commander of the 16th Armoured Battalion was humiliated by the poor performance of his men. The Ethiopians reported losing 150 men killed. Captured Somali T-54/55s were triumphantly put on display in Dire Dawa, along with other weaponry including armoured personnel carriers, rocket launchers and trucks.

Elsewhere it did not go so well for the Ethiopians. Their 3rd and 4th Divisions were routed. After a brief tank battle they abandoned the Kara Marda Pass, and the Somalis took Jijiga east of Harar on 14 August 1977. In the process they overran five military camps in the area. The battlefield was left littered with the Ethiopian 3rd Division's US-built M41 and M47 tanks and M113 armoured personnel carriers. Most of these were captured intact, suggesting the crews had run away rather than fight. Witnesses also saw several knocked-out T-34s, but the Somalis claimed these had been supplied to the Ethiopians by South Yemen. A news crew was shown a few dead bodies and no prisoners, suggesting the Ethiopians had abandoned their positions. The victors then pushed on through the mountains to Harar on the road to Addis Ababa.

By this point the Somali lines were very over-extended and they looked to the Soviet Union for resupply – but instead, the Soviets switched sides, having decided that an ally on the Red Sea would be much more useful to them than one on the Horn of Africa. In Mogadishu, the Somali capital, President Major General Siad Barre was furious. Not only did the Soviets know his entire order of battle, they had trained his army so knew precisely how it would fight. The Soviet bloc duly stepped in to help Ethiopia and provided advisers, instructors, troops, tanks and artillery. Committing 12 per cent of the Soviet Union's strategic airlift capacity, men and equipment were flown in from Angola, Cuba, South Yemen and the Soviet Union. The equipment included artillery, rocket launchers and approximately 500 tanks. Men and weapons were also shipped in by sea. A Soviet contingent, some 1,500 strong, was commanded by General Vasily Petrov, first deputy commander of Soviet ground forces. The Cubans sent around 15,000 ground troops under General Ochoa. Some of these were sent to defend Dire Dawa and Harar.

In light of Ethiopia's other wars against the separatists, Petrov was of the view that the Ethiopians, bolstered by the Cubans, needed to launch a knock-out blow against the Somalis as soon as possible. Ethiopian tank crews were hurriedly trained to use their new Soviet tanks and the much-reinforced Ethiopian Army conducted a major counter-offensive in February 1978 involving 120 T-54 and T-62 tanks. These forces were directed by the Soviet general Grigory Barisov, who was Petrov's chief of operations. Barisov had been an adviser to the Somali military until he was expelled in November 1977.

The Soviets successfully airlifted an entire Ethiopian division over the mountains and landed it behind the Somalis besieging Harar and at Jijiga. These forces included seventy Cuban BMD-1 airborne combat vehicles and ASU-57 airborne assault guns. The surprised Somalis were swiftly surrounded and suffered 3,000 dead. Jijiga was recaptured on 5 March 1978 and three days later the humiliated Somalis announced they would withdraw from Ethiopia, having abandoned much of their heavy equipment. By 14 March they had gone.

In total, the Somalis lost 8,000 men, three-quarters of their tanks and half of their aircraft. They were left with just fifty T-34s and thirty T-54s, as well as about 150 armoured personnel carriers. The Ethiopians, though, were distracted by the on-going Eritrean and Tigrayan insurgencies and the guerrilla war in the Ogaden dragged on for another two years. Nonetheless, the Ethiopian Army was now convinced that the Soviet doctrine of the massed tank attack was a war winner.

Ethiopia had some 400 tanks which it deployed during the conflict that saw the Eritreans doggedly fighting for independence, but the tanks did little to counter the Eritreans' growing military confidence. After the Ethiopian Revolution in 1974 the Marxist guerrillas of the Eritrean People's Liberation Front withstood the Ethiopian Army's offensives in 1976, 1978 and 1979. Another offensive known as the Red Star campaign was launched in 1982. In January of that year 90,000 Ethiopian troops were deployed to Eritrea to join 30,000 already there, to form the 2nd Revolutionary Liberation Army. When these forces attacked the Eritreans they were repulsed with heavy losses and the offensive had ground to a halt by April 1982. This set the tone for the next eight years.

In neighbouring Tigray province the Ethiopians launched seven offensives between 1975 and 1983 against the Tigrayan People's Liberation Front. These offensives were not successful either. By 1983 the Tigrayans claimed to control 85 per cent of the countryside. Then, in February 1984, the Eritreans took Tessenai and Ali Didir. After overrunning garrisons on the Red Sea coast, they won a major victory at Marsa Teklai on 24 March

1984, taking 3,000 prisoners, including the Ethiopian deputy regional commander.

The Soviet Union's response was further massive logistical support for Ethiopia. Armoured personnel carriers, tanks and jet fighters poured in. Amongst these deliveries were about forty T-55s and a similar number of armoured cars, half of which were battlefield replacements. During the summer of 1985 some 50,000 Ethiopian troops with their new equipment successfully captured an important Eritrean line of communication from the key town of Barentu to Sudan. To the northeast they then launched their Red Sea counter-offensive on 10 October 1985, pushing the Eritreans back to their 'Golden Trench' defences around Nacfa in the provincial region of Sahel. The fighting then reached a stalemate.

By the late 1980s the Ethiopian Army had built up its strength and was ready to deliver a knock-out blow. Armoured units totalled thirty-two tank battalions equipped with 750 tanks comprising 600 T-54s, 100 T-62s, 20 T-34s and 30 M47s. They also had more than 650 tracked and wheeled armoured personnel carriers for their mechanized infantry. These were deployed to support the 1st Revolutionary Army in eastern Ethiopia, the 2nd in Eritrea and the 3rd in Tigray. The 4th was deployed in the Ogaden until the Ethiopian-Somali rapprochement. By contrast the Eritreans had a single tank brigade operating captured T-54s. However, for all its armoured might, the Ethiopian tanks seemed to make very little difference on the battlefield. In reality, much of this equipment was poorly maintained and not all of it was operational. Crew proficiency was similarly a problem. Furthermore, the highly mobile guerrillas always seemed able to outwit the ill-coordinated Ethiopian tank battalions.

For the Ethiopians 1988 marked an unwanted turning point, when the war began to go truly against them, with humiliating defeats at Afabet, Keren and Inda Selassie. At the beginning of the year the Eritreans and Tigrayans were making significant advances, despite their paucity of tanks. By March 1988 the Tigrayans had taken three towns and scored a victory at Wukro, 50 kilometres north of Makelle, defeating the Ethiopian 32nd Brigade. Worse was to come.

Shortly after, on 19 March 1988, in a 48-hour battle, the Eritreans took Afabet, the Ethiopians' regional military command centre in southern Sahel. Afabet was defended by three Ethiopian infantry divisions, supported by the 29th Mechanized Brigade, totalling about 18,000 men. These forces were completely routed, with the Eritreans capturing 6,000 prisoners, fifty tanks, sixty pieces of artillery and three Soviet military advisers. The rest were either killed or deserted. The mechanized brigade resisted for a time, then withdrew on Afabet, only to get caught on the open road by Eritrean artillery. Once trapped, the column was quickly destroyed.

The carnage was terrible. One of the defeated Ethiopian units was the crack 'Nadaw' Division, and the Eritreans were amused that its name meant 'Destroy'. Some of the captured tanks were found to be still operational and were absorbed into the Eritreans' armoured brigade. Smiling Eritreans were photographed driving away one of the T-54s 'liberated' at Afabet. Also amongst the booty were 130mm howitzers and multiple rocket launchers, which were also pressed into service.

The Eritreans then laid siege to Keren, south of Afabet, and in the subsequent fighting 1,800 Ethiopian troops were killed. Apart from the Eritrean capital, Asmara, and the Red Sea port of Massawa, which were still held by the Ethiopians, Eritrea was now liberated. In Tigray things went just as badly for the Ethiopians. At the end of March they abandoned Adigrat, leaving Tigray's largest city of 1.5 million people to the separatists. Hargere Selam, Mekoney and Adowa also fell. The Ethiopian 17th Division tried to make a stand at Axum, but on 27 March, after a seven-hour battle and losing 1,200 men, the Ethiopians scattered. By April the Tigrayans were almost entirely in control of the province.

From 13 to 23 May 1988 the Ethiopians launched a counter-offensive involving up to 100,000 men from Keren against the Eritreans. Once again the whole operation went horribly wrong, with the Ethiopians suffering 9,100 casualties and losing another fifty tanks. In Tigray they made little headway, other than retaking Adigrat. Undeterred, the Ethiopians planned their next operation, which was intended to reopen the road from Inda Selassie to Asmara. They gathered three divisions, including a veteran one redeployed from the Ogaden, numbering some 20,000 men with armoured support. When the Tigrayans counter-attacked at the end of December 1988, the Ethiopians were forced back to Inda Selassie with the loss of 3,000 men.

The Eritreans and the Tigrayans then defeated the Ethiopian 3rd Army at Inda Selassie on 19 February 1989, killing 3,000 and capturing 9,612. In the process they cut the road to the Red Sea and isolated the remaining Ethiopian forces in Eritrea. In Tigray, this forced government troops to evacuate Adigrat and the 15,000-strong Ethiopian garrison abandoned Makelle without firing a shot. The Ethiopian military was so thoroughly demoralized by the unending defeats that disgruntled elements launched a coup to oust President Mengistu. They failed and the resulting purge did nothing to help restore the military situation.

The Eritreans launched a conventional attack using tanks to take Massawa, and after three days of fighting defeated the 17,000-strong garrison and took 8,000 prisoners. By 10 February 1989 Massawa was firmly in the hands of the Eritreans. Mengistu fell from power two years later and Eritrea finally gained independence. Tigray was to remain part of Ethiopia, but this was poor compensation for the Ethiopians as they lost access to the Red Sea.

# Chapter 11

# The Struggle for Mavinga
## The Angolan Civil War, 1975–2002

While the Soviet Union and Cuba used Ethiopia as a rudimentary testbed for their armoured warfare doctrine in order to prop up an unpopular Marxist regime, they did exactly the same thing in Angola. After Angolan independence, Moscow and Havana threw their full backing behind the newly installed Marxist government in Luanda. Moscow poured in millions of dollars' worth of military equipment and sent its generals to take charge. This intervention, though, had far greater consequences than in Ethiopia, because the rebel UNITA guerrilla army enjoyed the support of not only South Africa but also America. This situation threatened to spark the Third World War. Despite the risks, Angola became engulfed in full-scale conventional warfare, with the well equipped Angolan military launching large-scale offensives every dry season.

A month-long Angolan government offensive in 1987 and a two-month UNITA counter-offensive the following year saw the largest battles ever fought in southern Africa. By this stage the 90,000-strong Angolan Army had ten tank battalions with 540 tanks, consisting of 300 T-54/55s, 90 T-62s and 150 T-34s. There was also a 28,000-strong Cuban Expeditionary Force supporting the Angolan government, but these troops were deployed in a static defence role. UNITA had about 65,000 regulars and militia.

Large numbers of Cuban troops first intervened immediately after Angolan independence. South Africa, backing UNITA, did not want the rival People's Movement for the Liberation of Angola (MPLA) taking power. Operating from occupied Namibia, South Africa sent four armoured columns north to try to oust the MPLA from Luanda, the Angolan capital, in 1975. They numbered 2,000 men, spearheaded by armoured cars, howitzers and mortars. In response, Cuba shipped in by air and sea a division of troops supported by ninety tanks. This force swiftly secured the streets of Luanda and Huambo in a show of strength.

Despite the arrival of the Cubans, there were initially few large-scale confrontations with the South Africans in neighbouring Namibia. The most serious occurred on 9–12 December 1975 when one of the South African columns killed 200 Cubans for the loss of four dead. Although they got to within several hundred kilometres of Luanda, the increasing Cuban build-up brought the South Africans to a halt and saved the MPLA. However, the country was left in a state of civil war, with South Africa regularly intervening in southern Angola. Neither side, though, was strong enough to deliver a knock-out blow.

Biding its time, South Africa launched a much larger armoured invasion of southern Angola on 23 August 1981. Operation Protea involved 11,000 men, 36 Centurion tanks, 70 AML-90 armoured cars, about 200 armoured personnel carriers, artillery, surface-to-air missiles and some 90 aircraft and helicopters. These were divided into three armoured columns that pushed towards Angolan urban centres. They ended up occupying 50,000 square kilometres of Angola's southern Cunene province. This operation also served to keep at bay the guerrillas of the South West African People's Organisation, allied with the Angolan government and fighting for Namibian independence.

In late 1983 and early 1984 the South African 61st Mechanized Brigade pushed deep into Angola to attack the SWAPO base at Cuvelai. The brigade consisted of armoured cars and armoured personnel carriers supported by heavy artillery. They killed 424 guerrillas and Angolan troops and captured twenty-five T-54 and PT-76 tanks. The South Africans suffered only twenty-one casualties and lost two armoured personnel carriers. Both were hit by Angolan tanks. The biggest surprise was that the Angolans brought their tanks into offensive action for the first time. Previously they had been used as static artillery, firing from fixed positions in defence of Angolan and SWAPO bases. On this occasion they had tried to surround the South African armoured columns. The Angolan government then deployed 200 tanks and 15,000 men, backed by fighter-bombers and helicopter gunships, to block UNITA at Cafunfo and Sumbe. This marked the high water mark of the rebels' push northwards; from now on they would have to fight to protect their southeastern strongholds.

The South African government was so alarmed by the Angolan armed forces' growing confidence that in September 1984 it conducted the largest military exercise since the Second World War. This was held in the northern Cape near the Namibian–South African border. It involved

11,000 men, spearheaded by tanks and supported by artillery, attacking 'enemy' positions in a large-scale set-piece battle. It clearly signalled to Angola and Cuba that South Africa was ready for a conventional war.

Despite this posturing, the Angolan government and its Cuban allies launched a massive armoured offensive, backed by helicopters and jets, towards UNITA's strategic base and airstrip at Mavinga in the summer of 1985. This base protected the road to their headquarters at Jamba. Should Mavinga be overrun, it would bring Jamba within range of Angolan and Cuban aircraft. It would also give SWAPO greater access to the border area. During August five motorized infantry brigades started pushing up from Cuito Cuanavale in order to reach Mavinga 120 kilometres away. Another four brigades struck out from Luena to cover the 350 kilometres to Cazombo, another UNITA stronghold. In all, eighteen Angolan Army brigades were involved in these operations, totalling in excess of 15,000 men. By 7 September 1985 they had reached the outer defences of both Cazombo and Mavinga. UNITA did not have enough men to hold both towns, so they abandoned Cazombo.

The South African Air Force, stationed in Namibia, was scrambled on 17 September 1985 and proceeded to bomb the Angolan armoured columns heading for Mavinga. South African pilot Lieutenant Colonel Pine Pienaar recalled 'Everyone returned safely and the next morning we learned that the enemy spearhead had been halted.' He and his colleagues then proceeded to shoot down Angolan and Cuban transport helicopters being used to bring forward reserves and supplies, as well as their helicopter gunship escorts. Given that the South Africans were prepared to risk their hard-to-replace aircraft in the face of Angolan surface-to-air missiles and jet fighters, this shows just how seriously they took the armoured threat. The South African air-strikes were conducted on three consecutive days and helped turn back the advancing Angolan armour.

The South Africans also committed ground troops to help save Mavinga. The 32nd 'Buffalo' Battalion, equipped with armoured cars, transport vehicles and artillery, drove on Mavinga from the south and intercepted the Angolan tank columns. The 1,200-strong 32nd Battalion was a mercenary force consisting of Angolans and Mozambicans led by white South African officers. When operating in Angola, South Africa claimed it belonged to UNITA. At least two further battalions were deployed to Angola, the 101st Kaokoland and 202nd Kavango, both of which were formed from Namibian recruits. Other such foreign units included the 44th Battalion, made up of white former Rhodesians, and the 201st Battalion, raised from Namibian bushmen.

After being bombed the Angolan Army blundered into a trap north of the Lomba river and its forces were heavily shelled by South African heavy artillery. They only just escaped, suffering serious casualties and losing a large amount of armour. British war correspondent Michael Hornsby, with *The Times*, reported:

> We must have seen at least 50 smashed trucks and the blackened hulks of a dozen or more Soviet-made armoured personnel carriers. In one small area some 20 Russian-made Zil trucks, one mounted with the multiple rocket launcher known as a Stalin Organ, had been destroyed.

With the help of South African firepower, UNITA contained the Mavinga offensive, destroying seventy-nine vehicles and capturing fifty-two. By 7 October 1985 the government forces had been defeated and the Soviet and Cuban officers with the attack force were flown to safety. UNITA claimed to have killed 2,300 government troops, while the government claimed 1,300 rebels. South Africa only listed twenty-three killed and these were all white.

Thanks to the very poor performance of the government forces, in late 1985 the Soviet general Konstantin Shagnovitch, an Afghanistan veteran and the highest-ranking Soviet officer to serve outside Afghanistan or Europe, assisted by the Cuban general Arnaldo Ochoa, arrived to take control of all forces in Angola. This caused alarm in South African intelligence, who feared the civil war would now swing in favour of the Angolan government. They had already appreciated that air mobility was key, not lumbering columns of tanks, and they assumed the Soviets would now adopt the same tactics in Angola.

However, Shagnovitch proceeded to ignore American experiences in the jungles of Vietnam and his own experience in the mountains of Afghanistan and decided to rely on overwhelming numbers of armour and infantry to crush UNITA. After all, such a strategy had brought Marshal Georgi Zhukov to Berlin, so it should work in Angola. Shagnovitch seemed to miss the point that he was fighting another counter-insurgency war, not a conventional one. His rigid doctrine and the poor command and control structure of the Angolan Army was not a recipe for victory.

Shagnovitch launched 20,000 troops with tanks and artillery against UNITA in 1986, with three armoured columns pushing on Lumbala, Mavinga and Munhango. In the face of constant guerrilla attacks his offensive soon ground to a halt. To assist UNITA, the South Africans deployed 3,000 men with seventy armoured vehicles in southern Angola. Another 30,000 troops were just across the border in Namibia ready to assist if needed. UNITA was likewise greatly helped by America's decision to supply state-of-the-art anti-tank and surface-to-air missiles.

Throughout the 1980s the Angolan government received millions of dollars' worth of Soviet military assistance, consisting of tanks, armoured cars, armoured personnel carriers, infantry fighting vehicles, artillery, ground attack aircraft and missiles. These included an estimated 150 T-55 and 35 T-62 tanks, as well as about 65 BMP-2 infantry fighting vehicles, 150 BTR-60 armoured personnel carriers and 40 BRDM armoured cars, which are thought to have been delivered in 1987, just in time for the summer campaigning season.

By the end of September 1987 the Angolan government forces were dug in along the Lomba river some 40 kilometres from Mavinga. UNITA, with the support of four South African battalions and the South African Air Force, attacked these positions on 1 October 1987, inflicting 2,000 casualties. The South Africans committed tanks for the first time and their artillery helped destroy a Cuban mechanized brigade. However, the following month government forces took the town of Cuito Cuanavale. The US Department of Defense was baffled by Shagnovitch's strategy, noting 'The Soviets have developed no specific doctrine to deal with the insurgency in Angola.' It went on to observe 'Their campaigns have mostly been large, slow-moving sweeps during the dry season aimed at destroying UNITA bases.'

Sensing an opportunity for a significant victory that could force the government to the negotiating table, UNITA, backed by 6,000 South African troops, launched an offensive against Cuito Cuanavale on 12 January 1988. Lying 200 kilometres northwest of Mavinga, it was the key to southeast Angola. It was also now the Angolan Army's main staging base and the best airstrip in the region. In February government forces counter-attacked but were repulsed. In the fighting that lasted six weeks the Angolan Army lost one brigade and had two others badly mauled. In April the South Africans committed their elite presidential regiment from the 82nd Armoured Brigade, but still neither side was able to prevail.

With the war steadily going against it, the Angolan government stated that it was ready to timetable a Cuban withdrawal, if the US and South Africa cut aid to UNITA. Talks commenced, but progress was slow. In the meantime, government forces fought to push UNITA back 70 kilometres east of Cuito Cuanavale. However, there were 3,000 South Africans in Cunene south of Ngiva and a further 6,000 in Cuando Cubango. In response to the South African presence in southern Angola,11,000 Angolan and Cuban troops advanced south towards the South African security zone in May 1988. The Cubans rushed in reinforcements, including the 15,000-strong 50th Mechanized Division, bringing the Cuban Expeditionary Force to well over 55,000 men. By 8 June 1988 this division was within striking distance of the Namibian border. It consisted of three infantry regiments, one tank regiment and an artillery regiment. Nineteen days later Angolan and Cuban forces killed twelve South African soldiers.

South Africa now faced the long-feared all-out conventional war and in response mobilized the 10th Division, which included the 81st Armoured Brigade, to defend Namibia. Clashes followed between the tanks of the South African 61st Mechanized Battalion and the Cubans, who lost a number of tanks and armoured personnel carriers. Luckily, behind the scenes negotiations had been continuing and in August 1988 the South Africans prudently withdrew from Angola. The Cubans agreed to be gone by July 1991. UNITA, though, vowed to fight on alone.

Knowing they must act before the Cuban withdrawal, government forces launched a two-pronged offensive against Mavinga on 23 December 1989. This involved more than 7,000 Angolan troops, with six motorized groups and a tank company. The weakness of the tank force seemed to indicate that the Angolans had finally accepted the fact that mobility was the name of the game. Nonetheless, Mavinga was not taken until 5 February 1990 and UNITA retook it sixteen days later. The Angolan civil war was to drag on for another twelve years, by which time UNITA was defeated simply by attrition.

South Africa supported anti-government forces not only in Angola but also in Lesotho and Mozambique. The activities of the South African-backed Mozambique National Resistance (Renamo) forced Zimbabwe to militarily assist the Mozambican Army during the 1980s. The Zimbabwe National Army (ZNA) was created in 1979 with the transition to black majority rule and the end of white-ruled Rhodesia. Its formation came with the amalgamation of Robert Mugabe's Zimbabwe African National

Liberation Army (ZANLA) and Joshua Nkomo's Zimbabwe People's Revolutionary Army (ZIPRA) guerrilla armies and the Rhodesian Defence Force (RDF).

During the late 1970s the RDF totalled just 10,800 men in its war against the guerrillas, with a further 15,000 Territorial Army and Police Reserves available. By 1979, when the conflict came to a close, the Rhodesian Army numbered 20,000. The amalgamation of the RDF, ZANLA and ZIPRA was expected to create a force of about 50,000, but the Zimbabwe National Army ended up 40,000 strong. By the late 1980s it had expanded by an additional 4,000 men and comprised seven brigades, one armoured regiment, one artillery regiment, one air defence regiment and twenty-three infantry battalions.

The ZNA inherited the Rhodesian armoured corps' vehicle fleet. This included the indigenously built Bullet and Crocodile wheeled armoured personnel carriers and the 'Vaporizer' reconnaissance vehicle (so named because that is what it did if it struck a mine), British-supplied Ferret and South African S/90 scout cars, French Eland armoured cars and German-designed UR-416 armoured personnel carriers. South Africa moved swiftly to destabilize the new state. The armoury at Inkomo Barracks near Harare was blown up on 16 August 1981, destroying 36 million dollars' worth of equipment. Attempts were also made to blow up the ZNA's armoured vehicles.

During the early 1980s China, which had at one time supported the various guerrilla armies, stepped into the breach to provide the fledgling ZNA with armour. Beijing shipped in thirty Type 59 and ten Type 69 tanks, plus thirty YW-531 tracked armoured personnel carriers. Zimbabwe also received ten T-34/85s and twenty Type 63 light tanks from China, as well as twelve T-55 tanks, twenty BRDM-1 scout cars and twenty BTR-152 armoured personnel carriers from North Korea. Chinese tanks and armoured personnel carriers were exported to a number of other sub-Saharan countries, including Congo, Sudan, Tanzania, Zaire and Zambia.

For much of the 1980s the Zimbabwean Army was deployed supporting Mozambican government forces. Most of Zimbabwe's trade passed through Mozambique to the ports at Beira and Maputo. In 1983 Renamo cut the Limpopo Valley railway. Mozambique's troops were notably ill-equipped, poorly led, underfed, badly paid and lacked transport. They numbered only 15,600 men, organized into seven infantry brigades, each with a tank battalion and a single tank brigade. These tank forces comprised ninety

T-54/55s and 195 ancient T-34s, but few of them were operable. Of far greater use were some 200 armoured personnel carriers, but again few of these were actually in service. Renamo was able to field 9,000 fighters trained and armed by South Africa, with another 3,000 in reserve.

Zimbabwe was forced to commit 13,500 troops to guard the vital 300 kilometre stretch of the Beira railway corridor from the port to the Zimbabwean border. This force, backed by armour and artillery, took the lead in an operation mounted to take Renamo's headquarters in 1985. Unlike in Angola, tanks did not feature heavily in the Mozambican civil war. Not until the negotiated peace in the early 1990s was the ZNA able to extricate itself from the Mozambican morass. Between 1982 and 1987 the ZNA also had to fight a guerrilla war in Matabeleland against South African-backed Shona rebels. This again did not involve tanks.

\* \* \*

The conflicts in Angola and Ethiopia on the whole showed exceptionally poor handling of tanks. In both instances they were used in a conventional role, in what were largely counter-insurgency wars against highly flexible and reasonably well-equipped guerrilla armies. For all the armoured muscle supplied by Moscow, it did the government forces no good. If anything, adherence to Soviet conventional warfare doctrine led to defeat.

# Chapter 12

# Tanks vs Toyotas

## The Chadian–Libyan War, 1978–1987

Bouncing out of the desert on 23 March 1987, a group of Toyota pick-up trucks carrying Chadian soldiers and tribesmen sped through the Libyan perimeter defences at the oasis of Ouadi Doum. They dashed through the minefields at such speed that the mines exploded harmlessly behind them. Rapidly overrunning massed tanks, artillery and rocket launchers, the Chadian forces drove through the camp and dismounted to engage the surprised garrison, which rapidly fled. The battle of Ouadi Doum heralded the beginning of the end for Colonel Muamar Gaddafi's involvement in Chad.

In the late 1980s Colonel Gaddafi's Libyan tanks had occupied northern Chad and paid a terrible price, losing at least three tank brigades as a result. Like Angola and Ethiopia, Libya had amassed a massive tank fleet, courtesy of the Soviet Union, consisting of some 2,200 T-54/55, T-62 and T-72 tanks. It also had a similar number of armoured personnel carriers. These were used to equip thirty-eight tank battalions and fifty-four mechanized infantry battalions, which could be deployed as an armoured division and two mechanized divisions. The former consisted of two tank and one mechanized brigades supported by an artillery regiment, while the latter had two mechanized and one tank brigades, plus an artillery regiment. The Libyan Army, around 60,00 men, did not have the manpower to employ all its equipment and more than half of the tanks were held in reserve in storage.

War had been endemic in Chad for the previous two decades, and it looked likely to continue if Chad failed to unite itself and if external powers continued to meddle. What had initially started as a revolution against the government in N'Djamena in southwestern Chad became a power struggle between Hissene Habre's government in the south and the Libyans and their allies, the Chadian opposition forces, in the north. The Chadian liberation movement, Front de Liberation Nationale du Tchad (FROLINAT), was formed in Nyala, Sudan, on 22 June 1966, which resulted in a long-drawn-out civil war. It was not until August 1977 that Goukouni Oueddei, one of FROLINAT's leaders, emerged as President of the Government d'Union Nationale du Tchad (GUNT), while Hissene Habre, another FROLINAT leader since 1973, became Minister of Defence.

Taking advantage of the Chadian civil war, Gaddafi, who had come to power in 1969, occupied the mineral-rich Aouzou Strip in northern Chad in 1973. Two years later he almost went to war with neighbouring Egypt. On 2 August 1972 Libya and Egypt agreed to create a unified United Arab Republic. After squabbling over power sharing, this was changed the following August so that each country remained independent. After the Yom Kippur War, in which Libya declined to help Egypt beyond the commitment of a single armoured brigade, relations between the two deteriorated to the point of armed hostilities.

Gaddafi was suspected of eyeing a considerable area of the Egyptian Western Desert with a view to annexing it. To achieve this, he was accused of fermenting civil unrest in Egypt in order to distract the Egyptian military. By early August 1975 Egyptian and Libyan tanks were facing each other across the border and towards the end of the month some minor clashes took place. Both countries then backed away from all-out war, even though Gaddafi expelled large numbers of Egyptian workers. At that time Libya had only one armoured and two mechanized brigades, whereas Egypt had two armoured and three mechanized divisions, so the odds for a Libyan victory were not favourable. Moreover the Egyptians were thoroughly battle-hardened.

Meanwhile the two Chadian factions continued arguing, leading to a power struggle in which Oueddei, backed by Libya, defeated Habre in December 1980 and forced him into exile. Two years later, in June 1982, Oueddei was driven into exile in Libya when Habre successfully fought his way back from Sudan. In May 1983 Oueddei, again with Libyan military support, invaded northern Chad, seizing Faya Largeau in July, and then prepared to march on N'Djamena. In August France, the colonial mother country, intervened with Operation Sparrowhawk, halting the Libyans at the 16th Parallel, which effectively cut the country in half. For a time it seemed there might be a confrontation between units of the French Foreign Legion and the Libyan Army, but the 16th Parallel was not attacked.

By 1985 there was military and political deadlock. Habre was secure in the south, with French troops and air cover guaranteeing his position below the 16th Parallel, which was dubbed the Red Line. Meanwhile Oueddei and his troops, the Forces Armées Populaires (FAP), were safeguarded in their mountain strongholds in the north by Libyan support. A perceivable shift occurred at the end of 1985 in Oueddei's GUNT, which was now opposed to Habre. At a meeting in August 1985 in Cotonu, Benin, GUNT attempted to bring about greater political unity. It also produced a document denouncing Libya's policy of interfering in GUNT's internal affairs and declared that it was prepared to negotiate with Habre.

The Libyans began to doubt Oueddei's leadership, noting that Achiek Ibn Omar, leader of the Conseil Democratique de la Revolution (CDR), did not take part in the meeting, and denounced its findings. Furthermore, Libya favoured Achiek because he was an Arab, despite the fact that he had been detained by them from December 1984 to December 1985. Oueddei was a Toubou, the same tribe as Habre. The military commander of the CDR, Adoum Manani, who was even closer to the Libyans, was against negotiating with Habre, and wanted Oueddei punished in the hope that the CDR would become Libya's principal ally. Libya's desire for a switch of allegiance was confirmed when fighting broke out between FAP and CDR forces, resulting in the CDR seizing the palm grove at Fada, the second most important FAP stronghold, sited in the Ennedi mountains in northeastern Chad. FAP tried to retake Fada, while Oueddei issued a communique from Tripoli again calling for negotiations. It was now clear that there was a civil war within a civil war.

On 17 October 1986 Oueddei telephoned Radio-France Internationale, saying he was a prisoner of the Libyans, but was still prepared to negotiate! Events then became somewhat confused as the Libyans either tried to arrest or kidnap him. Kailan Ahmet, the Paris spokesman for GUNT, confirmed the kidnap attempt. In the following gun battle two of Oueddei's bodyguards were killed and he was seriously wounded. Many Chadians in Libya were rounded up and fifty GUNT officials were held at the Libyan military camp at Mordoum.

Not surprisingly, FAP forces turned against the Libyans, who began to attack FAP's strongholds, with napalm being used against civilian targets. As a consequence, thousands of refugees fled south of the Red Line. On 24 October 1986 FAP – estimated to be about 3,000 strong – joined Habre's government forces under truce. The Libyans then systematically set about FAP's supporters. On 10 November 1986 they killed hundreds of civilians using tanks and Tupolev and Sukhoi aircraft in ground and air attacks on Gorma, Gouro and Ounianga in northern Chad. Those of the region's 2,000 inhabitants who were not killed fled into the mountains. The Chadian government compared the callous attack to the Nazis' savage massacre of French villagers at Ouradour-sur-Glane. Five days later, on 15 and 16 November 1986, after a two-day summit between French and African leaders in Togo, the Chadian government and GUNT's opposition forces decided to unite against the Libyan invaders. This marked a critical turning point in the civil war, heralding a new Chadian nationalism. Habre stated, 'we now have a common cause ... we are united to fight Libyan aggression'. At the summit President Mitterrand of France pledged logistical support, although Habre had hoped for French offensive air cover.

This alliance meant that the bulk of GUNT's 10,000-strong opposition forces joined the government's lightly armed regular army of 14,200. Against them, Libya could field an army of 55,000 men, backed by several thousand tanks and 489 combat aircraft. Because Gaddafi did not admit to the presence of his troops in northern Chad, war was not actually declared between the two countries. Libyan commitment to the Chadian opposition forces, as well as protecting the Aouzou Strip, consisted of 8,000 men, two tank battalions, two mechanized battalions, surface-to-air missile units, and air force units equipped with about five aircraft and three Mi-24 Hind helicopter gunships. With the defection of the GUNT coalition forces, the Libyans were left only with the support of the CDR, estimated at about 2,000 strong, and a number of other unspecified factions.

By December 1986 FAP was under attack by both the CDR and the Libyans, who committed several thousand troops supported by T-54 and T-62 tanks, MiG-23 fighters and Tupolev bombers. The hard-pressed FAP were forced back into the Ennedi and Tibesti mountains. The Libyans and their allies occupied northern Chad along a line running from Faya Largeau to Fada, where they were out of the reach of Habre's Forces Armées du Nord Tchadienes (FANT).

The local Libyan commander-in-chief, Colonel Mahmoud Riffi, decided to crush all FAP resistance in the north. He led one armoured column towards Bardai in the northwest, whilst another moved on Zouar, also in the northwest, just to the south of the Tibesti mountains. Both columns were beaten off with heavy losses in casualties and prisoners. The Libyans regrouped for another try. Habre decided to commit himself to assisting FAP and hoped to enlist French military aid. On 16 December 1986 the French military commander, General Jenou Lacaze, visited N'Djamena; he refused to commit French forces beyond the Red Line but agreed to drop supplies to the beleaguered FAP in the mountains. Several days later US transports arrived in the capital carrying the first consignment of 15 million dollars' worth of US military aid, consisting of light weapons, ammunition and uniforms. Habre pressed for the rapid liberation of the north because of the Libyans' systematic destruction of Chadian villages, so a number of FANT 'Toyota' Brigades were despatched northwards to fight alongside GUNT's troops.

On 28 December 1986 Riffi's forces attacked again and succeeded in taking the strategic town of Zouar just before the relieving FANT troops arrived. Two days later FAP, reinforced with FANT's anti-tank and anti-aircraft missiles, counter-attacked, capturing the town and driving the Libyan garrison into the nearby hills. To the east the Chadians scored another success on 2 January 1987 when Habre's forces recaptured Fada in the eastern Ennedi mountains, killing 784 Libyans and capturing a large number. Some of the captured vehicles bore CDR markings, but most of the equipment belonged to the Libyan Army. The Chadian government displayed 130 Libyan prisoners in N'Djamena on 13 January 1987 as proof of Libyan intervention and to show how far south their forces had pene-trated. The government claimed 113 of the prisoners had been captured in the fighting since December 1986, mostly at Fada, while the other seven-teen had been taken in the spring of 1986 and in 1983. It was rumoured Gaddafi was employing foreign mercenaries, and the prisoners included two men from Mali and two from Niger.

After the fall of Fada, the Libyans retaliated with air-strikes on Arada, Oum Chalouba and Kouba Oulanga, all south of the Red Line. French Jaguar jets from N'Djamena and Bangui in the Central African Republic struck back, putting the Libyan airstrip at Ouadi Doum in northern Chad temporarily out of action. The base consisted of a 3 kilometre-long aluminium runway surrounded by Soviet-manufactured weapons, barbed wire and minefields. The Libyans then raided the bases at Kalait near the oasis of Oum Chalouba and Zouar. They also launched a small ground sortie against Kalait, possibly with the aim of provoking the French, but were driven off.

Habre was now presented with the opportunity to try to roll the Libyans out of northern Chad with a pincer offensive from Zouar in the west and Fada to the east. He persuaded France, through General Saulnier, to give him some limited support, with the next objectives being Ouadi Doum and the base at Faya Largeau that was lost in 1983.

FANT and FAP had proved that they could defeat the Libyans in open battle and had gained the upper hand over the CDR in Bourkou, Ennedi and the Tibesti mountains. But they needed continued French air cover, with Fada being particularly vulnerable to Libyan air-strikes. The Libyans had other air bases in Chad and at Sangha just over the border. Most of northern Chad was within reach of Libya's East German-piloted Soviet-supplied aircraft.

On 9 January 1987 Oueddei held a news conference in which he claimed he was the 'Legitimate Chief of Chad' and affirmed his friendship with Libya, whilst calling on FAP to cease fighting. But FAP spokesman Maina Sanhaye, the southern leader Wadad Abdelkader Kamougue, Adoum Yacoub, head of the Army of National Liberation (ANL), the armed wing of GUNT, General Djogo, former GUNT chief of staff, and Colonel Kotiga, leader of the southern Codos, had all thrown their lot in with Habre. The following two days witnessed a number of skirmishes between Chadian and Libyan forces. It was only a matter of time before there was a major battle.

The fighting continued and on 15 January 1987 Chadian troops captured a Libyan command post in the northwestern Tibesti mountains. The next day the Libyans bombed Fada, Wour and Zouar. By now it was rumoured that the Aouzou Strip had been turned into a concentration camp for Chadian civilians. Five days later, on 21 January 1987, the Chadian government launched what it called a 'clean-up operation' in the area of Zouar, the scene of intermittent fighting since December. Chadian forces destroyed all the Libyan command posts in the area and Chad's Embassy in Paris issued a statement saying 'The enemy suffered heavy losses in men and materiel and was routed ... Zouar and the surrounding area are under the sole control of the Chadian national armed forces.' It also said the government was ready for direct talks with Libya to end the conflict.

Instead, Gaddafi airlifted 5,000 fresh troops to Ouadi Doum at the end of January ready for a counter-attack against FANT and FAP. He was confident that he could not only hold Ouadi Doum but also crush the developing threat. The air base, commanded by Colonel Khalifa Belkacem Mouftar, was essentially defended by an armoured brigade with 200 tanks and armoured personnel carriers. As far as he was concerned, there was no way the Chadian Toyotas could triumph over his armour. His tanks would simply blast them to pieces. What Gaddafi did not know was that the garrison was poorly led, motivated and disciplined. Base security was inadequate, as were the outer defences.

Habre's mobile units in their heavily armed Toyota trucks, known as 'Technicals', reminiscent of the British Long Range Desert Group during the Second World War, pre-empted the Libyans by attacking Ouadi Doum on 23 March 1987. To avoid the Libyan tanks and artillery the Chadian raiders sneaked up under the cover of darkness and overwhelmed the guards and the tank crews. In the fighting that followed, one-third of the garrison were killed or captured; the rest fled, leaving behind all their tanks, including T-55s and T-62s, many of them fully operational and loaded with ammunition, and armoured personnel carriers. Dozens of West German tank transporters, twenty jet fighters and several batteries of surface-to-air missiles were also seized. This massive haul of abandoned weaponry was worth an estimated $1 billion.

Major Assabah Ozi, the local Chadian commander, said they captured the base 'because they were better soldiers'. Chad's official radio said the base's capture removed 'one of the most important barriers to the liberation of the country'. The victory pleased both Paris and Washington: it justified the French refusal to provide air cover beyond the 16th Parallel, and it justified the Reagan administration's military aid to Habre's government. The Libyans counter-claimed that pro-Libyan forces had won a victory over Habre's forces between Ouadi Doum and Ouadi Namous, but made no mention of the loss of the air base – a defeat of the first magnitude. They simply contented themselves with daily high-level bombing raids in an effort to destroy some of the abandoned equipment.

Faya Largeau, the last Libyan stronghold, consisting of an oasis forming a 40 kilometre stretch of greenery, now seemed doomed. With the Chadian 'Toyota Brigades' controlling the desert and the Libyan Air Force reluctant to risk low-level attacks, it was difficult to see how the base could be kept resupplied. Furthermore, Libyan morale had been dealt a severe blow. The Chadian forces began to move on Faya Largeau, but on 27 March 1987 the 2,500-strong garrison fled under the cover of a sandstorm. The Libyan defeat was complete, leaving them in possession only of the Aouzou strip.

On 4 and 5 April 1987 one-fifth of the estimated 2,000 Libyan troops operating against Chad from inside northwestern Sudan began to withdraw. The Sudanese had made it clear they would not tolerate the Libyans' presence any longer, and this was the first stage of a complete pull-out supervised by the Sudanese armed forces and scheduled to take a week. Habre visited America on 20 June 1987, where he was rather fancifully dubbed by the press a 'New Rommel'. There he gained the favour of President Reagan, who extended US aid. In just three years US assistance went from almost nothing to more than $30 billion.

Gaddafi's aspirations of forcing Chad into a 'Greater Libya' crumbled. The war had been felt at home due to the steady flow of casualties and the numbers of reservists that had been called up. There were periodic border area shortages of basic food stuffs because lorries had been commandeered to ferry supplies to the demoralized troops in Chad. There were also rumours of dissent within the Libyan Army, and a Paris-based expert stated 'There is growing discontent in the Libyan Army, the only sector that poses a real threat to his [Gaddafi's] authority, and it is possible that Chad could be the straw that breaks the camel's back.'

Chadian government forces took control of the town of Aouzou after defeating a Libyan force of 3,000 on 8 August 1987. It took the Libyans until the end of the month to recapture it, launching costly frontal assaults involving 15,000 troops backed by T-55 tanks. Then, early in September the Chadians launched 2,000 men into Libya as far as the strategic air base at Maaten al-Sarra. There, in an exact rerun of the events at Ouadi Doum, they defeated the ill-prepared 2,500-strong garrison, which was supported by a tank brigade and artillery. The Chadian Toyotas brought with them French-supplied anti-tank missiles to deal with the Libyan armour. The Libyans lost 1,713 dead, 312 captured, 70 tanks, 30 armoured personnel carriers, 22 rocket launchers and 26 aircraft. Unable to retrieve the heavy equipment, the Chadians blew it up, along with the runway, before withdrawing back over the border.

During the course of 1987 the Chadian government claimed to have captured more than 800 tanks and armoured vehicles, taken twenty-three aircraft and destroyed another twenty-eight, as well as missile and radar systems. In all, they destroyed weaponry worth $1.5 billion. Gaddafi was furious at the dismal performance of the Libyan Army and his generals were left scratching their heads trying to work out how Toyota trucks had defeated an entire armoured brigade yet again.

After the series of embarrassing defeats at Zouar, Fada, Ouadi Doum and Faya Largeau, Gaddafi was faced with two options: withdrawing completely from the Aouzou Strip and remaining on the defensive, or staying and counter-attacking. Although the fighting came to an end, with a cease-fire introduced on 11 September 1987, he did not withdraw from the Aouzou Strip until 1994. Local knowledge and determination counted for as much as heavy weaponry during the Chad-Libya War. Ironically, Colonel Gaddafi failed to learn a very important lesson from this conflict, because in 2011 Libyan rebels employing Toyotas defeated his regular armed forces using very similar tactics and finally ended his 42-year rule.

# Chapter 13

# The Hard Way

## The Soviet-Afghan War, 1979–1989

Essentially, the Soviet intervention in Afghanistan was a rehash of Operation Danube, the invasion of Czechoslovakia in 1968. Airborne assault forces were tasked to swoop into Kabul, the Afghan capital, while motor rifle divisions dashed over the border to support them. The mistake Moscow made was in thinking that Afghanistan was Czechoslovakia; certainly the Afghans were not going to roll over so easily. Initially, the Soviet military intervened to help a coup intended to topple President Hafizullah Amin and install in his place a pro-Moscow Marxist government under Barak Karmal.

The Afghan Army had an impressive paper strength of 80,000 men, organized into ten infantry divisions supported by the four armoured divisions, an artillery brigade, three mountain infantry brigades, three artillery and two commando regiments. The army could also draw on 150,000 reservists. The air force numbered about 10,000, equipped with 169 combat aircraft, with another 12,000 reservists. The gendarmerie fielded about 30,000 police and militiamen equipped with small arms. Quite who these forces would support was unclear.

Lieutenant General Viktov Paputin flew to Kabul on 2 December 1979, followed a week later by 1,500 men deployed to the strategically important Bagram air base just to the north of the capital, where they set about neutralizing President Amin's tanks. The Afghan Army's armoured units were equipped mainly with T-54/55s, with some T-62s stationed around the capital. T-34/85s were also employed for infantry support. The T-62 force was usually based at Pul-e-Charki, the site of a notorious prison near Kabul. Soviet advisers immobilized them by removing the batteries for 'winterisation' storage.

The Soviets struck on 24 December 1979. Bagram was secured in five hours and the troops were reinforced to 5,000 men. The key support weapons for the air assault forces were the ASU-85 assault gun and the BMD-1 airborne combat vehicle. The following day the main Soviet force, consisting of local motor rifle divisions, crossed the border. Directed by the Soviet 40th Army headquarters at Termez (now independent Uzbekistan), the 360th and 201st Motor Rifle Divisions drove on Kabul via the strategic Salang tunnel. The 357th and 66th Motor Rifle Divisions crossed the border at Kushka (now independent Turkmenistan), occupying the key cities of Khandahar to the southwest and Herat to the far west.

Two days later Soviet paratroops advanced on Kabul itself, although *Spetsnaz* Special Forces had already secured most of the city's main administrative buildings. The Darul Aman Palace was then assaulted by the airborne troops. President Amin managed to gather some soldiers still loyal to him and part of an Afghan tank regiment and destroyed a number of the Soviet airborne vehicles. They lost eight tanks whilst defending the Darul Aman Palace. The President, his family and advisers were subsequently killed, possibly executed by the *Spetsnaz*.

The Afghan Army's response to the Soviet intervention was mixed and many units were unable or unwilling to resist, although the 8th Afghan Division fought and lost 2,000 men for its trouble. On the whole, most Afghan units – whose loyalty to the government was already questionable – were simply disarmed and the army's manpower dropped by 50 per cent. The Soviets also relieved the Afghan Army of its anti-tank and anti-aircraft missiles in 1980, following desertions with this equipment.

Despite Afghan military resistance being largely ineffective, by the New Year Soviet casualties amounted to 6,000. By mid-January 1980 the 54th Motor Rifle Division had moved into Afghanistan and the 40th Army's forward headquarters was established in Kabul. The Limited Contingent Soviet Forces Afghanistan (LCSFA) numbered 85,000 men, with another 30,000 just across the border. That April the Soviets signed a stationing of forces agreement with the new Afghan government, leaving the LCSFA firmly in control. The country was divided into seven military commands under the de facto control of Soviet generals. The scene was now set for the Soviet-Afghan War.

The following year the Soviets shifted from using unreliable Afghan Army units to small air-mobile Soviet forces, although the Afghan commando brigades were also employed until they were worn down by casualties. The Soviets launched their Panjsher 3 and 4 offensives in September 1981 and the following year were again using large sweep operations employing ground forces, with Panjsher 5 being launched in April-May, followed by Panjsher 6 in September, all of which failed to crush Ahmad Shah Massoud's troublesome guerrillas. Major large-scale operations continued throughout that year.

In 1982 Soviet occupation forces remained largely the same, with the commitment of 95,000 men, supported by 150 aircraft and some 600 helicopters. Casualties by this stage numbered 5,000 dead and up to 10,000 wounded. In sharp contrast, the Afghan Army, largely due to desertion, had dropped from 80,000 to just 25,000 men (with divisions at only battalion and brigade strength), supported by 23,000 very unreliable police and militia units. In the face of this growing security problem, the LCSFA deployed three motor rifle divisions, one airborne division and one air assault brigade, totalling an impressive 115,000 men. By 1984 the Afghan Army's total armed forces were estimated at just 46,000. Organisation was roughly the same as in 1979, with an additional infantry division and a mechanized infantry brigade.

Afghan armour acted as a poorer cousin to the Soviets' armoured units, particularly their tank battalions. Equipped with older vehicles and deemed unreliable, they were often relegated to static guard duties, particularly in Kabul and the other major cities, where they still managed to cause trouble. In 1979 the Afghan Army fielded some 860 tanks and 400 armoured personnel carriers, with four armoured divisions consisting of the 14th (which mutinied in Ghazni in July 1980), the 4th, the 7th and the 15th, although the latter three were really only of brigade strength.

Throughout the war the Afghan Army suffered a continual drain in manpower due to desertion. After the invasion it dropped significantly and by 1985 could muster at best 40,000, but it had an annual loss rate of 10,000 through failure to answer the call-up, desertion, disease and combat casualties. Nonetheless, constant tank replacements by the Soviet Union meant that Kabul's tank fleet stood at about 300 T-54/55s and T-62s.

In 1981 the Mujahideen captured a BMP-1 from the Afghan 7th Armoured Brigade, and its crew sometimes took it into action alongside the guerrillas. On 10 September 1983 the seven-man crew of an armoured personnel carrier armed with anti-aircraft guns from Spin Boldak camp near the Pakistani border came over to the Mujahideen with their vehicle. T-55A '517' captured in Paktia province in 1983 also saw limited action with the Mujahideen. Along with two other tanks, in December 1983 it was used unsuccessfully to attack the town of Urgun. During the Soviet withdrawal, increasing numbers of tanks and AFVs began to fall into Mujahideen hands as the outlying towns were abandoned, and the captured vehicles were often daubed with graffiti and religious slogans.

Despite Soviet and Afghan government forces possessing superior armoured firepower, Afghanistan's geography never favoured armoured combat and its conduct was invariably to the detriment of the Communist troops involved. Although lacking heavy anti-tank guns, the Mujahideen were able to exact a significant toll on the armoured units and Afghanistan soon became littered with their rusting victims. Their main anti-tank weapon of choice was the Soviet (or Chinese copy) rocket-propelled grenade (RPG). Mujahid Hamid Walid, one of the guerrillas' best RPG-7 gunners, personally knocked out twelve armoured vehicles and numerous trucks. Walid, who always wore a black Soviet aircrew helmet into action, was killed on 23 July 1983 whilst engaging a Soviet convoy on the Ghanzi highway. Despite his bravery, his luck simply ran out.

Much cruder methods were also resorted to, including Molotov cocktails and home-made bombs. One trick the Mujahideen employed was to dig a deep trench across a narrow mountain road and then cover it. Once the leading tank had fallen in, blocking the way, the Mujahideen would then smear mud over the tank's driver slits before dousing the vehicle in petrol. The crew then faced a terrible dilemma: they could sit tight and hope the flames did not take hold, or bale out to face inevitable death. The guerrillas also became adept at customizing very large anti-tank mines.

Mujahideen courage seemed to have no limit when tackling enemy armoured vehicles. Throughout the whole war government forces and the Soviets lost large numbers of armoured fighting vehicles and these losses continually increased. The Mujahideen excelled at ambushing and trapping convoys. In the Panjsher valley – site of numerous Soviet offensives – the Mujahideen ambushed a big convoy on the road from Sangana to Khenji; it included four T-55s, more than a dozen BTR-60s and fifteen lorries, some of which plunged into the river bordering the road. In Khenji itself an abandoned tank, an armoured personnel carrier, several lorries and an Afghan Army mess truck bore testimony to the ferocity of the attack.

In May–June 1982 at Shawa, halfway up the Panjsher valley, half a dozen Soviet BTR-60s were knocked out and a tank was left stranded in the middle of the river by guerrillas armed with RPGs. Also, a T-72 reportedly had its turret blown off by a home-made mine at Bazarak. During continual harassment and ambushes through the period June–December 1983, the Mujahideen accounted for about 273 armoured fighting vehicles.

A brief survey illustrates the constant drain on resources faced by the government and Soviet armoured formations, and the large number of ambush actions fought. In June 1983 Mujahideen and collaborating armed forces personnel blew up thirty tanks at Shindand air base. Between July and August fourteen Soviet tanks were destroyed in Farah province, while in August an attack on a Soviet military post at Chakri, southeast of Kabul, saw two tanks damaged and a garrison of eighty men massacred. Also during August 1983 a further two tanks were knocked out in Kandahar province.

Between 3 August and 3 September 1983 the Mujahideen launched seven attacks on a convoy passing through Logar en route for Paktia province, destroying thirteen armoured vehicles, thirty-two trucks and six oil tankers. Another convoy of some 2,000 vehicles, passing through Hairtan Port to Khuln, was attacked on 18 August 1983 while crossing the Soviet-Afghan border over a newly constructed bridge on the Amu Darya river, losing two tanks and a jeep. The convoy continued to advance with helicopter gunships flying cover, but they failed to disperse the guerrillas. Two more tanks and several vehicles had to be abandoned after being set alight. Other clashes in the province accounted for another five tanks at Khullam and Samahan. In 1985 the Mujahideen's six-month kill average was 180 tanks and 530 other vehicles; however, during the first six months of 1986 government and Soviet forces lost 380 tanks and 1,120 other vehicles, representing a considerable increase.

By 1987/1988, despite suffering continual losses, the government, with ongoing Soviet resupplies, still managed to retain a powerful armoured force, consisting of 450 tanks and 440 armoured personnel carriers. The majority of the Soviet armoured fighting vehicles deployed in Afghanistan, such as the main battle tanks and large rocket launchers, proved to be ungainly and almost useless against the guerrillas' ambush tactics. Ultimately, though, the critical difference was not in the hardware but in the endurance of both sides.

Operation Magistral in 1987 was the last major offensive conducted by the Soviet Union during its ill-fated intervention in Afghanistan. The battle for Khost, initiated to lift the siege and cut the Mujahideen's supply routes from Pakistan once and for all, was probably the bloodiest of the war. Orchestrated by the Soviets to prove the Afghan Army's fighting capabilities, it involved 24,000 Afghan and Soviet troops sent to rescue the 8,000-strong garrison trapped by up to 20,000 Mujahideen. Brigadier Mohammad Yousaf, head of the Pakistani Inter-Service Intelligence's Afghan Bureau supporting the Mujahideen, recalled in his memoirs:

> Khost was surrounded by mountains in which sat the Mujahideen. All around were a series of defensive posts and minefields, with a substantial garrison at Tani. The Mujahideen were particularly strong to the south and southeast of the town, with their outposts overlooking the plain ... the totally exposed airfield ... was seldom used by the Afghans as we could bring it under fire so easily that they often resorted to parachute dropping of supplies.

The rising Soviet death toll in Afghanistan and the influence of public opinion back home finally began to affect Soviet policy. President Mikhail Gorbachev announced in mid-1986 a limited withdrawal as a sign of good will in the ongoing peace negotiations. This move naturally concerned the Afghan President Najibullah and was met with scepticism by the West. This view was reinforced in October 1986 when units with no tactical value pulled out. Nonetheless, Gorbachev made it clear he wanted to leave Afghanistan as soon as possible.

In the face of an imminent Soviet withdrawal, the Afghan government decided that it must at all costs avoid the loss of Khost and sever the rebels' supply routes. Ostensibly an Afghan operation, the relief was commanded by Major General Shahnawaz Tani (although he was to be subordinate to the Soviets) and Interior Minister Major General Mohammed Gulabzoi. On the Soviet side, General Valentin Varennikov, Senior Military Adviser to Kabul, oversaw the operation, with operational control in the hands of Lieutenant General Boris Gromov, commander of the Soviet 40th Army.

The drive on Khost had to be forced along 122 kilometres of guerrilla-infested road, through the Satu Kandau Pass and down the Zadran valley. The Mujahideen, although lacking heavy weapons, had plenty of rocket-propelled grenades to make the passage of the relief force highly dangerous. The outlying Afghan Army posts in the area – consisting of Tora Ghara mountain, Badam Bagh, Khost air base, Sinaki and Nadar Shah Kot fort, all of which were directed by Soviet advisers – were all awkward to defend.

Initially employing only Afghan troops, the offensive commenced on 18 November 1987 but immediately ran into tough resistance in the Shamal

Valley and elsewhere along the route. With the Soviets providing air support, on 24 November the Afghans captured positions in Ghalgai, Dara, Makhuzu, Sarooti Kandau and Shini Ghakhe. A month later, on 28 December, the Soviets claimed to be within 9 kilometres of Khost, while the guerrillas claimed to have halted them some 48 kilometres away. That same day a further attack on Saranai failed and Soviet paratroops lost sixty-three men as they withdrew, hotly pursued by the vengeful Mujahideen. The Khost garrison again attempted to break out, reaching Ismail Khel 10 kilometres to the west, before being driven back once more.

Khost was finally relieved on 30 December 1987 when trucks bearing 4,500 tonnes of supplies rumbled into the town. By 20 January some 400 trucks had got through, bringing 18,000 tonnes of much-needed provisions. This operation cost the Afghan and Soviet Armies dearly. According to the Mujahideen, between 18 and 29 December 1987 the Afghan Army lost 1,000 dead, possibly 2,000 wounded and 346 taken prisoner. Approximately 110 armoured vehicles were destroyed, including forty-seven tanks, as well as seven aircraft. The Soviets suffered very heavy casualties by normal standards, with at least 900 killed and wounded. Reports of Mujahideen casualties ranged from 150 to 1,500 dead, with possibly 2,000 wounded. Ironically, as soon as the bulk of the government/Soviet relief force withdrew from Khost, the Mujahideen simply resumed their blockade.

*   *   *

Once more, as in Angola and Ethiopia, tanks proved ineffective against well equipped and motivated guerrilla armies. Even with the backing of considerable air power, the Soviet Army was ultimately unable to prevail. It withdrew two years later leaving the Afghan government to struggle on alone for a number of years. In Afghanistan, like Africa, the terrain was simply not suitable for conventional mechanized warfare. Just as the Americans had come to rely on helicopters in Vietnam, so had the Soviets in the Hindu Kush.

# Chapter 14

# Middle Eastern Blitzkrieg
## The Iran-Iraq War, 1980–1988

At the beginning of the Iran-Iraq War in 1980 the two sides threw very sizeable tank forces at each other with gusto. However, what started as an Iraqi blitzkrieg soon bogged down into a terrible war of attrition, in which neither side showed any great flair with the employment of armour. As the conflict progressed, the Iranian Army became increasingly reliant on infantry, as did the Iranian Revolutionary Guard Corps. On paper, Iran had a very large tank fleet of about 2,000 vehicles, most of which had been purchased from Western sources, although the Shah was beginning to diversify. Before the Iranian Revolution, he ordered 875 British-built Chieftain Mk 5Ps and 1,200 *Shir Iran* ('Persian Lions' – Challengers with Chobham armour), but did not receive the latter. The Iranians began the war with 707 Mk 3/3P and Mk 5/5P Chieftains, 187 improved Chieftains and 40 Chieftain Armoured Recovery Vehicles. Initially Iran was also equipped with 250 British Scorpion light tanks.

The Iranians also had considerable numbers of American-built tanks, including 640 M47s and M48s. The 90mm-armed M48, like its predecessors, was under-gunned and had many design faults. The better armed 105mm M60A1 helped to rectify this and in 1980 Iran had 460 of them. The Iranian Army also deployed a number of American self-propelled guns, including the 175mm M107, the 155mm M109 and the 8in howitzer (203mm) M110. Iran's mechanized and motorized units were equipped with 2,000 armoured personnel carriers, consisting of the American M113 and the Soviet BTR-40/60/152 series. Despite this very impressive inventory, the Iranians lacked trained crews and mechanics, meaning that large numbers of these vehicles were held in storage. After the revolution, armoured corps officers were persecuted for their loyalty to the deposed Shah and their Western attitudes. Many had undergone British and American training.

In Iraq Saddam Hussein commenced the conflict with 2,850 tanks, including 50 T-34s and 1,850 T-55/T-62s. The Iraqis also deployed the 115mm-armed T-62 and had fifty of the newer T-72s, although this number steadily rose. Saddam then turned to France, buying the French *Char de Combat* AMX-30 main battle tank, which was also supplied to Libya and Saudi Arabia. Iraq also purchased the French *Cannon Automateur de 155mm* GCT self-propelled gun, mounted on the AMX chassis. Both Iraq and Iran used the Chinese Type 59 (copy of the Soviet T-54/55) and Type 69 (copy of the Soviet T-55) tanks. Other light AFVs in the Iraqi armoury included the Soviet PT-76, of which it had about 100. In total, Iraq fielded about 1,900 armoured vehicles of the BTR-40/50/60/125 series, as well as the Soviet BMP-1 infantry combat vehicle.

Before the war Iran had about four armoured divisions, each consisting of two armoured brigades containing two armoured battalions, one mechanized battalion, one artillery battalion and an engineer company. At the time of the Iraqi invasion, they were able to field only a single armoured division on the key southern front. In addition, they had two mechanized infantry divisions. By 1984, due to substantial losses and constant reorganisations, Iran had just three mechanized divisions, each of three brigades, totalling nine armoured and eighteen mechanized battalions. The following year Iranian armour strength included 300 Chieftains, 200 M47/M48A5s and 250 M60A1s, as well as 200 Type 59, T-54/T-55 and T-62/T-72 tanks captured from the Iraqis. In 1986–1987 Iran still had three mechanized divisions equipped with 1,000 tanks but it is doubtful whether many of these could be put into action.

To begin with, Iraq had four armoured divisions, two mechanized divisions, one independent armoured brigade and a Republican Guard mechanized brigade. This force had expanded by 1984–1985 to six armoured divisions (each of one or two armoured and one mechanized brigade), five mechanized/motorized infantry divisions and two armoured Presidential Guard brigades. Saddam Hussein's tank force in 1985 included 200 T-54/T-55s, 1,000 T-62s, 600 T-72s, 400 Type 59s, 200 Type 69s and 100 Romanian M77s, as well as the French AMX-30s. By 1986–1987 his formations were down to five armoured divisions and three mechanized/motorized divisions, but he still managed to retain a powerful tank fleet of 4,500 vehicles. Only a fraction of this number, though, were combat ready.

Both sides lost armour at a rapid rate and in large numbers, showing how vital replacement sources were and how this dictated the use of armour, in

Marines advance, supported by an M48 Patton during street fighting in Hue, Vietnam, 1968.

American troops examining a knocked-out North Vietnamese Army PT-76 amphibious light tank.

An Israeli M48 Magach taking on ammunition somewhere in Sinai in 1973.

A column of Israeli M48 Magachs moving towards the Suez Canal during the Yom Kippur War.

Israeli Centurions supported by armoured infantry firing on Syrian tanks on the Golan Heights, 1973.

Syrian T-54s knocked out on the Golan Heights.

More Syrian T-54/55 tanks destroyed whilst fighting the Israelis.

The business end of an Israeli Centurion. This tank was a firm favourite with the Israeli armoured corps thanks to its reliability and its ability to remain operational even after sustaining considerable battle damage.

uth Vietnamese soldiers with a damaged
orth Vietnamese Type 59 captured in 1972
uth of Dong Ha during the North's Easter
ffensive.

e Ethiopian Army captured this Somali T-54
ak during the Ogaden War.

is T-54/55 came a-cropper in Ethiopia during the long and brutal civil war.

Mujahideen with a burnt-out T-34/85. At the time of the Soviet invasion, Kabul had about 200 of these tanks still in service.

(*Left*) A Mujahideen tank hunter. He is wearing a Soviet tank crew helmet, probably a trophy from one of his kills.

(*Right*) A resistance anti-tank team ambush a Soviet armoured vehicle with their RPG-7.

he British Chieftain tank saw combat with the Iranian Army during the Iran-Iraq War.

ug-in Iraqi T-55s. The war soon went from mobile to bogged-down.

Israeli Zelda M113 armoured personnel carriers in Lebanon.

An Angolan T-54. A number of these tanks were used to attack the UNITA stronghold at Mavinga.

addition to the usual terrain constraints. Furthermore, Iraq and Iran both employed their armoured forces in unimaginative ways and often in a cumbersome manner. During the initial invasion in September 1980, in which the Iraqi spearhead consisted of mixed armoured units, they ended up with several hundred tanks and armoured personnel carriers stranded south of Abadan. The lack of Iranian air cover was notable from the start. On 12 October 1980 the Iraqis used pontoon ferries to get their tanks across the Karun river north of Abadan with little or no interference from the Iranian Air Force. It was only when the Iraqis became embroiled in Khorramshahr that they lost more armoured vehicles. Even in 1982, with the Iranian counter-offensive, Iraqi armour was still able to use the Khorramshahr highway with impunity.

By February 1983 Iran had captured 1,460 Soviet-built tanks and armoured personnel carriers, many of which they were able to recondition through the acquisition of Soviet engines. The Iraqis, though, always managed to obtain adequate replacements. At the beginning of June 1984 Iraq deployed hundreds of tanks on the southern front in anticipation of an Iranian offensive, including T-72s, some of them apparently on brand-new tank transporters. They lost forty-five tanks and armoured personnel carriers, mainly to Iran's Chinese-manufactured recoilless rifles and Soviet rocket-propelled grenades, during the Iranian Operation *Fatim Zahra* and the Battle for Highway 6 north of Basra in March 1985.

Fear of Iranian anti-tank weapons resulted in sixty Iraqi tanks on the same front forming a laager, despite the fact they had the upper hand. The Iranians seem to have had an abundance of RPGs and the Iraqis captured large numbers of them, including one batch of more than thirty-four launchers. This may be accounted for by the fact that in 1978 the Shah's government was operating an RPG-7 factory and it was still in production in March 1982.

In December 1985 the Iranians amassed assault craft and pontoon bridging equipment ready for their assault on the southern Fao peninsula, dubbed Operation *Val Fajr 8*, on 9 February 1986. During the offensive Iraqi air support was poor and the Iraqi Air Force found few exposed targets as the Iranians had learnt from past experience the importance of dispersing and camouflaging their forces. After the failure of their counter-attack on 13–14 February 1986, the Iraqis used their tanks as artillery, wearing out some 200 tank gun barrels in the process. The Iraqi Air Force failed to cut the pontoon bridges over the Shatt al-Arab Waterway, and the

Iranians were able to reinforce their bridgehead with their own tanks and artillery.

When the Iranians recaptured Mehran during *Karbala 2* on 2 July 1986, the Iraqis lost at least twenty armoured vehicles. During the Iranian *Karbala 5* offensive in January–February 1987, their acquisition of large numbers of US anti-tank missiles cost the Iraqis more than ninety-five tanks and other armoured vehicles. On 7 April 1987 the follow-up operation, *Karbala 8*, destroyed dozens more Iraqi vehicles.

Iranian use of armour was notoriously bad, compounded by a lack of air cover, and their difficulties were exacerbated by the resupply problem. For example, thirteen Iranian tanks were knocked out by an Iraqi helicopter strike near Susangerd on 19 November 1980. By the end of 1980 the Iraqis had captured thirty-one Chieftains, as well as twenty-five M60s and forty-three assorted AFVs. In January 1981, during an abortive counter-attack south of Susangerd, the Iranians lost 100 tanks. In September that year, during Operation *Thamin Ul-A 'imma*, in which the Iranians lifted the siege of Abadan, they lost 150 of their M48A5s that were simply abandoned. This was probably down to poor crew training. Ironically, in 1987, working through a middleman in the Emirates, they bought the tanks back from the Iraqis, who had been unable to integrate them with their Soviet equipment. Another 196 tanks were lost on 22 March 1982 in Operation *Fath Ul-Mobin*, launched west of Dezful and Shush.

The replacement of war losses was a problem for both sides, and new arms had to be secured from a variety of sources. In February 1981 reports from London and Washington indicated that Iraq had received about 100 T-55s from East Germany, or Poland, via Saudi Arabia. To circumvent the US arms embargo, Iran turned to a number of Eastern and Western European countries, as well as to Israel, Syria, Libya and North Korea. In July and October 1981 Israel sent tank spares and ammunition for Iran's US-supplied equipment, while on 14 July 1981 Libya began shipment of 190 vitally needed replacement tanks after training 200 Iranian tank crew. Also in July there were indications that a Soviet-Iranian agreement had been reached over training officers and providing technicians.

After successfully expelling Iraq's invading forces, Iran needed arms on a systematic basis, as the current ad hoc nature of its supplies was severely hampering the effectiveness of its operations. In February 1982 Iran made it clear that it would accept Soviet weapons and advisers. Syria's role as a middleman was enhanced and in March that year the volume of arms through Syria increased, including Soviet engines for captured Iraqi tanks. In the US the government turned a blind eye to private companies exporting spare parts to Iran. One American company regularly sent goods marked 'Tractor Engines' from Boston to Tehran. This continued until a customs officer with a military background noticed that the engines were equipped with superchargers. They were being used as replacements for the engines in Iran's M60s. By the end of 1982 North Korea had supplied Iran with 150 T-62s.

Initially, the Soviet Union ceased its arms shipments to Iraq, but the Iraqis simply turned to France. By the end of 1980 Iraq had acquired more than 100 AMX-30 tanks and scores of light armoured cars equipped with anti-tank missiles. During 1985–1986 France was still supplying Iraq, which took delivery of self-propelled guns, anti-aircraft systems and armoured recovery vehicles. The US exchanged weapons with Iraq for four years, despite the policy of neutrality. Pentagon officials are said to have negotiated as far back as 1982 to swap artillery for Soviet helicopters and armoured vehicles.

China was likewise quick to capitalize on the Iran-Iraq War. It exported up to 2,500 Type 59s and Type 69s between 1982 and 1989, many of which went to Iraq and Iran. The Chinese signed a contract in 1981 with Saddam to supply up to 600 Type 59s. The year after, this was followed by another deal for 400 Type 69s. All deliveries were completed by 1986. Initially, Iraq ordered up to 200 Type 69-Is armed with the smoothbore 100mm gun, which were delivered via Saudi Arabia in 1983. These were followed by Type 69-IIs. Iran also obtained about 400 Type 59/69s.

Throughout the eight-year-long Iran-Iraq War the tactical use of tanks on both sides was poor. Regardless of the unfavourable terrain, neither side seemed able to organize and conduct large-scale armoured operations effectively. When Iraq first invaded Iran, its armoured formations –schooled in Soviet doctrine, led by largely British-trained officers – did exhibit some blitzkrieg characteristics. The Iraqis deployed large columns of up to 100 tanks, which in at least one instance were moved around on tank transporters because of the unsuitable roads. But lacking infantry support, particularly those trained for street fighting, the invasion bogged down around the cities and nothing came of their opening armoured thrusts. Coordination and cooperation between infantry and armour on both sides was extremely poor.

Iran's armour usually operated as independent brigades in support of the regular army, the *Pasdaran* (Islamic Revolutionary Guard Corps) and the *Basij* (Popular Mobilisation Army). Inter-service rivalry and poor communication between these organisations greatly hampered effective planning, with predictable results. Increasingly, the *Pasdaran* and *Basij* relied on massed human-wave attacks using teenagers to capture their objectives. The army's commanders were understandably horrified by the resulting loss of life.

Iraqi air power made it difficult for the Iranians to operate effectively, even on a divisional level. Without adequate air cover, Iran could not concentrate its armour, nor did it ever have sufficient numbers to do so. The Iranians proved particularly inept in the tactical siting of their tanks, which resulted in them being easily knocked out. Most of Iraq's armoured divisions ended up committed to static defence roles near Baghdad and Basra. Generally, both sides resorted to using their tanks as mobile artillery or pill-boxes.

# Chapter 15

# Beirut and Back

## The Arab-Israeli War, 1982

The fifth Arab-Israeli War involved Israeli armoured columns charging headlong into two Syrian armoured divisions. Israeli planning for the invasion of Lebanon to counter the terrorist activities of Yasser Arafat's Palestinian Liberation Organisation (PLO) started in late 1981. The IDF intended to deploy some six-and-a-half divisions, with about 75,000 men, 1,240 tanks and 1,500 armoured personnel carriers. Troops were also kept on the Golan Heights to deter the Syrians from attacking the vulnerable base of the IDF advance. Notably, making its debut was the Israeli-built Merkava tank. For the attack on Lebanon, the Israelis deployed 180 Merkava Mk Is, which were to perform well, unlike the accompanying M113s or Zeldas.

The PLO had approximately 15,000 men in Lebanon. The bulk of them were organized into three conventional brigades, with the Yarmouk Brigade stationed on the coast, the Kastel Brigade in the south, and the Karameh Brigade on Mount Hermon's eastern slopes, in an area known to the Israelis as Fatahland. To fend off the IDF's armour, the PLO had only about sixty tanks, plus some heavy artillery, mortars and truck-mounted rocket launchers. The tanks were largely old T-34/85s that were really only useful as static pill-boxes. One of the biggest menaces to Israeli armour were the young Ashbal ('Lion Cubs') or 'RPG kids' recruited by the PLO, who would remain hidden until the last minute.

The rival Syrian-backed Palestinian Liberation Army had two brigades plus some smaller units deployed in Syria and Syrian-occupied Lebanon. A third brigade was in Jordan. Their total strength was about 4,000. They were armed and equipped as regular troops, effectively part of the Syrian armed forces, so were not available to support PLO operations. Likewise, the 2,100-strong Saiqa faction of the PLO also answered to the Syrians.

To complicate matters for the Israeli planners, the Syrian Army had about 30,000 men with 712 tanks deployed in two main areas of Lebanon.

In the strategic Bekaa Valley running down the eastern side of the country was the 1st Armoured Division, comprising the 91st and 76th Tank Brigades with 160 tanks each, supported by the 58th Mechanized Brigade with forty tanks, and the 62nd Independent Tank Brigade with another thirty-two tanks. In the Beirut and Shouf Mountains area guarding the important and vulnerable Beirut–Damascus Highway was the 68th Tank Brigade with 160 tanks, the 85th Mechanized Brigade with thirty-two tanks and an infantry brigade with another thirty-two tanks. All in all, this was a formidable-looking tank force that the Israelis would have preferred not to tangle with.

Israel's strategy for Operation Peace for Galilee was to push its tanks up the Lebanese coast, bypassing the major PLO centres and cutting off their escape route through the Bekaa. Only then could the PLO be destroyed piecemeal. On the central front the old Crusader fortress of Beaufort Castle was an important initial objective. Overlooking southern Lebanon and northern Israel, it had been a PLO artillery observation post for years.

Lebanon had gained independence from France in 1943. Just five years later, with the creation of Israel, thousands of Palestinian refugees poured northwards and crossed into southern Lebanon. For twenty years they lived in refugee camps, dreaming of an independent state of Palestine. Then in 1968 Beirut became the headquarters of the PLO, the umbrella organisation for the different political factions dedicated to the overthrow of Israel. The PLO set up bases in southern Lebanon to carry out cross-border terror operations in Israel. Largely unwillingly, the Lebanese were dragged into the Arab-Israeli conflict.

Lebanon was fractured along factional lines during the civil war of 1975–1976. The PLO was unable to keep out of this internecine warfare and was soon fighting Lebanese Christian militias. At the height of the conflict Syria despatched its PLO faction (known as Saiqa) and the Palestinian Liberation Army to fight alongside the Muslim forces. In turn, the Christians supported the Syrian-Lebanese peace plan, but the PLO refused to cooperate. Syria sent troops, sanctioned by the Arab League, to help the Christians and prevent the PLO establishing a state within Lebanon capable of resisting Syrian aspirations. The Syrians also consolidated their military presence in Beirut and the Bekaa Valley. After the 1979 Camp David accord between Israel and Egypt, Syria's relations with the PLO improved and the Syrians withdrew from the coast. Despite this, by 1981 Syria still controlled two-thirds of the country and refused to withdraw.

Israel launched Operation Peace for Galilee on 6 June 1982, invading Lebanon along a 100-kilometre front. The Israelis were clearly hoping for a repeat of the Six Day War as they could not afford a protracted conflict. The invasion was only intended to force the PLO out of southern Lebanon, but at the same time it seemed highly unlikely that a confrontation with the Syrians could be avoided in the Bekaa, Beirut, the Shouf mountains and along the Beirut-Damascus Highway.

Major General Yekutiel Adam's Task Force West, formed by Brigadier General Yitzhak Mordechai's 91st Division, was to push up the Mediterranean coast towards Beirut. Lieutenant General Amir Drori's Task Force Centre, employing the 36th and 162nd Divisions, was to advance along the slopes of the Lebanon Range. Lastly, Major General Avigdor Ben Gal's Task Force East potentially had the toughest task, which was to clear Fatahland and the Bekaa. His forces comprised the 90th and 252nd Armoured Divisions, plus two major ad hoc formations.

At 1100 hours the three brigades of Mordechai's Ugda 91 crossed the border to the west. Under the cover of artillery and air-strikes, Israeli Centurions pushed north, supported by paratroops acting as infantry riding on the Zeldas. Amphibious armoured landings were also conducted all along the Lebanese coast. By nightfall Task Force West had isolated Tyre and was halfway to Sidon. The following day, in the centre, it took the Israelis three hours to overcome a regular Palestinian battalion and six T-34 tanks at the PLO's Nabatiyeh camp. This was discovered to contain a large number of international terrorists, who were undergoing training. In total, Israel rounded up about 1,800 foreign terrorists from twenty-six countries in southern Lebanon. Task Force East, struggling along the mountain tracks, made slow progress in the face of determined PLO tank-hunter teams and supporting Syrian artillery fire.

On 8 June the Israelis moved to secure Tyre and Sidon, while some of the amphibious assault forces moved on Damour, just south of Beirut. Israeli tanks and armoured personnel carrier-borne infantry came into contact for the first time with Syrian armour and artillery at Jezzine, where they were supporting a Palestinian Liberation Army brigade. The Syrians had reinforced the town with a tank battalion and a commando unit. Both the Syrians and Israelis had orders not to fire on each other, but fighting soon broke out. The Israelis claimed all of the Syrians' T-62s for the loss of eight tanks. Once beyond Jezzine, the Israelis were soon heading for Syrian positions around Lake Qaraoun. On the eastern flank they ran into well dug-in Syrian T-62 tanks, which opened fire. In response the Israelis called up their anti-tank helicopters.

The day after, near Joub Jannine northeast of Qaraoun, Israeli armour encountered a Syrian/PLO force armed with Sagger anti-tank missiles. These hit three armoured personnel carriers and a Centurion before Israeli artillery fire silenced the Sagger teams. On 9 June PLO artillery killed Major General Adam, commander of Task Force West, when his field headquarters was hit. Inevitably, the Israeli advance was now threatening Syria's hold on Lebanon and the Israelis planned to sever the Beirut–Damascus Highway, which would cut off the Syrian forces.

Seizing the initiative, the Syrian 58th Mechanized Brigade and 1st Commando Battalion at Ein Zehalta, in the Shouf Mountains, ambushed an Israeli column of M60 Patton tanks at 2300 hours. First, they pinned down the Israelis, who were descending a steep road, with prolonged shelling. Then the Syrian commandos and T-62 tanks got amongst the Pattons, causing heavy casualties. The only way to extricate them was with air cover, but this could not be guaranteed because of the Syrian surface-to-air missile defences sited nearby in the Bekaa. Instead, supporting Israeli artillery dropped anti-personnel shells right on top of their own tanks and the Pattons were eventually able to withdraw. Ein Zehalta was subsequently taken by an Israeli paratrooper battalion flown in by helicopter.

It was clear that the situation would lead to an escalation in the fighting with Syria. Indeed, the Syrian president Assad's forces in the Lebanon were facing a crisis. War had not been officially declared, but those units in Beirut were in danger of being isolated. Syria was suddenly faced with the prospect of losing its foothold in Lebanon altogether. Assad's brother Rifaat urged him to send more surface-to-air missiles to Zahle in the Bekaa to counter the Israeli Air Force, though Defence Minister General Mustafa Tlas opposed this, as his intelligence suggested the Israelis would probably knock them out. Regardless of the general's advice, more batteries were despatched. The main battle for the Bekaa took place in the air.

On the ground in the Bekaa it was the Syrian armoured forces that bore the brunt of the Israeli assault and suffered as a result. Syrian tank crews performed far better than in 1967 and 1973, this time often fighting with great tenacity and skill when standing their ground. On day five half of the Syrian 1st Armoured Division was destroyed around Lake Qaraoun at the southern end of the valley. This enabled the Israelis to consolidate their hold along the Bekaa–Joub Jannine line. However, one Israeli tank battalion drove into the assembly area of the 58th Mechanized Brigade and became trapped. It was unable to escape until the following day and had to leave behind a number of M60s.

The Syrian 3rd Armoured Division also suffered a bloody nose in the Bekaa on 11 June. The T-72 tanks of its 82nd Armoured Brigade came up against the Merkavas of the 7th Armoured Brigade. The Syrians blundered into the Israeli positions and within minutes nine of their tanks had been knocked out. The Merkava's armour proved invulnerable and although they were hit many times, no crew were killed. Major General Avigdor Ben Gal recalled, 'To our great satisfaction, we saw that the T-72s burn just like any other tank.' Capture of a T-72 would have been a windfall for Western intelligence agencies and the Syrians tried unsuccessfully to prevent the Israelis from removing one of them. Although a cease-fire with the Syrians, that included the PLO, came into effect on 12 June, sporadic fighting continued.

The Syrian 85th Mechanized Brigade, equipped with T-55 tanks and BTR and BMP armoured personnel carriers, attacked Israeli armour south of Beirut on 14 June in an attempt to stop the IDF cutting its communications with Damascus. It got to within 100 and even 50 metres, and fought stubbornly until all its equipment was lost. Although this proved the Syrians' ability to stand and fight, squandering their forces in this way did not say much for their leadership or tactics. Although many of the Syrian Army's units had been severely battered in the often-fierce engagements with the IDF, the bulk of them in the Bekaa were able to withdraw to the vicinity of the Damascus Highway. Nonetheless, the Syrian armoured corps had been unable to stop the Israeli tanks and the Syrian tank forces passed their anti-tank mission over to Syrian anti-tank helicopters and commando forces.

In the Bekaa on 22 June Syrian surface-to-air missile sites were again attacked by the Israeli Air Force. At Damour the IDF captured 5,000 tons of arms and ammunition, including anti-aircraft missiles. By the end of June the IDF had collected 4,170 tons of ammunition, 764 vehicles, 26,900 light weapons and 424 heavy weapons. Somewhat ironically, in August Israel sold $50 million worth of captured Syrian and PLO arms and ammunition to Iran.

The IDF besieged the PLO in Beirut until mid-August 1982, when they finally agreed to quit the city; some 14,400 Palestinian fighters and Syrian soldiers withdrew, including the remains of the 85th Mechanized Brigade and the Palestinian Liberation Army. The PLO left by sea, while the Syrians and their allies were given safe-conduct along the Beirut–Damascus Highway.

Syrian Army losses are believed to have been up to 1,200 dead, approximately 3,000 wounded and 296 taken prisoner, as well as almost 500 armoured vehicles. The PLO lost 1,500 dead and an unknown number of wounded; more importantly, they also lost their entire infrastructure in Lebanon, including all their personnel files. Operation Peace for Galilee cost the IDF 368 dead and 2,383 wounded in six weeks of fighting.

The Syrian Army caught up in the fighting lost 200 T-62s, 125 T-54/55s, nine T-72s and 140 armoured personnel carriers. The Israelis found that at least 200 of these were in salvageable condition. Afterwards, Syria went on a massive armoured vehicle buying spree. In the early 1980s they ordered 800 BMP-1s, as well as large numbers of T-72 tanks and BTR-80 armoured personnel carriers. Then, in the early 1990s, the Syrians ordered 252 T-72 tanks from Czechoslovakia and another 350 from Russia. Israel meanwhile had gained a valuable security buffer in southern Lebanon to supplement its Golan Heights defences.

*Chapter 16*

# Uncle Sam's Final Showdown
## The Gulf War, 1990–1991

After President Saddam Hussein's disastrous and fruitless nine-year war with Iran, in the late 1980s he decided to distract public attention away from the economic and political failings of his regime by embarking on a new foreign adventure: to reclaim Iraq's lost province – oil-rich Kuwait. The pretext for the invasion was a spurious row over oil production, but it served its purpose and tension was rapidly cranked up. Saddam's Medina and Hammurabi Armoured Divisions, two powerful Republican Guard Corps units, invaded Kuwait on 2 August 1990. The following day the Tawakalna Republican Guard Armoured Division moved to secure Kuwait's border with Saudi Arabia, sealing the country from the outside world.

President Bush instigated Operation Desert Shield, a massive multi-national effort to defend Saudi Arabia. Major General Houston's US 82nd and Major General James H.B. Peay III's 101st Airborne Divisions arrived in August 1990. The US 24th Infantry (Mechanized) Division under Major General Barry McCaffrey was the first heavy formation to deploy to the Gulf in September 1990, with its 1st and 2nd Brigades. This was followed by Brigadier General John Tilelli's US 1st Cavalry Division and Major General Thomas Rhame's US 1st Infantry (Mechanized) Division in December that year. All these units had come from America and, with the exception of the 3rd Armoured Cavalry Regiment, were equipped with the M1 or IPM1 Abrams tank armed with a 105mm gun. Due to the collapse of the Warsaw Pact and the negligible threat posed by the Soviet Union, Washington was able to redeploy Major General Ronald Griffith's 1st Armored and Major General Paul Funk's 3rd Armored Divisions from Germany to bolster Desert Shield. All these units were equipped with the newer improved M1A1 tank with a Rheinmetall 120mm M256 gun.

By late January 1991 there were well over half a million US personnel in theatre. The number of US ground forces committed to Desert Shield, and the subsequent operations Desert Storm and Desert Sabre under General H. Norman Schwarzkopf to liberate Kuwait, was staggering: approximately 260,000 troops equipped with some 2,000 M1A1 tanks and 2,200 M2 and M3 Bradley infantry fighting vehicles, supported by 500 artillery pieces plus 190 Apache and 150 Cobra attack helicopters. There were also 90,000 Marines with 250 M60 tanks, 250 Light Armoured Vehicles, 430 amphibious assault vehicles and 160 aircraft.

Britain committed 35,000 men under Lieutenant General Sir Peter de la Billiere, including the 1st British Armoured Division under Operation Granby. This division included the 7th Armoured Brigade or 'Desert Rats', with two regiments of FV4030 Challenger Mk 3s, and the 4th Armoured Brigade with another regiment, totalling 160 tanks, commanded by Major General Rupert Smith. The division's three mechanized infantry battalions were each equipped with forty-five new FV510 Warrior mechanized combat vehicles. The two reconnaissance units were equipped with a range of vehicles based on the Scorpion.

France contributed 14,000 men, as part of Opération Daguet under Lieutenant General Michel Roquejoffre, who commanded the French Rapid Reaction Force. They comprised Foreign Legion, Marine infantry, helicopter and armoured car units. The main formation was the 6th Light Armoured Division with forty AMX-10C armoured fighting vehicles under Brigadier General Mouscardes. It should be noted that French divisions are smaller than their NATO counterparts and are typically reinforced brigades. However, the 6th Division was augmented with reinforcements that included the 4th Dragoon Regiment, a tank unit equipped with forty-four AMX-30B2 tanks, from the French 10th Armoured Division. Although the AMX-30B2 was old and due to be replaced by the Leclerc, it was more than able to deal with most Iraqi tanks.

The Kuwaiti Army in exile consisted of three or four brigades, totalling 10–15,000 men, equipped with more than sixty Chieftain and M-84 tanks. The principal armoured unit was the 38th Kuwaiti Armoured Brigade, dubbed the 'Al Shadid' (Martyrs). This brigade had lost twenty-two of its eighty Chieftains during the Iraqi invasion. The 35th Kuwaiti Mechanized Brigade was equipped with M113s. Saudi Arabia contributed two main forces: the regular Saudi Arabian Armed Forces (SAAF) and the Saudi Arabian National Guard (SANG). By 1991 the SAAF totalled 67,500 men, and the army or Royal Saudi Land Forces (RSLF) fielded 40,000 of them, organized into two armoured and four mechanized brigades (including the

10th Armoured Brigade and the 8th, 10th, 11th and 20th Mechanized Brigades), one infantry brigade and one airborne brigade, equipped with 550 tanks (including 300 French AMX-30s and 250 American M60s) and 1,840 combat vehicles, armoured personnel carriers and armoured cars. SANG totalled 55,000 men with 35,000 active and 20,000 tribal levies, equipped with 1,100 American V-150 Commando armoured personnel carriers.

The largest Arab contingent came from Egypt, with 47,000 troops consisting of the 3rd Mechanized Division (with about 200 M60s and 300 M113 and M109 self-propelled guns) and the 4th Armoured Division (with about 250 M60s and a similar number of M113 and M109 self-propelled guns). Syria committed 19,000 men, consisting of one airborne brigade and the 9th Armoured Division (with 250 T-62 and T-72 tanks plus BMP infantry fighting vehicles). Both Egypt and Syria stated their troops were only deployed to defend Saudi Arabia, though this policy was to change. Qatar also provided an armoured battalion equipped with about twenty-four French-supplied AMX-30 tanks. In total, the Coalition gathered half a million men from thirty-one countries armed with 3,400 tanks and 1,600 pieces of artillery, while the Allied air forces included 1,736 combat aircraft and 750 support aircraft.

Despite this massed array of military hardware and calls by the United Nations for Iraq to withdraw, Saddam Hussein refused to leave Kuwait. In the face of such obstinacy the Coalition prepared its plans for a ground war, but first, under the guise of Operation Desert Storm, Coalition fighter-bombers hunted down every piece of Iraqi military equipment they could find. By early January 1991 Western intelligence reports suggested that Saddam's forces deployed in the Kuwaiti theatre of operations, encompassing Kuwait and southern Iraq, numbered approximately 540,000 men, equipped with 4,000 tanks, 2,700 armoured personnel carriers and other armoured fighting vehicles and 3,000 pieces of artillery. This force included the 150,000-strong elite Republican Guard Corps. These figures were based on the assessment that forty-three Iraqi divisions were in the Kuwaiti theatre of operations. On the face of it, this was a formidable fighting force that would not be easy to defeat.

The Iraqis had considerable but somewhat mixed experiences of armoured warfare. In 1973 the Iraqi 3rd Armoured Division had been committed in support of the Syrians, but performed fairly poorly, losing 140 tanks to the Israelis. This was followed by nine years of war with Iran between 1980 and 1988. However, tactical use of tanks on both sides was at best unimaginative. Nonetheless, within the Iraqi armed forces Saddam's Republican Guard Corps had gained a particularly tough reputation. While hardly comparable to Hitler's elite Waffen-SS, during the Iran-Iraq conflict the Guard had formed a strategic reserve, acting as a 'fire brigade' that was sent to any front that was in need of bolstering. It fought on almost every front and in most of the major battles, expanding from one armoured brigade in 1980 to three armoured, one infantry and one commando brigades by 1987. Four years later it was claimed that the Corps consisted of seven whole divisions. Whenever the Guard appeared Iraqi morale was greatly improved, as was their combat performance.

Despite the impressive numbers, the truth was that neither the Iraqi Army nor the Republican Guard had been given time to recover from the gruelling conflict with Iran. In 1990 Iraq was still equipped with Brazilian, Chinese, Czech and Russian armour, much of it poorly serviced and in desperate need of spares. Saddam's armoured forces were equipped with some 5,500 tanks, comprising 2,500 Russian T-54/55s, 1,500 Chinese Type 59/69s, 1,000 Russian T-62s and 500 T-72s, as well as 8,100 armoured personnel carriers consisting of Russian BMP-1/2 infantry fighting vehicles, BTR-50/60/152s and MTLBs, Czech OT-62/63s, Chinese YW-531s, American M113s and Brazilian EE-11s. These forces were supported by 500 Russian-supplied self-propelled guns of the 122mmm, 152mm and 155mm calibre, and 3,200 pieces of artillery and multiple rocket launchers.

The bulk of the Iraqi tank fleet consisted of the tried and tested Soviet-supplied T-54/55, T-62 and T-72 range of tanks – all of which were decidedly long in the tooth by 1990. The T-72 was the Iraqi Army's most modern tank during Desert Storm, although it was a good ten years older than the US Abrams. A few Iraqi-upgraded Russian T-54/T-55 or Chinese Type-59/69 tanks with additional frontal arc armour (giving a greater degree of protection against high-explosive anti-tank rounds) were encountered by Coalition tanks during the fighting. Some of the Iraqi T-62s had also been modified in a number of areas. It was unknown if they had any fitted to fire laser-guided missiles via the 115mm gun.

The Americans had very good intelligence on the T-55/62 and even the T-72 in part due to the Arab-Israeli Wars. The Israelis first fought the T-54/55 in 1967 and the T-62 in 1973. During the Six Day War the Arabs lost 1,072 tanks and about another 2,000 in the Yom Kippur War, and many were passed on to the US for intelligence analysis. The guns of both tank types performed poorly in long-range exchanges (over 1,500 metres), and while the T-62's 115mm U5-T smoothbore gun was effective, crew performance was hampered by the cramped conditions. Likewise, their excellent armour was compromised by the location of internal fuel and ammunition stores (adding greatly to the risk of internal detonation, even from a glancing hit). The Soviet-designed tanks also had a tendency to overheat in the desert, thereby aggravating the already severe problem of crew discomfort.

Combat experience had already shown that the 105mm/M68 tank gun firing armour-piercing fin-stabilized discarding-sabot (APFSDS) projectiles was capable of penetrating the frontal armour on early T-72s. The Abrams' 120mm had the added advantage of firing the M829 APFSDS-T (T = tracer) round with a depleted uranium penetrator. This meant that the M1A1 and the 105mm-armed M60 could easily deal with the cream of the Iraqi armour. In fact, the US Department of Defense was almost ecstatic over the Abrams' performance in the Gulf. Likewise, the British Challenger's 120mm gun could knock out enemy tanks at 2,500 yards and beyond, and with its excellent thermal sights it was just as effective at night. Its Chobham armour was also enhanced by the addition of extra armour packs on the front and sides.

General Schwarzkopf knew that speed was of the essence with the ground war. He had to conduct two envelopments, the first around Kuwait to prevent the Iraqi garrison escaping, and a second, much larger, one to prevent reinforcements reaching Kuwait. He also needed to secure Kuwait's vital oilfields as quickly as possible – there were three major areas in the northeast and four to the south. Saddam's generals planned to use oil as an environmental weapon that would enhance their defences and funnel their enemy's tanks into predetermined killing zones. Once Schwarzkopf's attack started there was every chance that Saddam would open the valves in Kuwait's oilfields to form vast oil lakes, and then dynamite the oil-heads to create seas of fire and choking smoke. This would greatly impede Schwarzkopf's tanks and jets; it would also hide any Iraqi troops massing for a counter-attack. He fully understood that his tanks had to dash forward as fast as possible to try to prevent this, but ultimately it would prove to be an impossible task.

Schwarzkopf's ground offensive, dubbed Operation Desert Sabre, envisaged an enormous encircling operation that would not only encompass Kuwait but also a vast area of southern Iraq stretching up almost to the city of Basra. Although King Fahd was commander-in-chief of the Saudi armed forces, operational control of all Arab forces came under his nephew, His Royal Highness Lieutenant General Khalid bin Sultan. The Egyptian and Syrian forces were also committed to the offensive, on the proviso that they were not used inside Iraq.

Three commands were deployed on the eastern third of this enormous front. Joint Forces Command North, made up of the units from Egypt, Syria and Saudi Arabia, and led by Lieutenant General Prince Khalid bin Sultan, held the portion of the line east of 7th Corps. To the right of these forces was Lieutenant General Walter E. Boomer's US 1st Marine Expeditionary Force, which had the 1st (Tiger) Brigade of the US Army's 2nd Armored Division as well as the US 1st and 2nd Marine Divisions. On the extreme right Joint Forces Command East anchored the line on the Gulf, and consisted of units from all six member states of the Gulf Cooperation Council. Like Joint Forces Command North, it was under General Khalid's command.

To the west the 18th Airborne Corps was to attack deep into Iraq to control the east-west lines of communication along the strategic Highway 8 and cut off Iraqi forces in and around Kuwait. Even further west, the French 6th Light Armoured and the US 101st Airborne Divisions were to conduct a massive western envelopment with a ground assault to secure the allied left flank and an air assault to establish forward support bases deep in Iraqi territory. The US 24th Infantry Division had the central role of blocking the Euphrates river valley to prevent the escape north of Iraqi forces in Kuwait, and then attacking eastwards in coordination with 7th Corps to defeat the armour-heavy divisions of the Republican Guard.

In the centre of the Coalition line, along the Wadi al Batin, Major General John H. Tilelli's US 1st Cavalry Division was to strike northwards into a concentration of Iraqi divisions, whose commanders remained convinced that the Coalition would use Batin and several other wadis as avenues of attack. In the meantime, 7th Corps would conduct the main Coalition effort, attacking east of the 18th Airborne Corps and west of Wadi al Batin, driving to the north and then east to find and destroy the heart of Saddam's ground forces, the armour-heavy Republican Guard divisions.

Desert Sabre was unleashed at 0400 hours on 24 February 1991. The relentless air attacks had already taken a terrible toll on Iraqi morale. Washington assessed that at least 150,000 Iraqi troops had deserted before Desert Sabre even commenced. Two Iraqi divisional commanders subsequently informed their British captors that they had received no orders for almost two weeks. As instructed, Joint Force Command East pushed towards Kuwait up the coast to form the anvil for the American, British and French thrust into Iraq, which was intended to trap the bulk of the Iraqi forces. The Saudis came up against the Iraqi 5th Mechanized Division, which was still recovering from the Khafji encounter, while the commander of Marine Central breached Iraqi defences further inland.

To the far west, as planned, General Mouscardes' French 6th Light Armoured Division, reinforced by the 2nd Brigade of the US 82nd Airborne Division, advanced to protect the far western flank. The 82nd was bolstered with forty-three of the army's M551A1 Sheridan light airborne assault vehicles in its air-droppable tank battalion. The French 4th Dragoon Regiment, normally part of the French 10th Armoured Division, was augmented by elements of the 503rd Combat Tank Regiment. French reconnaissance units consisted of the 1st Foreign Legion Cavalry Regiment and the 1st Spahis Regiment; they were able to conduct such offensive operations as they had strong anti-tank capabilities. They consisted of three squadrons equipped with the AMX-10RC $6 \times 6$ armoured car, armed with a 105mm gun, plus the Véhicule de l'Avant Blindé (VAB) $4 \times 4$ armoured personnel carrier. Both were ideal for the mad dash across the Iraqi desert. None of the newer tracked AMX-10P infantry combat vehicles were deployed to the Gulf. Mouscardes' men successfully moved to secure the Al-Salman air base. Pushing 60 kilometres into Iraq, they destroyed the Iraqi 45th Infantry Division, then formed a screen to protect the left flank of the 18th Airborne Corps assault. Fortunately for the French, they suffered few casualties with only three fatalities during combat.

To their east, 2,000 men of General Peay's US 101st Airborne Division were moved 113 kilometres into Iraq in a massive air lift involving 400 helicopters. There they established a forward operating base named Cobra. A further 2,000 men arrived by vehicle, then the division moved to sever vital roads along the Euphrates and Tigris valleys to isolate the Iraqi forces in Kuwait. Meanwhile the 18th Corps' US 24th Infantry Division under General McCaffery, supported by the US 3rd Armoured Cavalry Regiment, raced north to link up with the 101st Airborne Division and on 25 February swung right to attack the northernmost Iraqi Republican Guard positions. The 3rd Cavalry Regiment was the only tank unit in America equipped with the M1A1 Abrams and was the first US unit to take on the Iraqis, with an engagement on 22 January 1991.

Meanwhile, US armoured columns raced to trap the Republican Guard and stop them escaping northwest towards Baghdad with their armour. Initially, the Guard's commanders thought the 7th Corps was driving on Kuwait City, not on the Guard itself. The intention had been that the Iraqi 12th Armoured Division would act as the immediate tactical reserve, while the Guard forming the strategic reserve came to the rescue. When the Guards realized what was happening, they desperately attempted to stop the 7th Corps from breaking through to their rear. Three armoured divisions, the Medina, Hammurabi and Tawakalna, deployed by the road running parallel to the Iraqi–Saudi pipeline. The scene was now set for the battle for Kuwait City and the battle of the Basra pocket.

In mid-January 1991 it was assessed that facing General de la Billiere's British 1st Armoured Division were seven Iraqi divisions, consisting of the 20th, 21st and 25th Infantry Divisions, with the 6th, 12th and 17th Armoured Divisions and the Tawakalna Republican Guard Division in reserve. By the end of January the Iraqi 16th Infantry Division had joined the front-line forces and their reserves were bolstered by the 26th and 36th Infantry Divisions. On paper, this was a formidably daunting force. However, the front-line divisions did not have any air cover and were suffering daily under the air-strikes. Britain's armoured forces were about to become involved in some fierce tank battles.

As part of Operation Granby, the British 1st Armoured Division, commanded by Major General Rupert Smith, came under the US 7th Corps and was part of the great armoured left-hook that attacked the Iraqi Republican Guard formations. Smith's two armoured brigades, the 4th and 7th, under Brigadiers Christopher Hammerbeck and Patrick Cordingley respectively, were to alternate spearheading the advance. In the vanguard of General Smith's assault were two armoured reconnaissance units. The British Army had continued its love affair with its cavalry regiments and remained wedded to the concept of reconnaissance by force. They were to dash forward across the barren desert landscape and probe the Iraqi defences that had withstood air attacks and the preliminary artillery and rocket bombardment. Their highly dangerous job was to draw enemy fire to help locate positions that needed neutralizing as the division rolled forward. The firepower of these reconnaissance forces was quite considerable.

These units consisted of the 7th Armoured Brigade's A Squadron, 1st The Queen's Dragoon Guards and the divisional formation 16th/15th The Queen's Royal Lancers Regiment. Whilst most countries opted for wheeled vehicles to conduct this role, the British Army had developed a unique family of tracked armoured fighting vehicles. The two main variants were the FV101 Scorpion and the FV107 Scimitar light tanks; armed with 76mm and 30mm guns respectively, these were known as combat vehicle reconnaissance tracked or CVR(T)s. The headquarter elements were also equipped with the anti-tank Striker variant and Spartan armoured personnel carrier, both based on the Scorpion chassis. Also in support were Sultan command vehicles, Samson recovery vehicles and Samson ambulances, all of which are again Scorpion derivatives.

The light armour was to precede the heavy tank regiments. These consisted of the 7th Armoured Brigade's Royal Scots Dragoon Guards, which had been reinforced by elements of the 14th/20th King's Hussars, the 17th/21st Lancers and the 4th Royal Tank Regiment, plus the Queen's Royal Irish Hussars tank regiment, also reinforced by units from the 17th/21st Lancers. The 4th Armoured Brigade's tank units comprised the 14th/20th Hussars Tank Regiment, reinforced by A Squadron, the Life Guards, and elements of the 4th Tank Regiment. The Royal Scots Dragoon Guards and the Queen's Royal Irish Hussars had four tank squadrons with fifty-seven Challenger tanks and 670 men, while the 14th/20th King's Hussars had three squadrons with forty-three tanks and 650 men. The squadrons each had four tank troops, each with three tanks, plus two in the HQ and administration troop.

Late in the afternoon of 24 February 1991 the 7th Corps launched the central Coalition thrust and the US 1st Infantry Division breached the Iraqi defences. The battered and bruised Iraqi 48th Infantry Division in the mouth of the breach was estimated to have lost 98 per cent of its tanks – in other words, it was wiped out as a fighting force. To the left of Marine Central, the Egyptian-Syrian Joint Force Command North was directed to breach the Iraqi defences in the centre of the Iraqi border. The Egyptian 3rd Mechanized Division spearheaded the advance. The day after, the two brigades of Smith's 1st Armoured Division, preceded by Lynx attack helicopters, were to pour through the US 1st Infantry Division's breach. Swinging right, the British were to attack the 12th Armoured Division, held in tactical reserve, in order to protect the 7th Corps' thrust towards the Republican Guard. This Iraqi division had been estimated to number 13,000 men equipped with up to 300 T-55 and T-62 tanks.

At 1515 hours on 25 February the 'Desert Rats' of Brigadier Cordingley's 7th Armoured Brigade, spearheading the 1st Armoured Division, began to advance into Iraq, passing through the US lines. They were to thrust eastward into Kuwait. Facing them were elements of the Iraqi 12th Armoured Division, which was now believed to be about 65 per cent combat effective; of its 250 tanks, only 115 were operational. However, it was anticipated that the Iraqi 12th and 48th Divisions would remain in place, supported by an unidentified Iraqi brigade. It was clear that the going would not be easy.

Attacking a series of objectives codenamed after metals, the brigade destroyed two Iraqi tanks at 'Copper', a position believed to be defended by fourteen enemy tanks. The British Challengers' 120mm guns accounted for at least five further Iraqi T-55s and six armoured personnel carriers. Moving on to 'Zinc', which possibly contained an Iraqi brigade with up to 100 tanks, the 7th Armoured Brigade attacked in the darkness. All the Iraqis could do was fire back at the muzzle flashes as they counter-attacked with almost fifty vehicles. Daybreak revealed another ten Iraqi armoured vehicles knocked out in the desert sands. On the night of 25/26 February Brigadier Christopher Hammerbeck's 4th Armoured Brigade was also involved in a confused engagement with about twenty Iraqi tanks for 'Copper South'. The next day, with the 4th Brigade continuing their advance to the south, the 7th Brigade pressed on and the Iraqis lost another nine T-55s to British gunnery.

Hammerbeck's 4th Armoured Brigade attacked objective 'Brass', accounting for thirty tanks and almost fifty armoured vehicles; in total, it knocked out sixty tanks and ninety armoured personnel carriers. During Desert Sabre the 1st Armoured Division accounted overall for 200 Iraqi T-62s, 100 armoured fighting vehicles and 100 artillery pieces. British Army Air Corps Lynx helicopters also destroyed at least four T-55s and seven other armoured vehicles, with a number of other probable hits. This said much for superior British training and firepower.

The Saudi and Kuwaiti forces were almost in Kuwait City by 26 February, heralding the beginning of the end for the remains of the Iraqi Army in the Kuwaiti theatre of operations. The US Marines were on the outskirts, whilst the 18th Corps was in the Euphrates Valley and the 7th Corps was making progress against the Republican Guard. Nonetheless, units of an Iraqi armoured division decided to stand and fight in Kuwait City, perhaps with the intention of buying time for their retreating comrades. Liberation of the city followed a large-scale tank battle at the international airport, during which the Iraqi 3rd Armoured Division (a veteran not only of the Iran-Iraq War but also of the 1973 Arab-Israeli Yom Kippur War) lost more than 100 tanks. The US 1st Marine Division destroyed about 310 Iraqi tanks in total across Kuwait. The Iraqi defences now all but collapsed, as it became every man for himself. The Coalition victory was soon tainted by allegations that the fleeing Iraqis were needlessly massacred.

In truth, there was no 'Mother of Battles', as Saddam had threatened. Coalition forces only fought about 35 per cent of those Iraqi troops assessed to be in-theatre. The front echelon conscripts of Saddam's army were expendable, whilst his loyal Republican Guard largely managed to slink away with their tails between their legs, to wreak more havoc in the months following the cease-fire. Casualties for the Coalition were remarkably light. For example, America lost 148 killed in action and some 340 wounded, though there were also almost 100 non-combat fatalities. The British lost thirty-six dead, seventeen of them in combat, and forty-three wounded. Of these combat losses, friendly fire was a major contributor, with up to thirty-five US personnel killed and seventy-two wounded, and nine British killed and thirteen wounded by their own side.

While the Coalition fought to free Kuwait City, up to 800 American tanks from the 7th Corps' US 1st and 3rd Armored Divisions, as well as the 2nd Armored Cavalry Regiment, launched attacks on a Republican Guard division inside Iraq which lost 200 tanks. They then moved forward and engaged a second division. American Apache attack helicopters and A-10 Thunderbolt tank-busters also played a significant role. One Apache alone destroyed eight T-72s, and on 25 February two USAF A-10s destroyed twenty-three Iraqi tanks, including some T-72s, in three close air support missions.

In the envelopment the US M1A1 tanks easily outgunned the Iraqi T-72s and in a night engagement on 25/26 February the Guards' Tawakalna Armoured Division was largely destroyed without the loss of a single US tank. The Republican Guard, unable to stem the American armoured tide, tried to retreat. The next morning a brigade of the Medina Division, supported by a battalion from the 14th Mechanized Division, attempted to protect the withdrawal. The Medina Division found itself under attack from the US 1st and 3rd Armored Divisions, while the remnants of the Tawakalna were finished off by air attacks.

The Medina's armoured vehicles trying to flee were caught being loaded onto their tank transporters and were bombed by USAF A-10s and F-16 fighters. Along Route 8 Apache attack helicopters caught another eighty

T-72 tanks still on their transporters. Although not all the roads out of Basra were closed, the Coalition was determined that Iraqi tanks and artillery should not escape. The 7th Corps armour also fought the Republican Guard's Hammurabi Armoured Division 80 kilometres to the west of Basra. The US 24th Mechanized Division, having made a dramatic 240-kilometre drive northwards to join the US 101st Airborne Division on the Euphrates, also now swung right to block the Iraqi escape route. The six remaining Republican Guard divisions had been hemmed in overnight in a swiftly diminishing area of northern Kuwait and southern Iraq, with their line of escape northwards largely severed.

On 27 February the US 24th Mechanized Division attacked the Guard's Hammurabi Armoured Division, the Al Faw and Adnan Mechanized Divisions and the remnants of the Nebuchadnezzar Mechanized Division. They fled, with the Nebuchadnezzar Division possibly escaping over the Hawr al-Hammar Lake causeway. The 24th Mechanized Division also captured fifty Republican Guard T-72 tanks as they were fleeing north along a main road near the Euphrates. It was all but over for Saddam's Republican Guard.

Six disparate brigades with fewer than 30,000 troops and a few tanks were now struggling back to Basra. The Iraqis agreed to a cease-fire the following day whilst the British 7th Armoured Brigade moved to cut the road to Basra just north of Kuwait City. However, some troops continued to escape across the Hawr al-Hammar and north from Basra along the Shatt al-Arab Waterway. Brigadier Cordingley, commander of the 7th Armoured Brigade, noted, 'By 28th February it was clear that General Schwarzkopf's plan to annihilate the Republican Guard with a left hook through Iraq had failed ... The majority of the Iraqi soldiers were already on their way back to Baghdad.'

Saddam, firmly in control of Iraq's state media, had no need to acknowledge this terrible defeat. Victory was the reason for abiding by the cease-fire. Baghdad Radio announced 'The Mother of battles was a clear victory for Iraq ... We are happy with the cessation of combat operations as this would preserve our sons' blood and people's safety after God made them triumphant with faith against their evil enemies.'

Only a residual Iraqi threat remained by 30 February. Two Iraqi tank brigades were southwest of Basra, another brigade with forty armoured vehicles was to the south, and there was an infantry brigade on either side of the Hawr al-Hammar. In total, about eight armoured battalions, the remnants of those Iraqi forces deployed in and around Kuwait, were now trapped in the 'Basra Pocket'. Basra itself lay in ruins, and to the west and east marshes and wetlands made passage impossible. Despite the cease-fire, the US 24th Division fought elements of the Hammurabi again on 2 March after reports that a battalion of T-72 tanks was moving northward towards it in an effort to escape. The Iraqi armoured column foolishly opened fire and suffered the consequences. The Americans retaliated with Apache attack helicopters and two task forces, destroying 187 armoured vehicles, 34 artillery pieces and 400 trucks. The survivors were forced back into the 'Basra Pocket'. By this stage Iraq only had about 700 of its 4,500 tanks and 1,000 of its 2,800 armoured personnel carriers left in the Kuwaiti theatre of operations; with organized resistance over, the Iraqis signed the cease-fire on 3 March 1991.

# Chapter 17

# A Messy Balkan Divorce
## The Break-up of Yugoslavia, 1990–1991

Following Moscow's military interventions in Hungary and Czechoslovakia, Soviet-built armour did not see any further action in Europe until the very end of the Cold War. In the 1990s it was involved in extensive fighting during the violent decade-long break-up of Yugoslavia. At the start of the various wars of succession, the Yugoslav National Army (*Jugoslovenska Narodna Armija* – JNA) had 130,000 men under arms, with 1,635 tanks and 600 artillery pieces. Serbians constituted the army's largest ethnic group, providing more than 40 per cent of the manpower and 80 per cent of the officers and non-commissioned officers. Around 55,000 men were deployed in Croatia and 20,000 in Slovenia. The Croatian National Guard totalled 40,000, plus 15,000 armed policemen. The Slovene Territorial Defence Force numbered 35,000, with another 8,000 armed policemen.

The JNA's tank holdings included around 290 T-72s and M-84s (locally built T-72s) and 750 T-54/55s. From photographic evidence, most of the latter appear to have been T-55s as they lacked the ventilator dome. Although obsolete by modern-day standards, the T-54/55s provided valuable direct artillery support to the various warring factions. Around 550 elderly T-34s and Shermans were in storage. The JNA had nine armoured and eleven mechanized brigades. Each armoured brigade had three tank battalions with about thirty tanks divided into three companies. The mechanized brigades only had one or two tank battalions. In theory, the JNA's armoured forces should have easily rolled over the rebellious Croatians and Slovenes, who lacked heavy weapons.

The Croatian War of Independence, also known as the Croatian Homeland War, commenced on 17 August 1990. Simmering tensions escalated between the Croatians and Croatian-Serbians, with the JNA intervening on behalf of the latter. One of the first instances of tanks being used was when JNA armour helped Serbian militias drive Croatian police from their station at Dalj in early 1991. Tanks were then used to attack Dvor na Uni and Kostajnica. Eastern Slavonia, mainly under Croatian control, was flat and therefore idea for armoured warfare. During July 1991 the JNA used the 252nd Armoured Brigade to attack Vinkovci and Vukovar, and the latter was then besieged by units that included the Guards Mechanized Division. When a Serbian armoured battalion entered Borovo-Naselje, one of Vukovar's suburbs on the western banks of the Danube, in mid-September 1991, they were greeted by Croatian 64mm rocket launchers. In the street fighting that followed, the Serbians lost ten M-84 tanks and eighty armoured personnel carriers. In revenge, the Serbians began to shell the city. Vukovar was soon dubbed Croatia's 'Stalingrad'.

In the autumn of 1991, in what was dubbed the 'Barracks War', the Croatians seized JNA T-55s at Sibenik. More rugged than the M-84, the T-55 played an important role in the battles fought between the Croatians and Serbians. The Croatians camouflaged some of theirs with reddish brown and black, and painted the Croatian red and white chequerboard shield on the glacis and turret sides. They also seized many T-72s and M-84s. However, it took until October before the Croatians were able to operate a force of about 100 tanks and armoured vehicles.

At Karlovac, during the Barracks War, the JNA garrison tried to break out with their tanks, causing destruction in the town before being forced to return to base. They lost two tanks, including an ancient T-34/85, which lay abandoned at the roadside. By 22 September 1991 the Croatians had captured thirty-two barracks and military bases. In response, the JNA committed 15,000 men supported by 300 tanks, 700 armoured personnel carriers and 1,500 artillery pieces. Battles were fought on five different fronts in Croatia.

British mercenaries serving with the Croatian National Guard fought JNA T-55s at Osijek and Velika Pumpa in Eastern Slavonia. Sometimes the Serbian tank forces were not as formidable as they first appeared. In one instance at Osijek a group of twenty-five JNA T-55s plus a single T-72 turned out to contain only twelve real tanks: the rest were wooden dummies. At Velika Pumpa the Croatians and their allies had to rely on rocket propelled grenades and one-shot rocket launchers to fend off a force of seven T-55s and a T-72. They claimed to have knocked out four of the T-55s and the T-72.

In a show of force, JNA tanks were sent to the plains of Slavonia in the autumn of 1991 as part of a general offensive against the newly independent

Croatia. In Western Slavonia, during the bitter fighting for the city of Novska, the Croatian defenders did not succumb to the Serbians' superior firepower, instead stopping JNA T-55s in the streets using hand-held anti-tank weapons. One foreign volunteer recalled, 'Only the rear of the tank is vulnerable to light rocket launchers. But it's a dangerous game, and inevitably, we always lost one or two men in such attacks.' On one occasion at Novska a T-55 serving with a Serbian militia trying to escape trouble reversed into a deep concrete storm-drain and became stranded with its hull and gun almost vertical. It was caught in no-man's-land, and neither side was able to retrieve it until the fighting ended.

At Vukovar the Croatian defenders counter-attacked with T-55s retrieved from ex-federal barracks, but any gains were soon lost to the superior JNA forces. By this stage the 1,500-strong Croatian garrison was fending off a mechanized division and two armoured brigades totalling some 20,000 men. On 18 October the Serbians captured the Borovo-Naselje railway station, cutting the Croatian defence in half. The following day Serbian tanks and infantry captured part of Vukovar's southern suburbs. The garrison was not overwhelmed until 18 November 1991, by which time it had killed 5,000 Serbians and destroyed fifty tanks and 200 armoured vehicles. This battle sapped the strength of the JNA and exhausted its armoured forces. As a result, they were unable to take Osijek or Vinkovci. The former was defended by a few Second World War M36 tank destroyers and T-55s.

On the Dalmatian coast, the town of Zadar was one of the Serbians' strongholds, but the Croatian Tiger Brigade, supported by T-55s, thwarted them. This unit was issued with the best equipment available to the Croatian Army and was deployed as an armoured reserve all over Croatia. After being used in a conventional role in the short autumn campaign, the tanks of both sides were dug in and became static artillery. Later, in Bosnia-Herzegovina, Serbian T-55s were able to shell Sarajevo with impunity. In the spring of 1992 a force of thirty Croatian T-55s rolled into western Bosnia to secure lines of communication with the Bosnian-Croatians, resulting in fighting near Kupres. The 1st Guards Brigade of the Bosnian-Croat Army was armed with T-55s.

While the Croatian Homeland War dragged on until 1995, the fighting in other republics of the former Yugoslavia did not end until 2001. By that stage, Croatia had amassed 220 T-55s and Serbia maintained a force of more than 700; in contrast, Bosnia and Slovenia had fewer than 100 each. The T-55s serving with the elite Croatian Tiger Brigade were haphazardly over-sprayed with lime green, dark green and black, and their tiger's head emblem was applied to the turret on either side of the main armament. Similarly, tanks of the Bosnian-Croat Army's 1st Guards Brigade had a four-colour blotchy camouflage scheme, with white tactical numbers on the turret and glacis. A gold on black insignia was painted on the turret either side of the main gun.

The performance of the JNA's armour against Slovenian separatists during the brief Ten Day War was extremely poor. All attempts by the JNA to secure Ljubljana, Slovenia's capital, were stopped by the Slovene Territorial Defence Force. On the first day of the war, 27 June 1991, the Slovenes were involved in heavy fighting against the JNA's 4th Armoured and 140th Mechanized Brigades along the border with central Croatia. There was also moderate fighting against the 1st Armoured Brigade. Near the eastern border the 32nd Mechanized Brigade was also engaged. Two days later some of the first JNA T-55s to be seized were a dozen captured by the Slovenes at the Sentilj border post near Austria. These were quickly re-organized as the Slovene 7th Military District Tank Company and turned against the JNA. The Slovenes' territorial forces hand-painted the letters TO (*Teritorialna Obramba*) in white on their tanks.

Serbian armour captured at Rozna Dolina on 30 June 1991 was used to form the Slovenian 6th Military District Tank Company. The JNA's 4th Armoured Brigade lost a tank battalion after it was captured on 2 July. Attempts by two tank columns from the 1st Armoured Brigade to reach Ljubljana and Logatec were thwarted. The following day the elite Prole-arian Guards Mechanized Division was deployed from Belgrade to Slovenia. It was to drive along the Belgrade–Zagreb motorway towards Slovenia but the entire operation was soon abandoned after the tanks kept breaking down. A JNA armoured column consisting of a squadron of M-84 and T-55 tanks with supporting armoured personnel carriers crossed the Croatian border into Slovenia on 3 July. They headed for Brezice but were ambushed on the outskirts. Within two minutes the Slovenes destroyed an M-84 and two armoured personnel carriers. The tank was hit by anti-tank rockets, which took the turret clean off. It was the last time the JNA would intervene in Slovenia. A cease-fire followed and Yugoslavia formally recognized Slovenian independence.

The greatest failing of the JNA was that, although well versed in the use of armour, it used its tanks in penny packets. Furthermore, they were often poorly supported by infantry, especially when fighting in the close confines of urban surroundings. What really saved the Croatians and Slovenes was the Yugoslav version of the US M-72 light anti-tank weapon, known as the RBR M-80, and the German-made Armbrust rocket launcher. These prevented them from being overwhelmed by Serbian tanks and made the tank crews constantly fear enemy tank-hunters.

*Chapter 18*

# No Strings Attached
## Soviet Armoured Exports, 1948–1991

The tank battles fought during the Cold War were undoubtedly fuelled by the Soviet Union's enormous generosity. 'One previous owner, no strings attached': except when that previous owner happened to be Moscow, there were invariably strings attached. The fact that the tank was ancient, would not meet your operational requirements and would leave you heavily indebted did little to deter many Developing World countries desperate for weapons. From the Horn of Africa to Central America, the Soviet T-55 and T-62 main battle tanks became as ubiquitous as the Kalashnikov AK-47 assault rifle.

In the highly tense post-Second World War era the Superpowers remained cautious about coming into direct confrontation, but this did not prevent serious indirect meddling elsewhere in the world. Time after time Moscow was able to make good its allies' massive tank losses. The Soviets conducted a substantial resupply of Syria in 1982–1983 following Syrian military losses in Lebanon. Major resupply also took place in 1977–1979 in support of Ethiopia in its clash with Somalia, and during the Arab-Israeli Wars of 1967 and 1973.

At the height of the Cold War in the 1980s the Soviet Union exported billions of dollars' worth of arms. Intelligence experts watched with a mixture of dismay and awe as cargo ship after cargo ship left from Nikolayev stacked to the gunnels with military hardware and sailed to ports such as Assab, Luanda, Tartus and Tripoli. Much of this equipment came out of strategic reserves and was very old, or had been superseded by newer models, as in the case of the T-55 and T-62 main battle tanks. Soviet armoured vehicle exports also included wheeled and tracked armoured personnel carriers.

In many cases Soviet weapon shipments were funded through generous loans, barter-deals or simply gifted, and Moscow's arms industries rarely saw a penny in return. The scale of Soviet armour manufacturing at its height was just mind-boggling. The tank plant at Nizhniy Tagil was supported by at least three other tank factories at Kharkov, Omsk and Chelyabinsk, while armoured fighting vehicles were manufactured at seven different sites. During the 1980s the Soviets were producing approximately 9,000 tanks, self-propelled guns and armoured personnel carriers every year. The Soviet Union's East European Warsaw Pact allies managed another 2,500. Moscow exported almost 8,000 tanks and self-propelled guns and more than 14,000 armoured personnel carriers/infantry fighting vehicles to the Developing World during that decade alone. In effect, they exported two-and-a-half years' worth of production. The Soviets' ability to churn out such vast numbers of tanks meant that on at least two occasions they were able to save Egyptian and Syrian forces from complete disaster.

After the Second World War Czechoslovakia was permitted to produce the T-34/85 tank and SU-100 self-propelled gun, largely for export to the Middle East. The T-55 was then licence-built from the mid-1960s for domestic and export purposes, followed by the T-72 in the late 1970s. Czechoslovakia also exported upwards of 3,000 of its OT-64 armoured personnel carriers, Iraq being the biggest customer. Similarly, Poland built the T-34/85, T-54/55, T-62 and T-72. Additionally, Bulgaria and Poland manufactured the Soviet MT-LB multi-purpose armoured personnel carrier, numbers of which were exported to countries such as Iraq. Romania manufactured T-55s from the late 1970s.

By the 1980s the Soviet Union had a staggering 52,600 tanks and 59,000 armoured personnel carriers in its active inventory, with another 10,000 tanks and armoured personnel carriers in storage. After the Warsaw Pact force reduction talks in Eastern Europe, Moscow agreed to withdraw 10,000 tanks and destroy half of them. Warsaw Pact members also agreed to cut tank numbers by almost 3,000 without complaint. At the same time the Soviets began to field newer tanks such as the T-64B, the T-72M1 and the T-80, while retiring older model T-54/55s and T-62s. They also improved their infantry fighting vehicle forces by fielding large numbers of tracked BMP-2s, as well as improving the earlier BMP-1. The net result was that a huge surplus of armoured fighting vehicles became available to the Developing World.

In the Middle East the massive Soviet tank supplies to Egypt and Syria made sense in light of the good tank terrain and the fact that both countries were regularly embroiled in large conventional wars with Israel. These proved ideal testing grounds. In Africa and Central America, where Soviet allies fought interminable bush wars against well armed and well organized guerrilla armies, the tank was largely useless. It took the Marxist governments of both Angola and Ethiopia a long time to wake up to the fact that fighter aircraft and helicopters were much more useful. Then again, it is easier to train tank crews than jet pilots. All these wars were characterized by significant tank losses, many of them simply abandoned.

In the mid-1950s Egypt arranged a major arms deal with Czechoslovakia, sponsored by the Soviet Union, for 530 armoured fighting vehicles (230 tanks, mostly T-34/85s but also some IS-3s, 200 BTR-152 armoured personnel carriers and 100 SU-100 self-propelled guns). These were followed by 120 new T-54s. Some of this armour saw action in the 1956 Suez Crisis against the Israeli, British and French armies. During the period 1962–1967 the Egyptians received 290 T-54s, 25 IS-3s and 50 PT-76 light tanks, as well as hundreds of BTR40/50/60/152 wheeled armoured personnel carriers and SU-100 tank destroyers. Syria also benefited from this export bonanza and in the late 1950s took delivery of 200 T-34s, 150 T-54s, 80 SU-100s and 100 BTR-152s. In the early 1960s the Soviets began to supply Syria with additional T-54s and armoured vehicles, and by 1967 the Syrian Army had 750 tanks and 585 armoured personnel carriers.

When the Israelis invaded southern Lebanon in 1982 they found the Palestinian Liberation Organisation's armoury included old T-34/85 and T-54/55 tanks. The Syrian Army caught up in the fighting lost hundreds of tanks and armoured personnel carriers, including T-72 tanks. Moscow was not pleased that the very first T-72 had fallen into Western hands. Afterwards Syria went on a massive armoured vehicle buying spree. In the early 1980s Syria ordered 800 BMP-1s, along with large numbers of T-72s and BTR-80s. Then, in the early 1990s, the Syrians ordered 252 T-72 tanks from Czechoslovakia and another 350 from Russia. Cynically, the Soviets armed both North and South Yemen. In 1968 North Yemen received up to fifty refurbished T-54s and South Yemen thirty T-34s. In the mid-1980s North Yemen purchased $14 billion worth of weapons, including sixteen T-62 tanks. The two countries became a single republic in 1990 and total deliveries amounted to more than 800 tanks, 270 BMPs and 300 BTRs.

The Soviet Union was swift to make good Arab losses after the Six Day War. Most notably, Syria received the T-62 before Moscow's Warsaw Pact satellites and was even supplied with the BMP-1. The shattered Egyptian Army also enjoyed Moscow's generosity. Between 1967 and 1973 it was supplied with 1,260 T-54/55s and between 1971 and 1973 it received 400 T-62s. Moscow also supplied 550 BTR-152/60s and 150 BMP-1s. Czechoslovakia, at Moscow's behest, provided another 200 armoured personnel carriers. Once again, all this equipment was deployed against Israel during the Yom Kippur War, and the Israelis accounted for another 2,000 tanks. During the fighting and in its immediate aftermath the Egyptians and Syrians received additional tanks, which helped save them from complete defeat.

Throughout the Cold War Moscow's military aid to its Communist allies came at a severe price. Ultimately, it was a way in which the Soviets could exercise overt power projection and create dependency amongst many Developing World countries that lacked the technical ability to support Soviet-supplied weapons systems. Wherever there were Soviet weapons, there were invariably also Soviet advisers and technicians. It also meant that for decades the Soviet Union and America were able to fight a series of very bloody proxy wars without ever coming to blows directly.

In Africa, Libya unsuccessfully used Soviet arms against Chad in 1983–1988. Angola and Ethiopia were Moscow's most important regional allies and customers. In the late 1970s, when Ethiopia was at war with Somalia, the Soviets delivered 400 T-54/55 tanks. Ironically, Somalia had been a Soviet ally and had received 100 T-34/54, before they had fallen out. In the case of Angola, in 1986 Soviet arms supplies were to the value of $2 billion, and included tanks, infantry fighting vehicles and artillery. Two years later in 1988, when Cuban forces propping up the Marxist Angolan government were in the process of withdrawing, Cuba handed over forty T-54s to government forces. Likewise, Mozambique, also blighted by civil war, spent $1 billion on weapons, which included the PT-76 light tank.

In the midst of a bitter and bloody civil war in the mid-1980s Ethiopia also took receipt of T-55s and BTRs. By the end of the decade it had spent over $5.4 billion on weapons whilst its population starved to death. The delivery of equipment to the port of Assab for the 1985 campaign in Eritrea consisted of T-55 tanks and armoured personnel carriers. Three years later the writing was on the wall for Ethiopia's Marxist government after its forces suffered a series of defeats. By the late 1990s Ethiopia was assessed to have in excess of 350 tanks, all of Soviet origin, Angola had 200 and Mozambique around 100.

Cuba, Moscow's number one ally in Uncle Sam's backyard, received arms worth billions of dollars. During the late 1950s Cuba was sent T-34s, T-54s,

SU-100s and BTR-60s. Cuban armed forces subsequently saw action during the Angolan and Ethiopian civil wars. In 1983 shipments included 100 T-62s and Cuba ended up with some 1,500 tanks which it had little use for, except for re-export or deployment in Angola. By the 1980s much of Cuba's armour was ageing and Moscow sent limited supplies of T-62s, PT-76s, BTR-152s and BTR-60s as replacements. Similarly, in 1983 Nicaragua's Marxist government took delivery of 44 T-55s, 13 BTR-50/60s, 20 armoured cars and 150 artillery pieces. The following year they took receipt of another 150 tanks, which were followed by a further 1,200 vehicles in a massive deal worth $600 million. However, it was Soviet helicopters, not tanks, that helped the Nicaraguan government defeat the Contra rebels.

In Asia, both India and Pakistan received T-54 tanks from the Soviet Union in the 1960s, amassing 1,420 and 820 tanks respectively, which they used against each other in 1971. By the 1990s the Indians had about 500 T-54/55s and Pakistan had fifty T-55s plus 1,300 Chinese copies. India, with its massive armed forces, re-equipped with T-72 tanks and BMP-2 infantry fighting vehicles, which it subsequently manufactured under licence. By the mid-1990s India, in a permanent armed stand-off with Pakistan, had 1,100 T-72M1s in service.

Communist Vietnam, at loggerheads with all its neighbours in the wake of the Vietnam War, was strengthened in the mid-1970s by billions of dollars' worth of Soviet military aid. This included 200 T-62 tanks, 1,000 T-55s and 300 BTRs. T-54s were also delivered to neighbouring Cambodia and Laos, where Communist guerrilla forces eventually came to power. Vietnamese tanks rolled into Cambodia in 1978 and stayed for ten years. After the Soviet withdrawal from Afghanistan, Moscow poured in arms including T-62s and BTR-70s to prop up its puppet government. Afghanistan received almost 1,000 Soviet tanks, 550 tracked BMPs and 300 wheeled BTRs over the years – most of which ended up smashed and scattered over the length and breadth of the country.

Moscow also used middlemen, such as Cuba, Syria, Libya and North Korea, to deliver its arms. The latter began licensed production of the T-62 in the late 1970s, which continued until the mid-1980s. North Korea is also believed to have built the BMP-1. During the Iran-Iraq War North Korea was encouraged to supply Iran with T-62s, even though Iraq had long been a Soviet ally. Similarly, many Eastern European countries exported vast quantities of licence-built Soviet armour. Once Iran invaded Iraq, Moscow ended its 'neutrality' and began to supply Iraq again.

Communist China was never able to compete on anything like the scale of the Soviet Union's armoured vehicle exports. Its Type 59 tank, a derivative of the T-54, went into production in the late 1950s. During the Vietnam War the North Vietnamese were supplied with 700 Type 59s, Type 62 light tanks and Type 63 amphibious tanks (a copy of the Soviet PT-76). Inspection of Chinese Type 59s delivered to Pakistan showed a good finish, but the tanks lacked gun stabilisation and power traverse, which impacted on the rate of fire. It also had relatively poor armour, and its manoeuvrability was considered poor in some quarters. Pakistan is believed to have upgraded some of these tanks with a 105mm gun. Other customers included Albania, Cambodia, Iran, Iraq and North Korea. Pakistan subsequently obtained 400 Type-69/85s. The Chinese also exported their follow-on Type 69 tanks to Iran and Iraq.

Ironically, the Soviet Union's huge arms exports did not give Moscow any great strategic leverage. Egypt defected back to the American camp, while Libya and Syria became dangerous liabilities. In Africa none of the Marxist governments in Angola, Mozambique and Ethiopia was able to defeat the rebels, leaving their economies in tatters. Soviet support for Vietnam soured relations with China, while support for Cuba and Nicaragua aggravated America no end. Ultimately, it was economic not military assistance that many of Moscow's clients really needed. This was something it was unable to provide and the gifting of billions of dollars' worth of arms, including tanks, contributed to the collapse of the Soviet Union and bankrupted its arms industry.

*Chapter 19*

# Goodbye Tank: End of Days

By 1991 the tank's dominance of the battlefield was firmly over. Man-portable anti-tank missiles and rockets meant that individual soldiers were increasingly effective as tank-killers. Add to the mix ground attack aircraft and attack helicopters, and a tank crew's chances of survival had become thinner and thinner. Nonetheless, for almost fifty years after the Second World War, and up to the point when the Cold War ended, it remained a dominant factor on the battlefield. One tank clearly stands out.

The T-54/55 was easily the most successful tank of the Cold War and was involved in almost every single major conflict since the 1950s from Budapest to Baghdad. In fact, the T-54 series has seen more action than any other post-Second World War tank. Although it was rapidly outdated, the T-54/55 formed the backbone of the Warsaw Pact's tank forces and was widely exported around the world, seeing combat with numerous armies well into the early 2000s.

Remarkably, the T-54 was so popular that it even outlasted its successor, the T-62. It remained in production for over thirty years until 1981, by which time well over 70,000 had been built worldwide, easily outstripping the T-34 and making it the most ubiquitous tank of all time. In contrast, only 20,000 T-62s had been built when production ended six years earlier in 1975. One of the reasons for this was that the T-62 cost three times as much to produce and the only real advantage it could offer was its larger gun. All its other capabilities were broadly comparable.

While Moscow never released any official figures for T-54/55 production, it has been estimated that the Soviet Union alone built about 50,000. It was also manufactured in China, Czechoslovakia, Poland and Romania, resulting in approximately another 27,000, bringing total numbers to around 77,000. Some sources even put the total global figure as high as 100,000. This beats hands down T-34 numbers, even allowing for post-war T-34 construction by Czechoslovakia and Poland, amounting to about 60,000. This makes the T-54/55 the most widely used tank in history –

a quite remarkable achievement. However, despite its incredible track record, the T-54/55 remains overshadowed by almost every other Cold War tank. Indeed, the Soviet T-62 and T-72 achieved far greater notoriety during the numerous regional conflicts of the Cold War, and the subsequent wars after the collapse of the Soviet Union.

When the T-54 was developed, its designers drew on Soviet experience gained in Europe during the Second World War. What was needed was a tank that could be used for a shock massed attack, that would simply overwhelm an enemy and then exploit a breakthrough. If the Cold War had turned hot in Europe, the T-54's low profile would have been ideal on the open north German plain, but its low turret reduced main armament depression to just 4 or 5 degrees. In contrast, Western tanks could manage double that; furthermore, the larger fighting compartment in Western tanks ensured greater crew comfort and – just as important – a faster rate of fire.

The T-54/55 was never really intended to fight in the heat of the Middle East and it was there that its shortcomings became most apparent. The cramped fighting compartment became unbearably stifling in the desert, forcing Arab crews to drive round with their engine louvres open, leaving the tank vulnerable. The baking heat inevitably reduced crew efficiency, not least the accuracy of their gunnery. Choking dust also reduced visibility, forcing tank commanders to fight with their heads exposed. (This was not a drawback for Israeli tank commanders, who preferred to fight that way.)

Both the British-built Centurion and the American M48/60 Patton armed with a 105mm gun outgunned the T-54. In 1967 the Israelis' Centurions had better ammunition and an effective killing range of 2,000 metres, while the T-54, hampered by the primitive quality of its anti-tank ammunition, could only manage 1,000 metres. The T-54 used basic armour-piercing ammunition, a solid, full calibre shot made of steel that offered limited penetration at long range. Due to energy dissipation, the shot only had 50 per cent armour penetration compared to other more modern types of round. Although the armour-piercing rounds of the T-54/55 could cut through armour twice as thick as its own diameter, this was only achievable at close range. Therefore, the 100mm tank round could penetrate 200mm of armour; the trick, though, was to get close enough to make it effective without being destroyed in the process. At maximum range T-54/55 rounds tended to glance off the angles of the Centurion's armour.

The Soviets' later T-62 main battle tank fired a more sophisticated armour-piercing fin-stabilized discarding-sabot (APFSDS) round tipped with a dart or arrow, which concentrated the striking energy in one spot. This type of tank, though, was never available to the Arabs in great numbers. Israeli tanks fired similar armour-piercing discarding-sabot rounds, as well as high-explosive anti-tank rounds that forced molten metal into its target. Both types had distinctive narrow tips and, like the APFSDS, were designed to cut through hardened tank armour; they remained very lethal at longer ranges.

Some T-55s were fitted with infra-red search lights, and these gave the Arabs a decided advantage in night combat with the Israelis. Historian Max Hastings, who covered the Yom Kippur battles as a war correspondent, wrote:

Very fortunately for the Israelis, the Syrians neither exploited their Soviet night-vision equipment effectively, nor used smoke to cover their own advance, which could have been fatal for the defenders, who relied overwhelmingly on the eyes of their gunners to destroy the Arab tank columns.

The T-54/55 also offered the Arab armies some other advantages. Its low profile made it a smaller target compared to the Israeli tanks, and in addition its lighter weight meant it could cross ground that the heavier and slower Centurions and Pattons could not. However, geography also greatly hampered the T-54/55: in flat deserts, dunes and on the Golan Heights it proved to be vulnerable. During the Arab-Israeli wars tank commanders liked to fight from a 'hull-down' position, i.e. dug in or from behind a sand dune, thus exposing only part of the turret. But the T-54/55's limited depression meant that the tank had to be driven up the rise it was sheltering behind in order to engage enemy tanks coming down the opposite slopes. This gave the Israelis a notable advantage when the Arab tanks exposed themselves. Iraq's T-54/55s and Type 69s faced exactly the same problems. Nonetheless, the performance of the T-54/55 should not be underestimated. In 1973, in combination with other Soviet weapons systems, it came very, very close to overwhelming the state of Israel. It was only poor leadership and training, particularly on the Egyptian side, that enabled the Israelis to eventually turn the tide after suffering heavy losses.

The humiliating defeat of Saddam Hussein's army in 1991 was an embarrassment to Moscow and came as a shock to all the Soviet client states. It clearly showed that armies equipped with Soviet-era armour could not stand up to modern Western armies. In the last two major wars that involved the T-54/55 many of them were not actually Soviet-built but were foreign pretenders to the throne. During the Gulf War and the Iraq War many of the Iraqi T-54/55s encountered were Chinese-built Type 69s and Polish T-55s. Well, they say imitation is the greatest form of flattery.

The initial T-54/55 design appeared in the late 1940s, but had long since been obsolete once it was no longer an adequate tank-vs-tank weapon. The 1960s had been its heyday. Yet whenever it was called upon to fight on battlefields where there were no next generation tanks, it remained a valuable instrument of war. This was particularly so during the numerous 'bush wars' and regional conflicts fought during the Cold War, and indeed in the Balkan wars. By 1991, though, it was definitely no longer a front-line tank.

Just after the Gulf War ended some joker sprayed 'Soviet made shit' on the upper glacis plate of an Iraqi T-55 abandoned on the highway outside Kuwait City. It was an act of triumphant bravado. By this stage in the tank's long 45-year history this comment was a little harsh but essentially true. Ironically, this particular T-55, singled out by the eloquent graffiti artist, had not been built in the Soviet Union but in Poland. Coalition troops understandably had little time for such subtle nuances, and in any case it was designed in the Soviet Union. Imagine if this was one of the Polish tanks delivered in the early 1980s. Having survived the destruction of the Iran-Iraq War, it finally came a cropper in the battle for Kuwait. Like its predecessor, the T-34, when Soviet tank designers came up with the T-54/55, they produced an even more durable and long-lasting tank. The T-54/55 became omnipresent during the Cold War's many tank battles, making it the most ubiquitous tank in history.

# Cold War Armoured Units

This list of armoured units is far from complete, nor can it be considered 100 per cent accurate. Many countries, even years after a conflict took place, refused to officially confirm which forces were involved. Also, units were regularly reassigned. For the sake of brevity, tank battalions serving with infantry divisions are not generally included.

## First Indochina War, 1946–1954

*French Army*

1st Foreign Cavalry Regiment
1st Light Horse Regiment
5th Cuirassier Regiment

6th Moroccan Spahi Regiment
Far Eastern Colonial Armoured
   Regiment

## Arab-Israeli War, 1948

*Arab Armies*

Egyptian tank battalion
Iraqi tank battalion
Lebanese tank company
Syrian tank battalion

*Israeli Defence Forces*

8th Armoured Brigade
   82nd Tank Battalion
   89th Mechanized Battalion
7th Mechanized Brigade

## Korean War, 1950–1953

*North Korean People's Army*

105th Armoured Brigade (later
   Division)
16th Tank Regiment
17th Tank Regiment
42nd Tank Regiment
43rd Tank Regiment
104th Tank Regiment

106th Tank Regiment
107th Tank Regiment
109th Tank Regiment
203rd Tank Regiment
206th Tank Regiment
208th Tank Regiment

*Republic of Korea Army*

51st Tank Company
52nd Tank Company

53rd Tank Company
55th Tank Company

| | |
|---|---|
| 56th Tank Company | 58th Tank Company |
| 57th Tank Company | 59th Tank Company |

### United Nations Forces

*US Army*
6th Tank Battalion
70th Tank Battalion
73rd Tank Battalion
89th Tank Battalion (formerly
  8072nd Medium Tank Battalion)
1st Marine Tank Battalion

*British Army*
29th Independent Infantry Brigade
  8th King's Royal Irish Hussars
  1st, 5th and 7th Royal Tank
    Regiment
  5th Royal Inniskilling Dragoon
    Guards

*Canadian Army*
25th Infantry Brigade
A, B and C Squadrons Lord Strathcona's Horse

## Suez War, 1956

### Sinai

*Egyptian Army*
1st Armoured Brigade
2nd Armoured Brigade

*Israeli Defence Forces*
7th Armoured Brigade
27th Mechanized Brigade
37th Mechanized Brigade

### Suez

*British Army*
6th Royal Tank Regiment

*French Army*
7th Light Mechanized Division

## Vietnam War, 1962–1975

*Army of the Republic of Vietnam*
1st Armored Brigade
  20th Tank Regiment
  4th Armored Cavalry Regiment
  11th Armored Cavalry Regiment
  17th Armored Cavalry Regiment
    (trans to 3rd Inf. Div.)
2nd Armored Brigade
  14th Armored Cavalry Regiment
    (trans to 22nd Inf. Div.)

  19th Armored Cavalry Regiment
3rd Armored Brigade
  15th Armored Cavalry Regiment
  18th Armored Cavalry Regiment
    (trans. to 1st Armd. Bde.)
4th Armored Brigade
  12th Armored Cavalry Regiment
  16th Armored Cavalry Regiment

*Australian Army*
1st Armoured Regiment

3rd Cavalry Regiment

*US Army*
11th Armored Cavalry Regiment
D Company, 16th Armored
   Regiment
2nd Battalion, 34th Armored
   Regiment

1st Battalion, 69th Armored
   Regiment
1st Battalion, 77th Armored
   Regiment

*US Marines*
1st Tank Battalion
3rd Tank Battalion
1st Amphibious Tractor Battalion

3rd Amphibious Tractor Battalion
1st Armored Amphibian Company

*North Vietnamese Army*
202nd Armored Regiment

203rd Armored Regiment

# Six Day War, 1967

## Sinai
*Egyptian Army*
4th Armoured Division
7th Armoured Division
6th Mechanized Division

*Israeli Defence Forces*
7th Armoured Brigade
60th Armoured Brigade

## West Bank
*Jordanian Army*
40th Armoured Brigade
60th Armoured Brigade

*Israeli Defence Forces*
Bar Kochva Armoured Brigade
Uri Ram Armoured Brigade
10th Mechanized Brigade

## Golan Heights
*Syrian Army*
14th Armoured Brigade
44th Armoured Brigade

*Israeli Defence Forces*
Mendler Armoured Brigade

# Indo-Pakistan War, 1971

## West Pakistan
*Indian Army*
Unknown

*Pakistani Army*
1st Armoured Division
6th Armoured Division

# Yom Kippur War, 1973

## Sinai

*Egyptian Army*

4th Armoured Division
  3rd Armoured Brigade
  25th Independent Armoured
    Brigade
21st Armoured Division
  1st Armoured Brigade
  14th Armoured Brigade
  18th Mechanized Brigade
3rd Mechanized Division
  GHQ Reserve

6th Mechanized Division
  22nd Armoured Brigade
  113th Mechanized Brigade
23rd Mechanized Division
  2th Armoured Brigade
  116th Mechanized Brigade
  118th Mechanized Brigade

*Israeli Defence Forces*

143rd Reserve Armoured Division
  14th Armoured Brigade
  600th Reserve Armoured Brigade
146th Reserve Armoured Division
  11th Reserve Armoured Brigade
162nd Reserve Armoured Division
  217th Reserve Armoured Brigade
  460th Armoured Brigade

  500th Reserve Armoured Brigade
252nd Armoured Division
  8th Armoured Brigade
  14th Armoured Brigade (trans to
    143rd Division)
  401st Armoured Brigade
  460th Armoured Brigade (trans
    to 162nd Division)

## Golan Heights

*Israeli Defence Forces*

146th Armoured Division
9th Armoured Brigade
19th Armoured Brigade
20th Armoured Brigade
70th Armoured Brigade
240th Armoured Division

17th Armoured Brigade
79th Armoured Brigade
36th Mechanized Division
7th Armoured Brigade
188th Armoured Brigade

*Iraqi Army*

3rd Armoured Division
6th Tank Brigade

12th Tank Brigade
8th Mechanized Brigade

*Jordanian Army*

3rd Armoured Division
40th Armoured Brigade

92nd Armoured Brigade

*Syrian Army*
1st Armoured Division
51st Tank Brigade
40th Mechanized Brigade
3rd Armoured Division

Assad Republican Guard Tank
   Brigade
15th Mechanized Brigade
Plus 46th, 47th and 68th Tank
   Brigades

# Angolan Civil War, 1975–2002

*Angolan Army*
1st–10th Tank Battalions

*South African Defence Force*
81st Armoured Brigade
82nd Armoured Brigade

*Cuban Army*
50th Mechanized Division

61st Mechanized Brigade

# Ogaden War, 1977–1978

*Ethiopian Revolutionary Army*
Unknown

*Somali National Army*
16th Armoured Battalion
15th Motorized Brigade

# Iran-Iraq War, 1980–1988

*Iranian Army*
92nd Armoured Division

Two Mechanized Divisions

*Iraqi Army*
Saladin Armoured Division
3rd Armoured Division
6th Armoured Division
10th Armoured Division
12th Armoured Division
16th Armoured Division

37th Armoured Division
1st Mechanized Division
5th Mechanized Division
14th Mechanized Division
51st Mechanized Division

# Lebanon, 1982

*Israeli Defence Forces*
36th Armoured Division
90th Armoured Division
91st Armoured Division

162nd Armoured Division
252nd Armoured Division

*Syrian Army*
1st Armoured Division
   91st Tank Brigade

76th Tank Brigade
58th Mechanized Brigade

3rd Armoured Division
  82nd Armoured Brigade
  5th Mechanized Brigade

62nd Independent Tank Brigade
68th Tank Brigade
85th Mechanized Brigade

*Palestinian Liberation Organisation*
Two Tank Battalions

# Gulf War, 1991

## *Coalition Forces*

*US Army*
1st Armored Division
3rd Armored Division
1st Cavalry Division
1st Infantry (Mechanized) Division

24th Infantry (Mechanized)
  Division
1st Tiger Brigade (from 2nd
  Armored Division)

*British Army*
1st British Armoured Division
  4th Armoured Brigade

7th Armoured Brigade

*Egyptian Army*
4th Armoured Division
  2nd Tank Brigade
  3rd Tank Brigade
  6th Mechanized Brigade

3rd Mechanized Division
  8th Tank Brigade
  11th Mechanized Brigade
  12th Mechanized Brigade

*French Army*
6th French Light Armoured Division

*Royal Saudi Land Forces*
10th Armoured Brigade
8th Mechanized Brigade
10th Mechanized Brigade
11th Mechanized Brigade
20th Mechanized Brigade

*Syrian Army*
9th Armoured Division
  52nd Tank Brigade
  53rd Tank Brigade
  43rd Mechanized Brigade

## *Saddam Hussein's Forces*

*Iraqi Army*
3rd Armoured Division
6th Armoured Division
10th Armoured Division
12th Armoured Division
17th Armoured Division

37th Armoured Division
1st Mechanized Division
5th Mechanized Division
14th Mechanized Division
51st Mechanized Division

26th Independent Armoured Brigade

*Republican Guard Corps*
1st Hammurabi Armoured Division
2nd Medina Armoured Division
3rd Tawakalna Armoured Division
4th Al Faw Mechanized Division

20th Independent Mechanized Brigade

5th Baghdad Mechanized Division
6th Nebuchadnezzar Mechanized Division
7th Adnan Mechanized Division

## Slovenian War of Independence, 1991

*Slovenian Territorial Defence Force*
6th Military District Tank Company
7th Military District Tank Company

*Yugoslav National Army*
1st Armoured Brigade
4th Armoured Brigade
32nd Mechanized Brigade
140th Mechanized Brigade

## Croatian Homeland War, 1991

*Croatian National Guard*
1st Brigade Tigers
2nd Brigade Thunder
3rd Brigade Martens
4th Brigade

*Yugoslav National Army*
Guards Mechanized Division
252nd Armoured Brigade
329th Armoured Brigade

# Chinese Cold War Tracked Armour

**Note:** Due to space restrictions the following appendices do not include development histories of American, British, French and Israeli armour. This is also on the grounds that Chinese- and Soviet-built armour played a much greater role in many of the tank engagements of the Cold War. However, comparative analysis of the performance of Western armour is referenced throughout the text, especially in the case of the numerous Middle Eastern wars.

Initial Chinese perceptions of the utility of the tank were greatly influenced by their experiences in Korea and Indochina. In Korea the terrain had confined the North Korean tanks to the roads and they had proved vulnerable to enemy air attack. General Wei Guo-qing, the chief Chinese adviser to the Viet Minh in Indochina, had witnessed how they had defeated the French without recourse to tanks. China's most significant contribution to the Viet Minh's war effort had been artillery and anti-aircraft guns, not tanks. The French had employed the M24 Chaffee light tank and the M4 Sherman medium tank, which had given them little discernible strategic advantage. Many senior Chinese generals saw little scope for the tank in the 'people's war' against the capitalists. They were steeped in the tradition of the 'human wave' attack used during the Chinese Civil War and the Korean War. Besides, the neighbouring Soviet Union was a fellow Communist state so there was no threat from that quarter – or so the Chinese thought.

## Type 58 Medium Tank

After Mao Zedong and the Communists took power in China in 1949 they obtained several hundred Soviet T-34/85s, which were used to equip a single mechanized division. After some delay, the Chinese began to produce a copy designated the Type 58, though this was swiftly rendered redundant with the appearance of the T-54. It is not clear if the Chinese ever had a full manufacturing capability for the T-34/85 like the Czechs and Poles, or simply conducted sub-assembly and refurbishments.

## Type 59 Main Battle Tank

In the 1950s Moscow supplied the People's Republic of China with a number of T-54As. The Chinese subsequently built their own version, the 36-ton Type 59 main battle tank that appeared in late 1957. These were constructed by Factory N.617 in Baotou in Chinese Inner Mongolia. The Chinese selected the location because the city was built up around heavy industry, in particular steel. Furthermore, being close to Mongolia meant that it was remote. However, once Baotou became the site of a plutonium plant, the Chinese had to disperse their tank-building facilities for fear of nuclear attack by America or the Soviet Union.

The early model Type 59 looked almost identical to the T-54 but was not equipped with a main armament stabilizer or infra-red night-vision equipment. Later models were fitted with a fume extractor similar to that on the T-54A, an infra-red searchlight for the commander and gunner, plus a larger one above the main gun, with a laser range-finder just to the right of it. To arm the Type 59 China produced a copy of the D-10T tank gun but the Chinese designation for this weapon is not known.

Subsequent upgrades resulted in the Type 59-I and Type 59-II, the latter being armed with a 105mm rifled gun. Outwardly the Type 59-I was the same but featured a simplified fire-control system and a laser range-finder, plus a low-pressure engine alarm and an automatic fire extinguisher. Also, the cupola door cover and safety door cover were fitted with a hydraulic booster to improve opening and closing. On the Type 59-II the barrel was fitted with a distinctive fume extractor and thermal sleeve. The Chinese produced up to 700 Type 59 tanks a year by the 1970s, rising to a rate of about 1,000 a year by the early 1980s.

## Type 59 Armoured Recovery Vehicle

This consisted of a Type 59 with its turret removed. As it did not have a winch, it functioned purely as a tractor-towing vehicle. Armament was provided by a single 12.7mm machine gun. It is thought this ARV may have been a field modification rather than factory built.

## Type 62 Light Tank

A derivative of the Type 59 was the Type 62 light tank, developed to cope with China's harsher environments, especially hilly terrain and soft ground where the former could not operate. It was essentially a scaled-down version with slightly smaller dimensions and from a distance it was hard to tell the two apart. The layout was identical in both but the Type 62, armed with a shorter 85mm gun, had lower ground pressure and was 15 tons lighter than the Type 59. About 800 were built for the Chinese People's Liberation Army and around 500 for export.

## Type 62 Armoured Recovery Vehicle

Some examples of the light tank variant were converted into armoured recovery vehicles. It is not clear if these were production vehicles or simply field conversions.

## Type 63 Light Amphibious Tank

The Chinese Type 63 was based on the Soviet PT-76 light amphibious tank, so the hull and wheels bear no resemblance to the T-54. However, the Chinese version was noteworthy as it featured a turret similar to that on the Type 62 and was likewise armed with the same 85mm gun. Its roof, though, was flatter, had smaller commander/loader hatch mountings, no ventilator dome and single hand rails either side. About 1,200 were built for the Chinese Army and a number were exported to North Korea and North Vietnam.

Thanks to regular border wars with India and the Soviet Union, the Chinese had need of both the Type 62 and the Type 63. The frontier with India is dominated by the Himalayas so is not tank country. In contrast, the border to the northeast with the Soviet Union along the Ussuri river is very marshy territory, and light/amphibious tanks can operate there.

## Type 69 Main Battle Tank

A further development of the Chinese Type 59 was the Type 69 that appeared publicly in 1982, though it may, as its designation implies, have gone into service some years earlier. The differences in appearance between the two were minimal. It drew on the Soviet T-62, an example of which was captured in 1969, though it did not copy the latter's 115mm gun. The Type 69 had an infra-red/white light headlamp arrangement that differed from that on Soviet tanks.

It also had distinctive cage-like 'boom shields' or 'grid shields' on the turret sides and rear, as well as a bank of four smoke grenade dispensers on either side of the turret. The 'boom shields', consisting of metal louvres mounted 450mm from the turret, were designed to detonate HEAT warheads and developed as a result of experiences in the 1979 war with Vietnam. Side skirts were also fitted to protect the upper track. Another distinctive feature was a semi-circular protrusion on the bottom of the rear hull plate to allow for a new fan, copied from the Soviet T-62.

Although the Type 69 drew on improvements featured on the Soviet T-62, it remained closer to the T-54 in design. The Type 69-I was armed with a smooth-bore 100mm gun (which was slightly longer than the 100mm rifle-bore gun on the Type 59 and had a bore evacuator near the end of the muzzle), while the Type 69-II had the rifled 100mm gun and a different fire-control system. The first variant does not seem to have been very successful and was superseded by the second model after just 150 Type 69-Is had been delivered. A Type 69-III (or Type 79) was produced for the export market armed with a 105mm gun, but only just over 500 were ever built.

# Type 69 Specialized Variants

### Type 653 Armoured Recovery Vehicle

This vehicle was produced to provide battlefield support for the Type 69 main battle tank. Whereas the Type 59 ARV was only a towing vehicle, the Type 653 was much more capable. It could not only recover stranded tanks, but also conduct major repairs (such as replacing engines), remove obstacles and dig firing positions for tanks and artillery.

It comprised a Type 69 hull and chassis minus the turret; in place of the latter a fixed superstructure was installed to the left, while to the right was a hydraulic crane mounted on a 360 degree turntable situated in line with the driver's position. A hydraulic 'dozer blade could be fitted to the front. The main winch enabled it to haul up to 70 tonnes. The Type 653 required a five-man crew.

### Type 84 Bridgelayer

This likewise consisted of a Type 69 with its turret removed and replaced with a bridge-launching system. The bridge of light steel folded in half with one half lying on top of the other when in transit. This extended to 18 metres and could bridge a 16-metre gap, and could take wheeled and tracked vehicles weighing up to 40 tonnes. A hydraulically operated stabilizer blade was mounted under the front of the hull and this was employed during the last phase of bridgelaying; it could also be used as a 'dozer blade. The Type 84 required three crew, including the driver.

**Type 80 Self-Propelled Anti-Aircraft Gun**
This was the Chinese version of the Soviet ZSU-57-2. It utilized a modified Type 69-II equipped with an open-topped turret armed with twin 57mm cannon. It had a vertical range of 8,000 metres, though was only effective to 5,000 metres, and a horizontal range of 12,000 metres. The Type 80 had a six-man crew. During the 1980s the Chinese also built several prototypes armed with twin 37mm guns but these did not go into production.

\* \* \*

Considerable quantities of Type 59/69 tanks were cynically exported to both Tehran and Baghdad during the Iran-Iraq War. Pakistan also proved to be a major customer for both models, though these proved disappointing there, as well as Thailand and Zimbabwe. Small numbers of the Type 653 ARV were also supplied to Bangladesh, Iraq, Pakistan and Thailand. Drawing on these tank designs, the Chinese went on to produce the Types 79, 80, 85 and 90. The Type 85-II was also built for the Pakistani Army. China produced somewhere in the region of 10,000 Type 59/69s.

# Soviet Cold War Tracked Armour

Originally, the T-54 and the T-62 were designed to overwhelm the armies of NATO on the central plain of Germany if the Warsaw Pact ever stormed through the Fulda gap. As a result, they were squat, offering the lowest profile possible, the rationale being they would have to close with NATO's ground forces as swiftly as possible. In contrast, NATO's tanks were designed to keep the enemy at arm's length, so presented a much higher silhouette to give the tank gunners greater visibility and range. The low silhouette – and therefore much-reduced gun depression/elevation – of the T-54 and T-62 was to prove a distinct disadvantage when fighting amongst the sand dunes of the Middle East during the Arab-Israeli Wars.

## T-10 Heavy Tank

Despite the rise of the main battle tank, the Soviet Union persisted with heavy tanks for a number of years after the Second World War ended. The innovative IS-3, armed with a 122mm gun, appeared in the closing months of the Second World War and remained in service until the 1960s, though despite modifications it was unreliable. It was followed by the short-lived IS-4, which needed redesigning.

Just after the T-54 went into full production, in 1956 the Soviets pro-duced the largely forgotten T-10 Lenin heavy tank (or IS-10) armed with a 122mm gun. This looked very similar to the IS-3 and likewise had a round 'mushroom head' turret, giving the tank a low silhouette. It featured seven road wheels on either side and three return rollers, whereas the IS-3 had six and three respectively. This was presumably in an attempt to address some of the power-to-weight problems experienced by the T-10. The IS engine and gearbox had simply not been up to the job.

Ironically, although classed as a heavy, the T-10 was in fact lighter than the later American Abrams, the British Chieftain and the German Leopard. It proved to be the very last of the Soviet heavy tanks, and for good reason. The T-10 was flawed and by the 1960s did not meet the Soviet Army's developing all-arms tank doctrine. Despite armour of up to 270mm, its slow speed, limited ammunition stowage, low rate of fire and poor depression on the main gun greatly reduced its combat effectiveness. In particular, it meant that the T-54 had to slow down to allow the cumbersome T-10 to keep up. (The IS tanks suffered the same problem in supporting the T-34 in 1945.) The T-10 at 51 tons was 15 tons heavier than the T-54 and could manage at best 42kph compared to the T-54's 48kph.

The T-10 first appeared publicly in the November 1957 Moscow parade, but it was not long before it was relegated to a tank-destroyer role. It was evident that it could function as a long-range anti-tank support weapon, but as a spearhead tank it was just too slow. In addition, its thick armour might have made it suitable for local counter-attacks, but for little else.

Although possibly deployed in Warsaw Pact countries by the Soviet Army, the T-10 was never exported and did not see combat during the Cold War. Some sources suggest it was supplied to Egypt and Syria but there is no evidence to support this and they are probably confusing it with the IS-3M that was exported to Egypt in the 1960s and employed in the Six Day War. It is possible that some IS-4 and T-10 tanks were shipped to Egypt for evaluation by the Soviet advisory teams but never handed over, though this would have been pointless as the Soviets were phasing out their heavy tanks.

Although ultimately a dead end, the heavy tank legacy should not be underestimated. Soviet post-war heavy tank production amounted to about 9,000, of which around 1,000 were IS-3M/IS-4 and the rest were T-10 and T-10M. However, by this stage Soviet doctrine and tank design were firmly focused on the main battle tank as the key armoured vehicle of the Soviet Army. The T-54 remained firmly the heir apparent.

## T-54/55 Main Battle Tank

In the closing years of the Second World War the Soviet Union designed a new medium tank called the T-44 that sought to improve upon the highly battle-proven T-34/76 and T-34/85, which had carried the Red Army into the heart of Berlin. The T-44 appeared in only very limited numbers between 1945 and 1949, seeing service at the end of the Second World War and then during the Hungarian Uprising in 1956. In the meantime, it was followed by the T-54; the first prototype appeared in 1946, with production commencing the following year in Kharkov. It had a very distinctive mushroom-shaped turret that drew on the Joseph Stalin heavy tank and provided excellent shot-deflection surfaces. The all-welded T-54 hull consisted of three compartments: the driver's at the front, the fighting compartment in the middle and the engine/transmission at the rear.

The round turret was a one-piece casting with the top comprising two D-shaped pieces of armour welded together down the middle, and welded into position. The commander sat on the left of the turret, with the gunner on the same side but in a more forward position. The commander's cupola could be traversed through 360 degrees, with a single-piece hatch that opened forward with a single periscope on each side. A TPK-1 sight with a single periscope either side was mounted in the forward part of the cupola top. The loader sat on the right of the turret and had a periscope and a single hatch that opened to the rear. The driver sat at the front of the tank to the left and had a single-piece hatch that swung to the left. There were two periscopes forward of this hatch, one of which could be replaced by an infra-red periscope that was used in conjunction with the infra-red light mounted on the right side of the glacis plate. To the right of the driver was an ammunition stowage space, batteries and a small fuel tank.

The T-54 engine was mounted in the rear of the hull and the tank used an electrical start-up system with a compressed air system for back-up in cold weather. In contrast, the subsequent T-55 used a compressed air engine start-up system, with an electrical back-up. This was because unlike the T-54, the T-55 had an AK-150 air compressor to refill the air pressure cylinders.

The T-55 appeared in 1958 and was essentially the T-54 with a new turret that lacked the distinctive rooftop ventilator dome. It also had a new stabilizer, increased ammunition load (forty-three rounds, up from thirty-four), new running gear and a more powerful V-55 diesel engine that gave slightly more horsepower, but the maximum speed of 50km/h remained the same. The T-54/55 series had a torsion bar suspension system that consisted of five road wheels with a very distinctive gap between the first and second wheels. The drive sprocket was at the rear and the idler at the front. Neither the T-54 nor the T-55 had track return rollers. Similar to the T-34 tank, the T-54/55's all-steel tracks had steel pins that were not held at the outer edge and therefore travelled towards the hull. A raised piece of metal welded to the hull just forward of the sprocket drove the track pins back in every time they passed it.

The T-54 and the upgraded T-55 were both armed with a 100mm gun, with frontal armour of just under 100mm and a range of approximately

500 kilometres. On both types the fume extractor was very near the muzzle of the tank gun. The T-54 was produced in at least eight different variants, while the T-55 had up to a dozen variants, though outwardly the differences in appearance were minimal. Engineering variants included armoured recovery vehicles, bridgelayers, 'dozers and mine-clearers.

The T-54 gunner had to estimate range with visual adjustment dubbed 'Eyeball Mark I'. In contrast, American-built M48 and M60 tanks had accurate optical-prism range-finding systems that allowed zeroing-in on targets within seconds, while British-built Centurions used machine-gun tracer bullets to correct the main gun targeting.

The T-54/55 could ford rivers through the use of a snorkel. Two types were available, a thin one for operational use and a thick one for training. They took up to 30 minutes to fit and were blown off once the far riverbank was reached. The combat snorkel was mounted over the loader's periscope and when not fitted was stored disassembled at the rear of the hull or the turret.

Production of the T-55 is thought to have run at the Omsk tank factory until 1981, long after the T-62 had gone out of production. Poland produced the T-54 between 1956 and 1964 and the T-55 from 1964 onwards. The East German Army favoured the T-54 over the newer T-62 and declined to accept the latter when it came into service. Instead, they waited until the T-72 had been produced before they upgraded.

## T-54 Specialized Variants

### T-54-T Armoured Recovery Vehicle

This was the initial designation for the turretless T-54 armoured recovery vehicle, which appeared in the 1950s fitted with a very wide diameter snorkel tube to ford deep rivers. Subsequently at least half a dozen types of T-54/55 ARV were developed. Most had limited capabilities compared to their Western counterparts and were mainly intended to tow damaged vehicles off the battlefield. They were known as BTS or medium armoured towers.

The T-54-T and the T-55-T were the first models to enter service and performed a similar role to the T-34-T (B) ARV, though based on a more powerful chassis. They had a loading platform in the centre of the vehicle, with sides that could be folded down to permit unloading or loading of replacement engines or transmissions. A jib crane was also provided, along with a large spade mounted at the rear of the hull.

## BTS Armoured Recovery Vehicle

The *Bronetankoviy Tyagach Srdniy* (medium armoured tractor) or BTS-1 was the first version of the T-54 to be used as an ARV and consisted of a T-54A with the turret removed. There were at least four variants with different weight-lifting equipment. The BTS-2 was fitted with a winch and large anchoring spade at the rear to assist with tank recovery. It was also equipped with a small tripod jib crane. This ARV was produced in Czecho-slovakia as the WZT-1.

Appearing in the 1960s, the BTS-3 (also designated the SPK-12G) featured a hydraulic crane fitted to the front left of the hull, with a tele-scopic jib enabling the vehicle to lift tank engines and turrets. The vehicle was additionally equipped with a front-mounted BTU-55 'dozer blade, a rear-mounted spade and a winch. The BTS-4 was similar to the BTS-2 but with the crane pivoted on the left side of the hull with a telescopic jib.

On all the variants the vehicle commander was normally seated to the right at the front of the hull, served by a single-piece hatch that opened to the right. To the commander's left was seated the driver, who was provided with two periscopes for observation and a single-piece hatch cover. The mechanics normally rode in the cargo hold, though this was uncomfortable as it also contained their tools and the snorkel (when stowed), plus spare fuel drums.

## T-54/MTU-1 Bridgelayer

The *Mostoykladchik Tankoviy Ustroystvo* (MTU-1) entered service with the Soviet Army in the late 1950s and comprised a turretless T-54 carrying a 12-metre rigid bridge (capable of spanning 11 metres) mounted on a launch frame. The bridge was constructed from four box truss panels, with inner treadways for small vehicles and outer ones for tracked vehicles. When on the move, the inner treadway ramp sections were folded on top of the main treadways.

It took a maximum of 5 minutes to launch the bridge. When an obstacle that needed to be crossed was reached, the span was winched forward on the launching frame, employing a chain-drive mechanism, which was dis-engaged once the bridge was firmly lowered into position. The bridge could carry a load of up to 50 tonnes and following use, could be recovered from either end.

For protection the vehicle was armed with a 12.7mm DShKM machine gun. This was positioned between the two treadways in the centre of the hull. In order to lay the bridge, the weapon had to be removed. The MTU-1 bridgelayer only required a two-man crew. Late production models also utilized the T-55 chassis.

## T-54K Command Tank

This was the first standard command version of the T-54A (Model 1955) fitted with additional radio sets. Accommodating the extra communications equipment meant a reduction in the amount of ammunition carried. Other command models included the T-54AK and the T-54BK. The T54-AK-1, equipped with a second R-113 radio, was designed for company commanders. The AK-2 was for battalion and regimental commanders, as well as regimental chiefs-of-staff. On this variant the HTM-10 telescopic antenna mast increased the broadcast range.

## T-54/BTU 'Dozer

The T-54 could be converted into a universal tank 'dozer (*Buldozer Tankoviy Universalniy*) with the installation of a 3.4-metre wide 'dozer blade onto the nose plate. It was intended for emplacing tanks or breaching anti-tank obstacles. However, fitting the blade was time-consuming; it could take up to 90 minutes to attach it and up to 60 minutes to remove it.

## OT-54 Flamethrower

On this model the 7.62mm coaxial machine gun was replaced by the ATO-1 automatic flame thrower (derived from the Second World War ATO-41/42 which was hull-mounted in the T-34). Ammunition storage in the bow was altered to permit the tank to carry 460 litres of flammable liquid. This was fired using compressed air, providing up to twenty bursts a minute out to a range of 160 metres. Accepted into service in 1954, it was built in only very limited quantities. The T-54B was also used as the basis for a flamethrower in 1959 but on this variant the flame gun replaced the main armament.

## T-54 Mine-clearer

This variant consisted of a T-54 fitted with the PT-54 mine-roller system, which was very similar in design to the earlier P-34 system used on T-34/76 and T-34/85 tanks in the Second World War. A framework holding two sets of six serrated rollers was fixed to the front of the hull. The rollers were aligned with the tank's tracks, so the area between the tracks remained uncleared. The modified PT-54M featured sets of five rollers rather than six. Another version used two serrated ploughs which were lighter and did not impede the tank's cross-country mobility.

## SU-122 Tank Destroyer
In 1949, following on from their experiences with tank destroyers during the Second World War, the Soviets produced the SU-122 (also known as the IT-122). This comprised a T-54 chassis with a superstructure very similar to that of the T-34-derived SU-100 tank destroyer. Mounted in the front of the hull was a 122mm gun with very limited traverse and elevation. The SU-122s were withdrawn from service in the late 1950s and reconfigured as armoured recovery vehicles, which NATO designated M1977. This was achieved by simply removing the gun and covering the mantlet aperture in the glacis plate.

## ZSU-57-2 Self-Propelled Anti-Aircraft Gun
The ZSU-57-2 was one of the first-generation Cold War self-propelled anti-aircraft guns and was first seen publicly in the late 1950s. It comprised twin S-60 guns mounted in an open-top turret on a shortened T-54 tank chassis. While the vehicle commander and the four gun crew operated from the turret, the driver was seated on the left-hand side at the front of the hull. The engine was the standard T-54 tank engine and the running gear was very similar but with one less road wheel either side. While the road speed was comparable to that of the T-54, the reduced weight of 28 tons gave a better overall performance.

The guns had a range of 4,000 metres with an elevation of up to 85 degrees. Although principally an anti-aircraft weapon, the ZSU-57-2 was also deployed to devastating effect in a ground-support role and was very effective against lightly armoured vehicles and troops caught in the open. It was deployed in the Soviet Army purely as a line-of-sight weapon, and there was little attempt to upgrade it with tracking and fire-control radar. Nonetheless by the late 1970s the ZSU-57-2 was still in service with well over a dozen countries.

## ZSU-23-4 Self-Propelled Anti-Aircraft Gun
The follow-on ZSU-23-4 was a vastly more versatile weapon and it was equipped with radar for both target acquisition and fire control, enabling it to operate in a wide range of climatic and visual conditions. This made it one of the most potent low-level anti-aircraft systems in the world. The crew of four comprised a commander, driver, radar operator and gunner, but while the large turret provided plenty of room, the armour was very thin.

This self-propelled gun, named Shilka, was first seen in the mid-1950s. It was combat-tested during the Yom Kippur War in 1973 and proved to be one of the most effective low-level air defence systems used against the Israeli Air Force. The radar could detect targets out to 20 kilometres and the system could be fired while the vehicle was moving. One flaw with the radar was that when engaging targets below 60 metres altitude, it suffered from 'clutter' (background interference). The quadruple-mounted 23mm cannon offered a maximum rate of fire of 1,000 rounds a minute for each gun, though the normal rate of fire was much lower at about 200 rounds a minute, fired in fifty-round bursts per barrel. As the gun calibre was smaller, the effective range against low-flying aircraft was around 2,500 metres.

Overall, the ZSU-23-4's layout was similar to that of the ZSU-57-2, but it was not mounted on a T-54 chassis; instead the lower chassis and running gear were largely identical to the PT-76 amphibious tank, with the same engine and transmission. While the vehicle performance was similar, the ZSU-23-4 was not amphibious. It was used to replace the ZSU-57-2 in the Soviet Army and the front-line units of other Warsaw Pact armies. Four ZSU-23-4s equipped every Soviet tank and motor rifle regiment, with a total of sixteen per division.

# T-55 Specialized Variants

### T-55 MTU-20 Bridgelayer

The MTU-20 was based on the T-55 chassis rather than the T-54. It entered service in the late 1960s as a replacement for the MTU-1. It carried a 20-metre bridge (capable of spanning 18 metres), the ends of which folded back to lie on top of the bridge to reduce the overall length when in transit. Like its predecessor, it took just 5 minutes to deploy or recover and only required two crew to operate.

### T-55 IMR Combat Engineer Vehicle

The *Inzhenernaia Maschina Razgrazheniia* comprised a turretless T-55 with a hydraulically operated crane that could traverse through 360 degrees. The crane could take a pair of pincer grabs for lifting or a small bucket for digging. Night operations were facilitated by the provision of a searchlight mounted on the crane. An armoured cupola with observation windows provided protection for the crane operator. At the front was a 'dozer blade that could be used in either straight or V configuration. The IMR first appeared in the early 1970s.

### T-55K Command Vehicle

The T-55K carried less ammunition than a regular gun tank in order to accommodate additional communications equipment and a generator. This enabled it to act as a command tank, of which there were at least three versions featuring different radios. The K1 and K2 carried two R-132 or R-123M and one R-124 radios. The T-55K3 was equipped with three radios (one R-123M, one R-124 and one R-130M), plus a 10-metre antenna. Subsequent variants were dubbed the T-55AK and T-55MK.

### T-55/BTU 'Dozer

The BTU-55 utilized a redesigned and lighter type of 'dozer blade, at 1.4 tonnes compared to the BTU's 2.3 tonnes, and it was the more commonplace of the two. It was also slightly quicker to fit and remove than the earlier design. Notably there was no bulldozer variant for the T-62, though the T-64 and T-72 could incorporate a 'dozer blade for self-emplacement.

### OT-55 Flamethrower

The AT-200 flame-gun was used to arm the T-55 flamethrower. The flame gun was again installed in place of the coaxial machine gun and was fired by one of twelve pyrotechnic cartridges carried by the tank. While fuelled by the same quantity of flammable liquid as the earlier OT-54, the subsequent OT-55 had a longer range, at 200 metres. This was the most common Soviet flamethrower tank and was used by the Soviet Army and Soviet naval infantry.

### T-55 Mine-clearer

The T-55 was modified in 1959 to take the PT-55 mine-roller system. Attachment fittings were welded to the hull front to take the 6-tonne PT-55, which had only four rollers in each section, and so cleared a narrower path. Its weight was such that the rollers were only installed when the tank was specifically on mine-clearing operations. The PT-54/PT-55 took approximately 5 minutes to detach and could survive the blast of ten swept anti-tank mines.

The KMT-4 tank-mounted mine-clearing plough was introduced in the 1960s. It comprised a 600mm wide cutting device with five cutting tines mounted at an angle in front of each track. These were lowered by hydraulic ram and simply ploughed up mines for removal rather than detonating them. This was followed by the KMT-5 design that combined both plough and rollers. The rollers were a new design, with only three rollers per section. Both had a quick-release mechanism that allowed the driver to drop them rapidly. However, the plough and rollers could not be used simultaneously unless the ground was very flat, so were deployed according to the type of ground or minefield they were required to clear. The KMT-4/ KMT-5 were compatible with the T-55 and T-62.

### T-55 BMR Mine-clearer

In the 1980s the Soviet Army deployed to Afghanistan a turretless T-55 mine-clearing vehicle. This was believed to be a variant of the M1977 Armoured Recovery Vehicle (*see* below) converted to take a mine-clearing plough with the KMT-5 or KMT-7 roller system. The driver was seated on the left with the commander to his right. The latter was served by a cupola mounting a 12.7mm machine gun, while on the right side of the hull was a bank of smoke grenade dischargers firing forward. In Afghanistan the BMR mainly deployed its mine-clearing rollers, to avoid the ploughs tearing up the country's rudimentary roads to the extent that wheeled vehicles could not use the cleared paths.

### SU-130 Tank Destroyer

In the 1950s T-55 chassis were used to create the IT-130 tank destroyer armed with a modified 130mm M-46 field gun. It was similar in appearance to the SU-100 but only a small number were produced. It did not prove very successful and, like the IT-122, it was converted in the late 1950s into an armoured recovery vehicle known as the M1977 ARV. It was not equipped with winches or any other recovery equipment so was restricted to a towing role, thereby limiting its utility. During the 1980s some of them were used as ad hoc armoured mine-clearing vehicles.

## T-62 Main Battle Tank

The Soviet T-62 tank was designed at Nizhnyi Tagil; it was based on the T-55 and incorporated a number of its components, but had a longer and wider hull and a new turret. While the engine and transmission from the T-55 were retained, a larger diameter fan improved the cooling system. The suspension was the same as on the T-55 but the mounts were reconfigured to allow for the longer hull. As a result, the spacing for the road wheels on the T-62 was different from that of the T-55, with distinctive gaps between the third and fourth, and fourth and fifth road wheels. Likewise, a distinctive fume extractor was positioned two-thirds of the way up the barrel of the larger calibre 115mm gun.

Although there were more than a dozen different T-62 variants, including upgrades, the three key production models were the 1962, 1972 and 1975 versions. Although pre-production models of the T-62 were built in

A British Challenger with the Royal Scots Dragoon Guards in Iraq in 1991.

France's AMX-30 armed with a 120mm gun was used by the French, Saudis and Qataris during operations in 1991.

An M1A1 Abrams of the 3rd Brigade, US 1st Armored Division, races across the desert in northern Kuwait during Operation Desert Sabre.

An American column, protected by Abrams tanks and Bradley infantry fighting vehicles, prepares for the offensive.

More armour from the US 1st Armored Division. In the envelopment of the Republican Guard the US M1A1 tank easily outgunned the Iraqi T-72.

Kuwaiti M-84 during Operation Desert Sabre.

Soldiers examine an Iraqi T-54 tank destroyed by the French 6th Light Armoured Division.

Lacking air support, much of Saddam's armour met this end.

his Iraqi tank was caught in the open.

ne crew of this Iraqi T-72 did a good job of camouflaging their vehicle, but it did not save them.

A destroyed Iraqi T-55 tank at Jalibah airfield.

The burnt remains of Iraqi BMP-1s.

This Iraqi T-72 was destroyed in a Coalition attack near the Ali Al Salem air base.

An Iraqi T-55 tank near the Basra-Kuwait Highway, the scene of one of the final Coalition attacks.

The debris of defeat: two Iraqi T-55 tanks abandoned on the Basra-Kuwait Highway near Kuwait City.

Abandoned T-55 and T-62 tanks on the streets of Addis Abba in 1991, at the end of the Ethiopian civil war.

Four Yugoslav National Army T-55s ambushed by Slovenian forces on the Italian border at Rožna Dolina in the suburbs of Nova Gorica in western Slovenia in 1991. That year the Soviet Union collapsed, marking the end of the Cold War.

1961, it was not seen publicly until 1965. Manufacture of the T-62 ran from 1961 to 1975, during which time around 20,000 were built, so nowhere near the T-54/55 total. The T-62 was supplied to more than twenty countries. Czechoslovakia and North Korea also built it for domestic and export purposes, the Czechs constructing around 1,500 T-62s during the period 1973–1978.

As in the T-54/55, the cast turret sat in the middle of the tank with the commander and gunner on the left and the loader on the right. Both had a single-piece hatch that opened to the rear and could be locked vertically. Instead of the T-54's twin hand rails on either side of the turret, on the T-62 there was a single, large hand rail on either side that could be used by tank riders or for hanging personal equipment.

The commander's cupola had four periscopes, two mounted in the hatch cover and two in the forward part of the cupola. The commander's sight, the TKN-3, was a day/night binocular periscope with an integral infra-red capability, mounted in the forward part of his cupola. For daylight use it had a magnification of × 5 and a 10 degree field of view, and in darkness it had a magnification of × 4.2 and an 8 degree field of view. The effective range when used with the OU-3GK searchlight was 400 metres. The handles of the sight were employed to rotate the commander's cupola and to operate the searchlight and target designation equipment.

The T-62's main armament was provided by a UT-5TS (2A20) 115mm smooth-bore gun fitted with a bore evacuator, which gave a maximum rate of fire of four rounds a minute at a standstill. Mounted coaxially to the right of the main armament was a 7.62mm PKT machine gun that had a practical rate of fire of up to 250 rounds a minute, fed by a belt containing 250 rounds.

Once fired, the main gun automatically elevated for reloading, however the turret could not traverse while the gun was being unloaded. An integral spent shell ejection system activated by the recoil of the gun ejected the empty cartridge case out through a trap door in the rear of the turret. The T-62 could carry forty rounds, with two ready rounds in the turret and the rest stored by the driver and in the rear of the fighting compartment. The gunner had a TSh2B-41u telescope with a rotating graticule for super elevation required for different types of ammunition and dual magnification, either × 3.5 with an 18 degree field of view or × 7 with a 9 degree field of view.

The T-62's main gun used APFSDS (armour-piercing fin-stabilized discarding-sabot) ammunition, which had a range of 4,000 metres. HEAT rounds gave a range of 3,700 metres, while HE could go out to 4,800 metres. The T-62 could match the Israeli guns but they were in short supply during the Yom Kippur War in 1973. The Egyptian Army had only about 100 T-62s whereas it had more than 1,600 T-54/55s.

Despite its limitations, the T-62's main gun caused a nasty surprise in the West as it appeared at a time when most NATO armies had chosen to standardize on the 105mm calibre. The Soviet 115mm gun was not only larger but also smooth bore, which was a major departure from the accepted rifled bore of the time. Nonetheless the T-62 was far from perfect; it suffered from thin armour, vulnerable ammunition and fuel storage, a poor gearbox in early models, a tendency to shed its tracks and generally poor operating conditions for the crew.

## T-64 Main Battle Tank

The T-62's bigger cousin, the T-64, appeared in the mid-1960s, but only about 8,000 were built and none was ever exported. The first prototype was finished in 1960, and the second three years later. The first production run was completed in 1966, with about 600 tanks all armed with the 115mm smooth-bore gun. These tanks suffered problems with the automatic loader, the power pack (particularly the transmission) and the suspension. Crucially, the improved T-64 featured an auto loader, which dispensed with the loader and therefore kept the size and weight of the tank down.

Another innovation on the T-64 that was less successful was the suspension. All Soviet medium tanks from the T-34 onwards had used five road wheels without any return rollers, so why the change was made to six very small road wheels and four return rollers on the T-64 is not readily apparent, though it was known that the T-62 had a tendency to shed its tracks. The T-64's design features appear to have failed, as the T-72 employed a completely different system, while modified T-62s were seen with T-72-style suspension, not that of the T-64.

Confusingly, the T-64 was very similar in appearance and layout to the T-72. The suspension consisted of six small dual road wheels (notably smaller than the six used on the T-72) and four track return rollers (the T-72 only had three), with the idler at the front and the drive sprocket at the rear. The tracks were narrower than the T-72's and the turret was slightly different. The driver sat in the front in the centre, while the other two crew were located in the turret, with the commander on the right of the gun and the gunner to the left.

The follow-on T-64A sought to iron out the early design faults and included the 2A26M2 125mm smooth-bore gun fed by an automatic loader. This tank went into service in 1969 and was first seen publicly the following year during the Moscow Parade. The 125mm gun was stabilized in both elevation and traverse, with the ordnance fitted with a thermal sleeve and fume extractor. It could fire up to eight rounds a minute and had a sighted range out to 4,000 metres employing the day sight and 800 metres employing the night sight. The 2A26 gun had vertical ammunition stowage, while the T-72 and T-80 were armed with a 125mm 2A46 gun with a horizontal ammunition feed system. The gunner selected the type of ammunition he wished to fire by simply pushing a button. It was a separate loading type, in that the projectile was loaded first, followed by the semi-combustible cartridge case; all that remained after firing was the stub base, which was ejected. The 125mm ammunition was common to the T-64, T-72, T-80 and T-90 tanks.

The T-64B's 125mm gun could also fire the AT-9 Songster anti-tank guided weapon, which was kept in the automatic loader in two separate parts, like standard APFSDS and HEAT-FS rounds, and loaded using the automatic loader. The 12.7mm anti-aircraft machine gun on the T-64 could be aimed and fired from within the tank. In total, around a dozen different T-64 variants were produced, including command and up-armoured tanks.

Whereas the Soviets had gone for designs that were easy to mass-produce with the T-54/55 and T-62, the latter's counterpart was much more advanced. As a result, while the T-62 was assigned to the motor rifle divisions, the newer T-64 served only with the armoured divisions. Somewhat ironically, the T-64 entered production only slightly earlier than the T-72, which was intended to replace the T-54/55 and T-62. The T-64, despite being a superior tank, suffered numerous teething problems that eventually consigned it to the scrapheap.

Although the T-64 served with the Soviet Groups of Forces stationed in the Warsaw Pact countries, it only saw combat against Chechen separatists. It only ever equipped the Soviet Army; after the break-up of the Soviet Union the Russian Federation kept 4,000 of them, while Ukraine ended up with 2,000. By 2013 Russia had scrapped all its T-64s, although Ukraine modernized some and kept them in service. None seem to have been exported.

The successors to the T-54/55 and T-62, the T-72, T-80 and T-90, were not produced in anything like the same numbers nor were they so widely exported, and the T-54/55 and T-62 retained their status as Moscow's tried and tested workhorses. Certainly the T-54/55 was the most widely used tank in the world – a record that is unlikely ever to be broken.

## T-72 Main Battle Tank

Confusingly, due to their shape the T-64, T-72 and T-80 all looked alike from a distance. The T-72 was a progressive development of the T-64 with improved suspension and a slightly different turret. The main difference was that the newer tank featured six large road wheels, whereas the T-64 had six rather small ones that are unlike those on any other Soviet tank. Like its predecessors, the T-72 was widely exported; it served with more than forty armies and saw combat in well over twenty different conflicts. Like many Soviet tanks, the T-72 was a great design. Two key features of the T-72 and its counterpart the T-64 were its powerful 125mm gun (deployed at a time when most of its adversaries were sporting 105mm guns) and its relatively light weight.

The 125mm gun fired APFSDS (armour-piercing, fin-stabilized discarding sabot), HE (high explosive) or HEAT (high explosive anti-tank) rounds and had an integrated fire-control system. This relieved both commander and gunner of some of their tasks, as well as increasing the probability of a first-round hit. This, of course, was a crucial capability in a tank battle.

The T-72 came about in part as an attempt to develop a simpler main battle tank as an alternative to the complicated, expensive and somewhat disappointing T-64. Through the 1960s a whole series of prototypes appeared, but the actual T-72 prototype was not completed until 1970. Essentially it drew on all its predecessors. It utilized the hull and turret layout of the T-64, as well as a similar drive train. The engine was an improved version of that used in the tried and tested T-62 and the cooling system was very similar to the one used in the T-55/T-62. All in all, it was a successful hybrid that brought together the best elements of all the Soviet Army's previous tanks.

The driver was seated at the front of the hull and used a single-piece hatch that opened to the right, in front of which was a single wide-angle TVNE-4E observation periscope. The other two crew members, as in the T-64, were seated in the turret, with the commander on the right and gunner on the left. The commander's contra-rotating cupola had a single hatch that opened forward, with two rear-facing TNPA vision blocks. In the front was a combined TKN-3 day/night sight with an OU-3 infra-red searchlight mounted over the top, and on either side of the combined sight were a pair of TNP-160 periscopes.

The gunner's hatch opened forward and had a circular opening for mounting the snorkel for deep fording. To the front of the gunner's hatch was another TNP-160 periscope, and a TNPA-65 vision block was installed in the hatch itself. In front and to the left of the gunner's hatch was a panoramic day/night sight, which was used in conjunction with the infra-red searchlight mounted to the left and in front of the sight. The gunner used the TPD-2-49 day sight and the TPN-1-49-23 night sight.

The suspension on either side consisted of six road wheels and three return rollers supporting just the inside of the track, with the idler at the front and the drive sprocket at the rear. The standard production T-72 was fitted with four removable spring-loaded skirt plates fitted on either side over the forward part of the track; in action, these were unclipped and sprang forward at an angle of 60 degrees from the side of the vehicle, giving some protection against HEAT projectiles.

The T-72 was powered by a V–12 piston multi-fuel air-cooled engine producing 740hp. It could run on three types of fuel – diesel, benzine and kerosene – with the driver being provided with a dial to set the engine for the type of fuel being carried. Later production models such as the T-72S were fitted with the much more powerful V-84 engine developing 840hp.

The main armament was the 125mm 2A46 smooth-bore gun fitted with a light alloy thermal sleeve and a bore evacuator. It could fire three types of separate loading ammunition: APFSDS with a maximum range of 2,100 metres, HEAT-FS with a direct fire range of 4,000 metres and HE-FRAG(FS) with an indirect fire range of 9,400 metres. The T-72 could carry a total of thirty-nine rounds of ammunition.

The T-72 went into production in 1972 and became fully operational the following year, but it was not seen in public until 1977. Around 20,000 were produced for both home and export markets. Some countries were also permitted to set up T-72 production facilities – though these were usually to assemble Soviet-supplied knock-down kits rather than building tanks from scratch. Nonetheless Moscow gave the T-72 design to a number of Warsaw Pact members so they could build the tank for their own armies and in some cases for the international export market.

As a result, the T-72 saw extensive action not only with the Soviets but also with numerous foreign armies, most recently in Syria during 2011–2020, where the Syrian Army struggled to quell a widespread rebellion. In fact, Syrian T-72s were first blooded against the Israelis in Lebanon back in 1982. They were also deployed by Colonel Gaddafi's regime in 2011 in an unsuccessful attempt to crush the Libyan rebels. Iran and Iraq also used the T-72 against each other during the Iran-Iraq War in the 1980s.

In contrast to Soviet tank designs, Britain never quite got it right until the Centurion and the Challenger. The Centurion was a bit of an aberration – drawing on all their experience during the Second World War, British tank designers actually came up with a very good tank that proved to be a major export success. In particular, the Israelis had great respect for the Centurion's tough capabilities and adapted it for their needs. Likewise, American tanks always tended to be slightly behind the design curve – the M4 Sherman greatly epitomized this. While the American range of Patton tanks were good, resulting in the M60, they still had their flaws. It was not until the advent of the Abrams that the Americans produced a truly dominant main battle tank. But the Soviets had got there first with the T-72. Its low silhouette in particular gave the T-72 a very sinister air. It was Soviet tank designers who pioneered the low-profile turret; normally, the bigger the main gun the bigger the turret, but on any tank the turret is the weak point as it is exposed and presents a ready target. The squat turrets of the American Abrams, British Challenger, French Leclerc and German Leopard tanks are taken for granted now, but it was the Soviets who pioneered the design with the T-72.

During the 1970s and the 1980s, at the height of the Cold War, this tank was seen as NATO's nemesis in central Europe. The fear was that Soviet armoured divisions would simply overwhelm the NATO armies and pour through the Fulda Gap. This never came to pass, but if it had, then Soviet T-72s would have been supported by Czech- and Polish-built T-72s in the forefront of the fighting.

The T-72 was intended as a cheap and cheerful way of replacing Moscow's existing workhorse tank fleet, comprising the T-54/55 and T-62. It went into service with the Soviet and Warsaw Pact armies throughout the 1970s and was also widely exported. In total there were at least fifteen Soviet variants. Serving with the Soviet Army, the T-72 saw very limited service in Afghanistan against the Mujahideen. Following the break-up of the Soviet Union, the T-72 saw action with the Russian Army in Chechnya,

Georgia and Ossetia. This, though, was in a counter-insurgency role for which it was never intended. The Russian Federation is believed to have inherited around 5,000 T-72s and a smaller number of T-80s. The T-90, a development of the T-72BM, did not go into production until after the demise of the Soviet Union so is outside the scope of this book.

While Poland and Czechoslovakia produced licensed T-72 tanks that were built to a better standard, they lacked the resin-embedded ceramic layer inside the glacis armour and the front turret. The Polish T-72 had thinner armour and the Russian, Czech and Polish versions suffered from lack of compatibility in parts and machine tooling. India undertook local production of the T-72M1 to equip the Indian Army in the late 1980s and early 1990s. The Yugoslavs also produced their own version, dubbed the M84, which they exported to Kuwait. Likewise, the Iraqis produced a copy known as the *Asad Babil* ('Lion of Babylon') – these were really kits put together from Russian spares, to get round UN sanctions. Subsequent versions included the Polish PT-91 Twardy and the Russian T-90.

## T-80 Main Battle Tank

The T-80, also armed with a 2A46 smooth-bore 125mm gun, was accepted into service just four years after the T-72. Like its predecessor, it drew on the design features of the T-64 but was greatly improved. The layout of the T-80 was generally similar to the T-64, with the driver's compartment at the front, a two-man turret in the middle, and the engine and transmission in the rear. There were, though, many detailed differences.

The T-80's rear hull top was different from the T-64's in that it had a distinct oblong exhaust outlet at the back of the hull. It tracks were also wider. The T-80 reverted to torsion bar suspension with six forged steel aluminium rubber-tyred road wheels and five return wheels on either side, with the drive sprocket at the rear and idler to the front. There were distinctive gaps between the second and third, fourth and fifth, and fifth and sixth road wheels.

Notably, the initial T-80 (1976) utilized the T-64A turret, but was replaced by the T-80B (1979), which was also equipped with the AT-8 Songster missile as featured on the T-64B. This was followed by the T-80BV (1985) featuring the T-64's explosive reactive armour and the much-improved T-80U (1985). However, the T-64 and its successor, the T-80, proved simply too costly to produce in large numbers. As the T-80 let itself down badly during the First Chechen War, the T-72 was replaced by the later T-90 (which had also been widely exported). By the late 1980s the Soviet Union had some 9,000 T-72s but just 2,500 T-80s. When the Soviet armed forces finally broke up, the Russian Federation had about 3,500 T-80s and Ukraine 345.

## PT-76 Amphibious Light Tank

During the Cold War the Soviets took their naval amphibious assault forces very seriously. Although more than half a million Soviet sailors had fought ashore during the Second World War, the Soviet fleet did not revive its naval infantry forces until the mid-1960s. These numbered about 20,000, though in the event of war would probably have been mobilized to three times this level. Moscow considered them an elite force, with the men receiving airborne, Arctic and mountain warfare training.

The Soviets, supported by their Warsaw Pact allies, ensured they had significant amphibious capabilities in the Baltic and Black Seas. Likewise, Soviet naval infantry operated with the Soviet Navy's river flotillas and with its Pacific fleet. A typical naval infantry brigade was equipped with medium and light tanks as well as wheeled armoured personnel carriers and was transported by the Alligator-class landing ship tank and Aist-class assault hovercraft.

At the forefront supporting their naval infantry was a distinctive amphibious tank. The Soviets knew that this would have a role forcing central Europe's major rivers should war break out there. The PT-76 *Plavay-ushchiy Tank* was first accepted into service in 1950 after being developed by the IV Gavalov OKB Design Bureau as the K-90. Around 7,000 of these light amphibious tanks had been built by 1967 when production finally came to an end. While it never saw combat with the Soviets, it was involved in some fierce fighting during the numerous Cold War proxy conflicts.

Interestingly, the PT-76 shared its heritage with some illustrious predecessors. The tank was armed with the 76.2mm D-56T anti-tank gun that was a development of the weapon used by the T-34/T-76 and KV-1 tanks during the Second World War. It had a maximum rate of fire of between six and eight rounds per minute, with a maximum range in the indirect fire role of around 13,000 metres. In addition, a 7.62mm SGMT machine gun was mounted coaxially to the right of the main armament. Many were also fitted with a 12.7mm DShKM anti-aircraft machine gun.

The tank's hull was of welded steel and was divided into three compartments, with the driver to the front, the fighting compartment in the middle and the engine at the rear. Unusually, the driver was seated centrally, with a single-piece hatch that swung to the right. The turret was of all-welded steel, with the commander, also acting as the gunner, seated on the left with the loader on the right. It had a single oval-shaped hatch that hinged forward and could be locked in the vertical. To the left of the hatch was a circular cupola housing three integral periscopes, which could be traversed by hand through 360 degrees by the commander. The commander also had an optical TSh-66 sight to the left of the main gun, while the loader had a periscope mounted in the turret roof forward of the hatch. The driver was also served by three periscopes mounted forward of his hatch cover.

The first production model was armed with the D-56T gun fitted with a multi-slotted muzzle brake. The subsequent and more common model was fitted with a double–baffle muzzle brake and a bore evacuator towards the muzzle. The PT-76B was fitted with a fully stabilized D-56TS and also had the benefit of an NBC (nuclear, biological and chemical warfare) system. The Model V-6 engine used in the PT-76 was one bank of that fitted to the T-54. The manual gearbox had five forward and one reverse gears and steering was of the clutch and brake variety. The torsion bar suspension comprised six road wheels with the drive sprocket at the rear and the idler at the front. The first and sixth road wheel stations had hydraulic shock absorbers and the steel tracks consisted of ninety-six links.

The tank was propelled through the water by two water jets mounted to the rear. Before entering water the crew had to erect the trim vane at the front of the hull and activate two electric bilge pumps, which were backed up by an emergency manual bilge pump. Steering the tank whilst in the water was simply done by opening and closing two hatches over the rear water jets.

A typical 3,000-strong naval infantry brigade was equipped with forty-four PT-76s, a similar number of T-72s (which started to replace the navy's T-55s in the mid-1980s) and 145 BTR-60/70 armoured personnel carriers. The Aist-class hovercraft was capable of lifting four PT-76s, one T-72 or 220 troops. A key unit was the Red Banner Northern Fleet's 63rd Guards Naval Infantry Brigade based at Pechenga on the Kola Peninsula. Its main role was to spearhead an invasion of Norway or Iceland.

Soviet Army tank and motor rifle regiments' reconnaissance companies were equipped with five PT-76s and three armoured personnel carriers, while each division had a separate reconnaissance company deploying a further five PT-76s. However, this light tank's limited utility meant that it was gradually replaced by T-54/55, T-62 and T-72 and even BMP-1/2 infantry combat vehicles. Because it was amphibious, it generally had no nuclear, biological and chemical warfare capability; further, it lacked night-fighting equipment and had very thin armour.

Nonetheless, the PT-76 saw extensive combat around the world, including in Africa and the Middle East, in the Indo-Pakistan conflict and during the Vietnam War. In fact, its most iconic moment occurred when the North Vietnamese used it to overrun the US Special Forces base at Lang Vei in 1968. The PT-76 ended up in the service of at least twenty countries, though Vietnam and Iraq were by far the largest recipients, receiving 250 and 100 respectively. The Chinese also produced a version known as the Type 63 but this had a very different cast turret. When the Soviet Union collapsed, the Soviet armed forces still had several hundred PT-76s and a number were serving with the Polish 7th Coastal Defence Brigade.

It is believed that the PT-76 was manufactured at the Kirov facility in Leningrad and the Volgograd Tractor Factory. Notably, many of this light tank's components were also used with the BTR-50 armoured personnel carrier, the SA-6 Gainful SAM system and the ZSU-23-4 self-propelled anti-aircraft gun.

## BTR-50 Armoured Personnel Carrier

In 1973 the Egyptian Army stormed across the Suez Canal to drive the Israeli armed forces from the Sinai desert. Amongst the armoured vehicles photographed rumbling over the pontoon bridges across the canal were Soviet-supplied BTR-50 amphibious tracked armoured personnel carriers. This model had originally been produced as a rushed job in response to the first generation of Western armoured personnel carriers, which had begun to appear in central Europe in the late 1950s. First seen in 1957, the open-topped BTR-50P was based on the PT-76 amphibious tank chassis.

The BTR-50 was designed to transport an infantry section or to carry artillery up to 85mm calibre that could be fired from the vehicle without offloading. The vehicle required two crew and could carry up to ten soldiers. Predictably the open variant left the passengers exposed and it was quickly followed by a version with an armoured roof, which was known as the BTR-50PK. Other variants included the BTR-50PA, armed with a 14.5mm KVPT or ZPU-1 machine gun, the BTR-50PU command vehicle, and some special purpose versions designed to carry electronic counter-measures equipment.

The BTR-50 was supplied to the Soviet and Warsaw Pact armies and was exported outside Europe, including to the Middle East. However, its major shortcoming was its lack of rear doors, which meant troops had to debus via roof hatches and over the sides, with predictable results when under fire. As a result, it was replaced by the BMP infantry fighting vehicle. Nevertheless, it still saw combat with, amongst others, the Egyptian and Iraqi armies.

The Czechs and Poles produced a modified version of the BTR-50PK dubbed the OT-62. This had improved road speed and range and a re-designed front compartment. The standard Polish version was designated the TOPAS 2AP; along with the PT-76 amphibious tank, it was deployed by the Polnocny class landing ship tank in support of Warsaw Pact naval assault forces.

## BMP-1 Infantry Combat Vehicle

One of the most innovative and revolutionary armoured vehicles to emerge from the Cold War was the tracked *Boevaya Mashina Pekhota* (BMP); this predated the American Bradley, the British Warrior, the French AMX-10 and the German Marder tracked infantry fighting vehicles. The BMP represented the first true mechanized infantry combat vehicle – essentially an armoured personnel carrier and tank hybrid. It was designed as a break-through vehicle and intended to help the Warsaw Pact cut its way through central Europe. This vehicle's key role was to ensure the swift and mass exploitation of a breakthrough of a lightly defended point in support of the infantry. In theory, the BMP was to charge forward, guns blazing, before disgorging its infantry to seize and hold enemy ground. Its 73mm gun and anti-tank missiles were designed to ensure that it could engage enemy tanks should the need arise.

The BMP-1 first appeared during the November 1967 Moscow military parade. The example seen there was believed to have been a pre-production model and it was followed by the initial production run of the vehicle known as the BMP Model 1966, though the main production variant was thought to be the Model 1970. The BMP first saw combat with the Egyptian and Syrian armies during the 1973 conflict with Israel. Subsequently it saw action with the Soviet Army in Afghanistan, with government forces in Angola, with the Iraqi Army, and with the Libyan and Syrian armies.

The vehicle consisted of an all-welded steel hull with a distinctive ribbed and sloping glacis plate. The driver was positioned at the front on the left and had a single hatch cover that opened to the right. He was served by three periscopes; the central TNPO-170 could be replaced by the TNPO-350B, which was vertically extendable and allowed the driver to see over the trim van when erected for amphibious operations. The troop compartment in the rear could transport eight soldiers, seated back to back with four on each side. Access was via four roof hatches or two rear doors, which had integral fuel tanks; each door also had a vision device, and the left door had a firing port.

The one-man turret was the same as that on the BMD-1 airborne combat vehicle. The gunner had a single hatch that opened forwards, and in front of this to the left was located a dual mode 1PN22M1 monocular periscope sight. Four additional observation periscopes served the turret gunner and a white light or infra-red searchlight was mounted on the right side of the turret. (Because it had a turret the public and media often mistook the BMP for a tank.) The turret housed the main armament: the 73mm Model 2A28 smooth-bore, low pressure, short recoil gun which weighed 115kg. This was served by a forty-round magazine located to the right rear of the gunner.

The gun fired a fixed fin-stabilized HEAT round with an initial velocity of 440m/s, accelerating to 700m/s once the projectile had left the barrel and the rocket motor cut in. This was the same round as that used in the SPG-9 infantry weapon and it had a maximum effective range of 1,300 metres. The PG-9 HEAT projectile fired by the 2A28 employed a small PG-15P stub casing to boost the projectile out of the barrel, at which point the PG-9V rocket motor ignited to supply the main source of propulsion. The HEAT projectile could penetrate up to 300mm of armour.

Mounted over the main gun was an AT-3 Sagger wire-guided ATGW launcher. A single missile was carried ready to fire, with two reloads in the turret, which were loaded via a rail through a hatch in the forward part of the turret roof. Mounted coaxially to the main gun was a 7.62mm PKT machine gun that was fed by a continuous belt of 2,000 rounds held in a honeycombed ammunition box mounted below the weapon. The turret traverse and gun elevation were electric but with mechanical controls in case of power failure.

The BMP's torsion bar suspension was made up of six rubber-tyred road wheels on either side, with the drive sprocket at the front, the idler at the back and three track return rollers. The first and last road wheel stations had a hydraulic shock absorber and the top of the track was protected by a light sheet steel cover. The track links consisted of the double pin type with water scoops between the housings. The BMP-1 was fully amphibious and was propelled through the water by its tracks. Variants of the BMP-1 were built by China, Czechoslovakia and Romania.

The Soviet Army had high expectations for the BMP's capabilities, but these were dashed in 1973. During the Arab-Israeli Yom Kippur War the Egyptians used the BMP exactly as the Soviet manual dictated. However, while the Soviet theory was all well and good, in the open tank ground of the Sinai the BMP proved ultimately to be vulnerable to Israeli tanks, anti-tank weapons and jet fighters. The 73mm gun proved to be largely ineffectual and the ATGW was difficult to control. To compound matters, Egyptian crew training was probably not as good as it could have been.

Soviet doctrine had to be rethought, resulting in the infantry dismounting about 300 metres from their objective, which was to be taken on foot under covering fire from the BMP gunner, supporting tanks and artillery. Despite this doctrinal rethink, in the intervening years the BMP saw combat in numerous wars around the world. Despite its limitations against enemy tanks, it provided infantry with a welcome force multiplier and set a trend that NATO followed.

## BMP-2 Infantry Combat Vehicle

Lessons gleaned from the BMP-1 inevitably led to the BMP-2. This first appeared in November 1982 in the Red Square parade, though it was believed to have already been in service for a number of years. While visually the BMP-2 was almost identical to its predecessor, one clear difference was the long thin barrel of the main armament, the Model 2A42 30mm cannon. This was housed in a two-man all-welded steel turret with the commander seated on the right and the gunner on the left. The gunner had a single rectangular hatch that opened to the front, with an integral rear-facing periscope and three fixed periscopes, two to the front and one to the left side. A total of 500 rounds were carried for the main armament.

In addition, the BMP-2 had a Spandrel AT-5 ATGW launch tube mounted on the turret roof between the gunner's and commander's hatches. As well as the infantrymen's small arms, the BMP-2 also normally carried an anti-tank grenade launcher and two surface-to-air missiles. The infantry compartment at the rear only had two roof hatches compared with the four fitted on the BMP-1, though access was normally via the two rear doors. It carried only six infantrymen compared to eight in the BMP-1.

Like its predecessor, the BMP-2 was fully amphibious. Just before entering water a trim vane stowed on top of the glacis plate was erected, the bilge pumps were switched on and the driver's centre periscope was replaced by the TNPO-350B. The upper part of the tracks had a sheet metal covering that was deeper than that on the BMP-1 as it was filled with a buoyancy aid.

From the late 1980s onwards a number of enhancements were carried out to production BMP-2s, most of which were retrofitted to earlier BMP-1s and BMP-2s. The latter were supplied to the Iraqi Army and were manufactured in India as the *Sarath* and in the former Czechoslovakia as the OT-90. The BMP-3, which featured redesigned road wheels and a higher hull profile, appeared just as the Soviet Union was collapsing. This up-gunned BMP had a turret-mounted 2K23 weapon system that comprised a 100mm 2A70 gun, a 30mm 2A72 coaxial cannon and a 7.62mm coaxial machine gun.

## MT-LB Multi-Purpose Tracked Vehicle

The versatile MT-LB by contrast started life in the late 1960s as a multi-purpose tracked armoured vehicle. In all, there have been more than eighty variants but its main roles were as an artillery prime mover, cargo carrier and armoured personnel carrier. Although slightly smaller than the BMP, it carried more men: three crew and ten infantry. Armoured protection, however, was rather less and the main armament was confined to one 7.62mm machine gun so it lacked any real firepower.

The MT-LB's hull was all-welded steel with the crew compartment at the front, the engine immediately behind, and the troop compartment at the rear. As with most Soviet armoured vehicles, the driver sat on the left and had a single-piece hatch, in front of which were three periscopes. The commander was located to the right of the driver and was served by a single-piece hatch and two periscopes. When in combat the commander also operated the turret.

The machine-gun turret was mounted above the commander's position and armed with a 7.62mm PKT machine gun. Like the turrets on the BRDM-2 and BTR-60PB, it did not have a hatch cover. The machine-gunner and the driver both had a windscreen in front of them, which during combat was protected by a flap hinged at the top. An aisle gave access from the front crew compartment to the personnel compartment at the back. The latter had inward-facing folding canvas seats for ten infantrymen. Two hatches over the top of the troop compartment opened forwards. Troops entered and vacated the MT-LB via two doors in the rear of the hull, both of which had a firing port. On each side of the troop compartment there was an additional firing port and vision block.

The standard torsion bar suspension consisted of six road wheels with the idler at the rear and the drive sprocket at the front. There were no track return rollers as the tracks rested on top of the road wheels. The vehicle was fully amphibious and was propelled through the water by its tracks. As with most armoured vehicles, just before entering the water a trim vane was erected at the front of the MT-LB and the bilge pumps were switched on. The MT-LB was not produced in such large numbers as the BMP but it entered service with the Soviet and other Warsaw Pact armies.

## ASU-85 Airborne Assault Vehicle

Following the Second World War the Soviets developed considerable airborne assault forces, known as the VDV (*Vozdushno Desantnaya Voyska*), which were supported by a series of armoured fighting vehicles that were air-portable and could be dropped by parachute. Key amongst these were the ASU and the BMD. The successor to the much smaller and less powerful ASU-57, the ASU-85 (*Aviadesantnaya Samokhodnaya Ustanovka*, or airborne self-propelled mount) that appeared in public for the first time in 1962 was the Soviets' main airborne assault vehicle. At 2.1 metres in height, the ASU-85 could be transported by air or parachute-dropped. Each Soviet airborne division had an assault gun battalion equipped with thirty-one ASU-85s. The Polish 6th Pomeranian Airborne Division also deployed it.

Based on the PT-76 tank, the ASU-85 had the same engine, transmission and running gear, and was roughly the same weight. It was not amphibious, having been adapted to the assault gun and tank destroyer role. The 2A15 85mm gun, which fired HE as well as AP rounds, was located just left of centre of the sloping glacis plate and had a traverse of 12 degrees and elevation of 15 degrees. The driver sat to the right of the main gun, with the other three crew members (commander, gunner and loader) behind. The vehicle carried forty-five rounds for the main gun and 2,000 rounds for the coaxial 7.62mm machine gun. The TShK-2-79 day sight or TPN1-79-11 night sight directed both the 85mm gun and the machine gun.

The only upgrade, dubbed the ASU-85 M1974 by NATO, appeared in the early 1970s. Intended to give the vehicle some measure of anti-aircraft defence, the upgrade consisted of the installation of a DShk-M 12.7mm heavy machine gun with 600 rounds, which meant that the main armament load was reduced to thirty-nine rounds.

## BMD-1 Airborne Combat Vehicle

The BMD-1 (*Boyevaya Mashina Desantnaya*) first entered service with Soviet airborne units in 1969 but was not seen publicly for another four years. Its main claim to military fame is that it spearheaded Moscow's invasion of Afghanistan in December 1979, helping to secure Kabul. Since then it was produced in three different variants, though the basic vehicle remained the same throughout.

This small APC had a crew of three and could carry four other passengers. Its main armament was the same as that on the BMP-1 ICV, the 73mm Model 2A28 smooth-bore, low-pressure, short-recoil gun weighing 115kg. This was loaded by an automatic forty-round magazine to the right rear of the gunner. It fired a fixed fin-stabilized HEAT round with an initial muzzle velocity of 400m/s, increasing to 665m/s once the projectile had departed the barrel and the rocket motor started. The projectile was the same as that used in the SPG-9 infantry weapon and had a maximum effective range of 1,300 metres. Traverse and gun elevation were electric with the usual manual controls for emergencies. The gunner was served by a dual mode 1PN22M1 monocular periscope sight mounted on the left side of the turret. Day mode magnification gave ×6 and a 15 degree field of view, while night mode offered ×6.7 and a 6 degree field of view.

Above the 73mm gun was a launcher rail for an AT-3 'Sagger' ATGW. Two missiles were carried inside the turret and were loaded via a rail through a hatch in the forward part of the turret. Controls for the Sagger were stored under the gunner's seat. When needed, these were locked in position between the legs of the gunner, who controlled the missile using the joystick in the usual manner. Mounted coaxially to the right of the main armament was a 7.62mm PKT machine gun. This was fed from a continuous belt of 2,000 rounds loaded into an ammunition box below the weapon. To catch the waste there was a cartridge and link collector mounted in the turret basket.

The hull of the BMD-1 was of welded aluminium. The driver was located at the front of the vehicle, seated in the centre just forward of the turret, and had a single hatch that opened to the right. Three periscopes were mounted forward of the hatch. The commander sat to the left of the driver and beside the commander's seat were the radio and gyrocompass. The bow machine-gunner sat to the driver's right and aimed the bow-mounted 7.62mm PKT machine guns using a TNPP-220 periscope sight. The two machine guns were mounted at either side of the front of the vehicle. Two semi-circular hatches were positioned on either side of the forward edge of the turret.

The BMD-1's turret had a single-piece forward-opening hatch to the left. The gunner had four periscopes, one mounted on each side and two forward of the hatch. The rear personnel compartment had a concertina-style hatch which opened towards the front.

The suspension comprised five small road wheels with the drive sprocket at the rear and the idler at the front, plus four track return rollers. The suspension combined a hydraulic system for changing the ground clearance and maintaining track tension with pneumatic springs; this enabled ground clearance to be changed from 100mm to 450mm. The BMD-1 was fully amphibious and was propelled through the water by two water jets at the rear of the hull. Limited numbers of BMD-1s were supplied to Angola, India and Iraq.

Soviet airborne or landing divisions were issued with 330 BMDs per division: three command versions with the divisional headquarters and three regiments with 109 BMDs each (ten command vehicles, nine BMDs without turrets and 90 basic BMD-1s). Initially the BMD-2 was issued at a rate of nine to each of the three airborne regiments.

## BMD M1979/BTR-D Airborne Combat vehicle

This was immediately distinguishable from the BMD-1 by its longer chassis, which had six (rather than five) road wheels and five (rather than four) return rollers, the lack of a turret and different hull top. This vehicle was first seen during the Soviet invasion of Afghanistan and was dubbed the BMD M1979 by NATO. Development of the BTR-D commenced in 1974, drawing on the automotive parts of the BMD-1. Like the latter, its hull was of all-welded construction. The glacis protection was increased using a dual slanted angle in the upper plates of the armour at the front.

The BTR-D was designed for a variety of roles, including carrying personnel, towing support weapons and maintenance support. It could carry ten infantry as well as the three crew, though the bow machine-gunners also normally deployed with the infantry. Some early models were fitted with a small one-man turret armed with a 7.62mm PKT machine gun. A number were also armed with a 30mm AG-17 automatic grenade launcher. A command post variant called the BMD-KShM with a 'clothes rail' radio antenna was also deployed to Afghanistan.

## BMD-2 Airborne Combat Vehicle

The BMD-2 that went into production in the late 1980s was essentially a BMD-1 chassis with a new turret equipped with a different main gun. Initially it was assessed that the BMD-2 was simply a rebuild of the earlier model, but it was in fact a new vehicle. While the chassis was almost identical to that of the BMD-1, the two-man turret was replaced by a one-man turret with the gunner being seated on the left and provided with a single-piece circular hatch opening to the front. The reduction of the crew from three to two meant the vehicle could carry five passengers instead of four.

The main armament consisted of a 30mm 2A42 dual-feed stabilized cannon with a 7.62mm PKT machine gun mounted coaxially to the right. This was the same weapon as that in the BMP-2 infantry combat vehicle. The BMD-2 carried 300 rounds of 30mm ammunition and 2,980 rounds of 7.62mm ammunition.

On the right side of the turret was a pintle that could take either the AT-4 Spigot ATGW launcher, which had a range of 2,000 metres, or the AT-5 Spandrel ATGW which had a range of up to 4,000 metres. The BMD-2 had only a single 7.62mm PKT bow-mounted machine gun, which was on the right side, while the left weapon port was removed.

## 120mm Airborne Self-Propelled Howitzer (2S9)

The 120mm SO-120 (2S9) *Anona* ('Anemone') self-propelled howitzer entered service in 1981 and was deployed in Afghanistan with Soviet forces fighting the Mujahideen. It was developed to meet the needs of the Soviet air assault divisions by providing an artillery and anti-tank capability. The Anona was armed with a turret-mounted 120mm breech-loaded 2A51 mortar with a 1.8 metre barrel. This had a fire rate of six to eight rounds a minute. Muzzle velocity was 560m/s for HEAT rounds and 367m/s for the artillery rounds. Ammunition was fixed and loading was done manually, although ramming was automatic. Once the round was in the feed tray an electric button was pressed and a rammer automatically seated the round in the chamber and closed the breech.

The 2S9 took just thirty seconds to come into combat and a similar time to come out of action. When deployed to a firing position, the suspension was raised to provide a more stable firing platform. The fighting compartment had stowage for twenty-five rounds of ammunition. Mounted below the rear of the turret was an ammunition loading hatch and mounted on top of the hatch was a device for loading ammunition from the ground directly into the fighting compartment. This permitted continuous fire without depleting the onboard ammunition supply.

The aluminium hull was a version of the BTR-D airborne ACV. The turret was located above the fighting compartment. The two-man turret was of welded aluminium construction with 16mm frontal armour. The turret roof had two hatches, one for the gunner and one for the loader; traverse was limited to 35 degrees either side. This vehicle lacked defensive weapons: it had no coaxial machine gun and there was no bow- or turret-mounted machine gun.

The tracks were the same as those used on the BMD-1 and the suspension was hydraulic with adjustable ground clearance of 100mm and 450mm. As in the BTR-D, there were six road wheels on each side and five track return rollers. Although it was never exported, a number of 2S9s were bequeathed to the Afghan Army when the Soviets withdrew in 1989.

## 122mm Self-Propelled Howitzer M-1974 (2S1)

The 2S1 122mm self-propelled howitzer, dubbed the M-1974 in the West, in fact entered service with the Soviet Army in 1971. Likewise, the 2S3 152mm, called the M-1973, also entered service that year. The Soviet military designation for the 2S1 (its industrial number) was SO-122, though it was more commonly known as the *Gvozdika* ('Carnation'). As both these vehicles had turrets they were commonly mistaken for tanks. (One way to tell them apart is that self-propelled guns normally have their turrets set at the rear of the hull rather than in the middle, which is normally the case with tanks.)

The M-1974 shared many of the same automotive parts as the MT-LB multi-purpose tracked armoured vehicle. The suspension system was similar to the MT-LB and consisted of seven road wheels with the drive sprocket at the front and the idler at the rear; it had no track return rollers. Its all-welded steel hull was divided into three compartments: the driver's compartment at the front on the left, the engine compartment behind the driver and the turret at the rear.

The main armament, designated the 2A31, was a modified version of the 122mm D-30 towed howitzer. This was fitted with a fume extractor and muzzle brake, and was held in position when travelling by a lock on the hull glacis plate. The latter was operated by the driver by remote control. The ammunition mix normally consisted of thirty-two HE, six smoke and two HEAT-FS armour-piercing rounds. It is believed around 10,000 2S1s were built for the home and export markets, with production coming to an end in 1991. This vehicle was widely exported to Africa and the Middle East.

## 152mm Self-Propelled Gun Howitzer M-1973 (2S3)

The main armament on the 2S3 self-propelled gun was the 152mm gun designated the 2A33, based on the towed 152mm D-20 gun howitzer but with a bore evacuator fitted just behind the muzzle brake. Depending on the type of ammunition used, this weapon had a maximum range of 24,000 metres. Just over thirty rounds complete with fuses were stored in the rear of the hull in three horizontal layers.

The large all-welded turret had a sloped front and sloped sides with vision blocks on each side. The commander sat on the left of the turret and the loader on the right. The commander's cupola could be rotated through 360 degrees and had a single hatch that opened to the rear. Mounted on the forward part of the hatch was a 7.62mm PKT machine gun that could be aimed and fired from inside the turret. To the left of this was normally mounted an OU-3K infra-red/white light searchlight.

The torsion bar suspension consisted of six dual rubber-tyred road wheels on either side, with the drive sprocket at the front, the idler at the rear and four track return rollers. The first and last return rollers only supported the inside of the track. About 10,000 of these self-propelled guns had been produced by the time the Soviet Union collapsed. The 2S3 notably ended up in service with the Hungarian, Iraqi, Libyan and Syrian armies.

## 240mm Self-Propelled Mortar M-1975 (SM-240 – 2S4)

The turret-less 2S4, 2S5 and 2S7 all consisted of a gun mounted on the top of the hull and all looked quite similar, though the 2S7 was by far the largest. In particular, the 2S4 and 2S5 used the same chassis and running gear. The Soviet 240mm self-propelled mortar was dubbed the M-1975 by the West, but was known as the SM-240 (2S4) by the Soviet Army, which tended to call it the *Tyul'pan* ('Tulip Tree'). The chassis was a modified version of that used in the SA-4 Ganef surface-to-air missile system.

The hull of the 2S4 was of all-welded armour construction giving the crew protection from small arms fire and shell splinters. The 240mm smooth-bore mortar was transported complete with its base plate on top of the hull in a horizontal position. The mortar could be hydraulically lifted by remote control to the rear of the vehicle so that in its firing position it faced rearward. Some forty mortar bombs were carried in the hull in two drum magazines that were off-loaded via a hatch in the roof. The mortar could fire conventional HE fragmentation bombs or an HE FRAG rocket-assisted projectile, which had an 18,000 metre range. Only about 400 2S4s were built and some were supplied to the former Czechoslovakia, Iraq and Lebanon.

## 152mm Self-Propelled Gun (2S5)

The 2S5, known as the *Giatsint* ('Hyacinth'), went into service in 1978 and had the same running gear as the 2S3. The long-barrelled 152mm gun, designated the 2A37 and fitted with a five-part multi-baffle muzzle brake, was mounted externally on the roof to the rear. It had a maximum range of 37,000 metres. The 2S5 had the same suspension and running gear as the 2S3 and 2S4. The chassis was of the standard all-welded steel construction with maximum armour of 13mm. The driver was seated at the front on the left and had a single-piece hatch that opened to the rear. In front of this were periscopes. The commander sat in a raised superstructure to the rear of the driver and had a cupola that could traverse through 360 degrees. The remaining three crew members were seated in a crew compartment at the rear of the hull and entered and exited via a ribbed ramp in the rear. This compartment was fitted with roof hatches and roof periscopes that gave fields of view to the sides of the vehicle.

Ammunition was of the separate loading type, i.e. separate projectile and propellant charge, and the crew were assisted by a semi-automatic loading system. This comprised an electrically driven chain rammer to the left of the breech, which folded back through 90 degrees to be parallel with the breech. A charge loading system was pivoted on the right side and had a projectile tray and charge tray. The ammunition was loaded into the trays and then swung upward through almost 90 degrees, where the rammer rams in first the projectile and then the charge. The 2S5 could carry thirty rounds, with the projectiles stowed vertically in a carousel device to the left of the rear compartment and the thirty charges to the right in three rows of ten. Finland was the only known export customer for this self-propelled gun.

## 203mm Self-Propelled Gun (SO-203 – 2S7)

This self-propelled gun came into service in 1975 with well over 1,000 being built. A fully enclosed crew compartment was at the front with seats for the commander and the driver. They were each served by a circular hatch in front of which were periscopes for forward observation. They also had windscreens that were covered by an armoured shutter hinged at the top when in action.

The 203mm gun was designated the 2A44 and was not fitted with a fume extractor or a muzzle brake. The gun operator sat at the rear on the left side with the elevation and traverse controls. He was served by a standard PG-1M panoramic telescope used in conjunction with the K-1 collimator. For direct fire he employed the OP4M-87 telescope. The weapon had an ammunition handling system that permitted a rate of fire of two rounds per minute, out to a range of 47,000 metres. At the rear of the vehicle was a very distinctive hydraulically operated spade that was lowered before firing started. In action, the 2S7 took up to 6 minutes to deploy, which was not ideal.

The V–12 liquid-cooled diesel engine was at the back of the crew compartment cab. To the rear of the engine was a second crew compartment that took four other personnel, with access to the vehicle via two circular roof hatches. The torsion bar suspension comprised seven dual rubber-tyred road wheels on either side, with six track return rollers, with the idler at the rear and the drive sprocket at the front. This self-propelled gun was deployed only by the Soviet Army and a few other Warsaw Pact countries.

## 152mm Self-Propelled Artillery System (2S19)

The 2S19 152mm self-propelled gun went into service just as the Soviet Union was collapsing. Its chassis was based on the running gear and suspension from the T-80 tank and the power pack from the T-72 tank. The main armament consisted of a turret-mounted long-barrelled 152mm gun, the 2A64, fitted with a fume extractor and muzzle brake. When in motion the barrel was held in position by a lock mounted on the front glacis plate. The turret was very large but could manage a 360-degree rotation.

# Soviet Cold War Wheeled Armour

## BRDM-1 Amphibious Scout Car

The BRDM-1 amphibious scout car went into service in the late 1950s. Notably, the BRDM Model 1957 had an open roof while the Model 1958 had an enclosed roof with twin hatches, and the latter became the standard production model. The BRDM-1's hull was of all-welded steel with the engine located at the front and the crew compartment at the rear. The driver sat on the left-hand side at the front with the commander on his right. Both had a hatch that swung forward and had a vision block for use when closed. There were also vision slits in the front of the hull.

There were two firing ports on either side of the hull and two large hatches in the forward part of the roof that opened rearwards. The rear of the crew compartment sloped at an angle of about 30 degrees and was fitted with a two-piece hatch that opened either side of the superstructure. There was also a firing port in each hatch. The vehicle was normally armed with a 7.62mm SGMB machine-gun pintle mounted on the forward part of the roof. Some were also fitted with a 12.7mm DShKM heavy machine gun mounted on the forward part of the roof with a 7.62mm machine gun mounted at the rear.

The vehicle had two belly wheels, located between the front and rear road wheels, that could be lowered to greatly improve its cross-country performance. Like most Soviet armoured fighting vehicles, the BRDM-1 was fully amphibious and was propelled through the water by a single water jet to the rear of the hull. A trim vane was stowed folded under the nose of the vehicle when not in use. The BRDM-1 ended up in service with about a dozen countries, including Afghanistan, Cuba, Mozambique and Sudan.

## BRDM-1 Anti-Tank Guided Weapons

The BRDM was modified as a guided anti-tank missile carrier and appeared in two versions. The first successful Soviet anti-tank missile was codenamed the AT-1 Snapper by NATO, but was known by the Warsaw

Pact countries as the 3M6 Schmel ('Bumble Bee'). This wire-guided missile was initially mounted on a modified GAZ-69 (later known as the UAZ-69) 2½-ton truck in which the quadruple launcher was completely unarmoured. On the BRDM-1 it was possible to provide a reasonable amount of protection for a triple mounting of the same weapon. The upper part of the rear hull of the BRDM was extended to take a retractable launcher for three Snapper missiles that stood clear of the hull top when in action and could be completely covered by sideways folding plates when not in use. One reload of three missiles was carried inside the vehicle.

The follow-on radio-guided missile, known to NATO as the AT-2 Swatter, was likewise mounted on the BRDM-1. Although only slightly smaller than the Snapper, it was possible to accommodate a retractable quadruple launcher that was fully protected when not in use by folding side and rear plates.

## BRDM-2 Amphibious Scout Car

The BRDM-2 appeared in the early 1960s and featured the same turret as that installed on the Soviet BTR-60PB and Czech OT-64 SKOT-2a armoured personnel carriers. However, a wide variety of turretless variants were also produced as platforms for various Soviet anti-tank guided weapons. On the standard BRDM-2 the armament comprised a 14.5mm KPVT machine gun with a 7.62mm PKT machine gun mounted coaxially to the right. A telescopic sight was mounted to the left of the main armament. The driver sat on the left-hand side in the front with the commander to his right. They were provided with a bullet-proof windscreen to their front which was covered by two armoured shutters hinged at the top. When the shutters were closed, the driver and commander were served by a series of periscopes around the front and sides of the vehicle. Entry was by two circular hatches immediately behind the commander and driver that opened vertically toward the centre of the vehicle.

As with its predecessor, the BRDM-2's central tyre pressure regulator system permitted the tyre pressures to be altered to suit the terrain. The driver was able to adjust individual tyres or all four while the vehicle was on the move. Also as with the BRDM-1, on each side of the vehicle, between the front and rear wheels, were two chain-driven belly wheels that could be lowered by the driver to improve cross-country performance and allow for crossing ditches. The suspension was formed by four semi-elliptical springs with telescopic dual action shock-absorbers mounted two per axle. Steering was hydraulically assisted on the front wheels, with the sealed brakes having air-assisted hydraulic actuators. The vehicle was fully amphibious. The BRDM-2 was exported to around fifty countries and saw extensive combat.

## BRDM-2 Anti-Tank Guided Weapons and Surface-to-Air Missile Systems

Variants of the BRDM were produced to carry the AT-2 Swatter, AT-3 Sagger and AT-5 Spandrel anti-tank missiles. The Sagger variant comprised a BRDM-2 with its turret removed and fitted with an arm, on top of which were mounted six AT-3 ATGWs. When on the move they were stored within the hull, but in combat the arm was raised above the hull, complete with overhead armour protection. The missiles could be launched from within the vehicle or from up to 80 metres away with the assistance of a separation sight. A total of eight missiles could be carried in reserve.

The Swatter variant had a quadruple launcher. A total of eight missiles were carried, including three in the ready-to-launch position. The Spandrel variant was in the past called the BRDM-3; it carried five missiles ready to launch above the turret with another ten in the hull.

The SA-9 Gaskin mobile surface-to-air missile system was based on a modified BRDM-2 chassis with its belly wheels removed. The original turret was replaced by a one-man turret with an elevating arm on either side on which were mounted two box-type launchers for the SA-9 fire-and-forget missiles.

## BTR-152 Armoured Personnel Carrier

The BTR-152 6 × 6 was developed after the Second World War as the Soviet Union's very first purpose-built armoured personnel carrier. It was manufactured in large numbers from 1950 and saw service with African and Asian armies. The all-welded steel hull showed close similarities with American and German wartime designs. Notably, significant numbers of the M3A1 4 × 4 scout car and M2 and M5 series of American half-tracks were supplied to the Red Army under Lend-Lease arrangements. Likewise, the Soviets captured large numbers of the Hanomag-built range of German half-tracks.

As with these latter vehicles, the BTR had a front-mounted engine with an open-top crew compartment for the driver and a troop compartment for up to seventeen soldiers. The driver and commander had separate glass windscreens that could be protected by steel hatches with vision blocks.

The infantry entered and exited the vehicle either via the open roof or through a single door in the rear plate of the hull. For defensive purposes the vehicle had six firing ports, three either side, and two more in the rear plate on either side of the door.

Initially the ZIS-151 2½-ton 6 × 6 chassis was used as the basis for the BTR-152, though later models utilized the ZIS-157. The six-cylinder in-line model ZIS-123 was a water-cooled petrol-type engine generating 110hp at 2,900rpm. The BTR-152's transmission layout was that of a conventional 6 × 6 commercial truck with the driveshafts leading to differentials on 'solid' axles. The gearbox had five forward speeds and there was a two-speed transfer box. The tyres had a pressure system that could be regulated by the driver to suit the ground conditions. Some BTR-152s also featured a front-mounted winch. Some vehicles were fully enclosed, such as the BTR-152U command variant, which had much higher sides to allow staff officers to stand up inside.

The normal armament comprised the standard 7.62mm machine gun or the heavier 12.7mm or 14.5mm machine guns mounted on the hull top. The BTR-152A-ZPU was an anti-aircraft variant armed with twin 14.5mm KPV machine guns in a rotating turret. Against aerial targets these were only effective to 1,400 metres. They also carried armour-piercing rounds for use against light armoured vehicles, which could penetrate 32mm of armour at 500 metres, but had a range of 2,000 metres against ground targets. Other anti-aircraft variants included the BTR-152D and BTR-152E.

Some of the vehicles supplied to the Egyptian Army were armed with the Czech Quad 12.7mm M53 anti-aircraft system, which comprised four Soviet 12.7mm DShKM machine guns on a Czech-designed two-wheel mount. A number of these ended up in service with the Afghan Army. Likewise, in 1982 the Israeli Army encountered BTR-152s being operated by the Syrian-backed Palestine Liberation Army; they were fitted with the towed twin 23mm automatic ZU-23 anti-aircraft gun in the rear of the troop compartment.

## BTR-40 Armoured Personnel Carrier

The BTR-152's smaller cousin, the BTR-40, was introduced in 1951 and was essentially a redesigned version of the American-supplied M3A scout car. It was based on the GAZ-63 truck chassis, but with a shorter wheel-base, and was a conventional four-wheeled-drive armoured truck with a frontal engine layout. In the event of chemical warfare one variant of this vehicle was tasked with a chemical decontaminant role, which included placing flag markers to warn of contaminated areas. A more conventional version was the BTR-40A/ZPU; this had an anti-aircraft role mounting twin 14.5mm KPV heavy machine guns in an open turret with a 360 degree traverse. These were manually operated and had an effective rate of fire of 150 rounds per minute.

## BTR-60 Armoured Personnel Carrier

The requirement to replace the non-amphibious BTR-152 was issued in the late 1950s. The heavy eight-wheeled amphibious BTR-60P entered service with the Soviet Army in 1961, since when it was supplied to armies throughout the world. It was built in Romania as the TAB-72. The BTR-60P was powered by two GAZ-49B six-cylinder, water-cooled, in-line petrol engines, developing a total of 180hp. The engines were mounted in the rear of the welded steel hull and drove all eight wheels, the front four being steerable. The BTR-60 series was fully amphibious and propelled through the water by a hydrojet system with a single controllable outlet at the rear. This gave a calm water speed of 10km/h (compared with 80km/h on land). During deployment in water a bilge pump was available, together with a trim vane that was normally carried flat on the nose plate.

The troop compartment (initially for fourteen but reduced in later models) occupied the centre of the vehicle, with the driver on the left and the commander on the right at the front. The troop compartment had no overhead protection but this was remedied with the BTR-60PA or BTR-60PK, which were fully enclosed with roof hatches, installed to supplement access through two small hatches on each side.

The final model, the BTR-60PB, was fitted with a small turret on the hull roof near the front, armed with a 14.5mm machine gun and a 7.62mm machine gun. The turret was identical to that fitted to the Soviet BRDM-2 reconnaissance vehicle and the Czech OT-64 armoured personnel carrier. While the BTR-60PB was built under licence in Romania as the TAB-71, the lack of easy access resulted in the Czech and Polish governments developing the SKOT (OT-64) series for their armies. Production of the BTR-60 series was completed in 1976, resulting in around 25,000 vehicles.

## BTR-70 Armoured Personnel Carrier

The follow-on BTR-70 first appeared during the November 1980 military parade in Moscow. The hull was of all-welded steel armour with improved protection over its front arc compared to the BTR-60. In addition, the nose was wider and the front gave added protection to the front wheels. While the BTR-70 was fitted with the same turret as its predecessor, some were fitted with the BTR-80 turret. Initial models of the BTR-70 were fitted with the same wheels and tyres as the BTR-60.

The two GAZ-49B engines were replaced by two ZMZ-4905 petrol engines, which developed 120hp each, compared to just 90hp each in the BTR-60. Both engines had their own transmission, with the right engine powering to the first and third axles, and the left powering the second and fourth axles. This meant that if one engine was out of action the vehicle could still move, albeit at a slower speed. The exhausts were less boxy than on the BTR-60. Whereas the BTR-60 could carry up to sixteen, the BTR-70's capacity consisted of two crew and nine passengers. Again Romania produced its own version, dubbed the TAB-77.

Although the BTR-70 was an improvement on the earlier BTR-60, it still had its problems, not least the inadequate means of entry and exit for the troops. Also, the two petrol engines were not very efficient and could catch fire. The Soviet Army first took delivery of the improved BTR-80 in 1984.

## BTR-80 Armoured Personnel Carrier

A key difference in the appearance of the BTR-80 was that a new hatch was installed between the second and third axles; the upper part of this opened to the front while the lower part folded down to form steps. This permitted troops to dismount much more quickly and with less exposure to enemy fire than in the earlier BTRs.

While the BTR-70 had three firing ports on either side of the troop compartment, the BTR-80 had its three firing ports angled to fire obliquely forward, thereby giving covering fire for the dead ground towards the front of the vehicle. There was also a single firing port to the right of the commander's bow position (also on the BTR-70), plus an additional firing port in each of the two roof hatches.

The two forward-firing ports were for the 7.62mm PK general-purpose machine gun, while the three firing ports on either side could accommodate the AKMS/AK-74 Kalashnikov assault rifle. Small arms carried by the crew consisted of two 7.62mm machine guns and eight 7.62mm AKMs or 5.56mm AK-74 and nine Type F1 hand grenades. For air defence they also normally carried two man-portable surface-to-air missiles such as the SA-14, SA-16 and SA-18.

A less visible change was the replacement of the two petrol engines with a single V-8 diesel engine developing 260hp, which provided a significant increase in its power-to-weight ratio. This meant a slightly improved road speed and better fuel efficiency, along with a reduced risk of fire.

While the one-man manually operated turret was similar to that fitted to the BTR-70 and the BTR-60PB, the 14.5mm KPV heavy machine gun had double the elevation of the earlier models. This meant it could deploy in an air defence role against low-flying aircraft and helicopters. Another visual difference from the earlier versions was that on the BTR-80 a bank of six electrically operated smoke grenade dischargers (81mm Model 902V) was mounted on the rear of the turret. This was operated from within the turret, and each grenade generated a smokescreen of up to 30 metres wide and 10 metres high.

Essentially, the BTR-80 and its predecessors were little more than armoured battle buses that provided protection from heavy machine guns only out to 100 metres. In the case of the BTR-80, on the frontal arc the armour gave protection against 12.7mm AP rounds at a distance of 100 metres; the upper hull only provided protection against 7.62mm AP rounds at a range of 100 metres, while the lower hull could withstand 7.62mm AP rounds from 750 metres.

*Appendix V*

# Warsaw Pact Cold War Tracked Armour

After 1945 the Soviet Union was keen to rearm its new-found allies in Eastern Europe, as well as emerging Communist governments around the world. By the time of the collapse of the Soviet Union in 1991 there were still thousands of foreign-built T-54/55s in service in Europe.

## Bulgarian MT-LB Multi-Purpose Tracked Vehicle

The MT-LB was manufactured in Bulgaria and Poland for many years. Notably, Bulgaria built it under licence for both domestic and export markets that included Iraq. Bulgarian variants featured a mortar carrier, which took either an 82mm or 120mm mortar in the rear of the hull.

## Czech T-54/55 Main Battle Tank

After the war Czechoslovakia was soon put to work producing the tried and tested T-34/85 medium tank and the SU-100 tank destroyer. Most of these were sent to the Middle East to equip the Arab armies in their wars against Israel. Then the Czechoslovaks began to build the T-54/55 for both domestic use and the export market, totalling at least 8,500 tanks. This was followed by the T-72. Between 1958 and 1966 Czechoslovakia produced 2,855 T-54As and 120 T-54AK command variants at the ZTS Martin tank plant. Also, from 1958 to 1982 the plant built 3,820 T-55As, 3,377 T-55s and 1,280 T-55AK1 command tanks. Many of these were sent overseas. By the early 1990s Czechoslovakia still had 1,547 T-54s and 1,543 T-55s in its tank fleet. While the Czech T-54 tanks were viewed as superior to those built by the Soviets, Moscow appears to have had a hand in their production. Notably, some surviving Czech T-54s were kitted out with Soviet-made electrics, gauges, optics and radio.

The Czechoslovak T-54/55s were modernized to produce the T-55AM2. The modifications included full-length track skirts that covered the upper part of the track. The 100mm gun was fitted with a thermal sleeve, and passive armour was added to the front of the turret (similar to that fitted on the Soviet T-62). Forward-firing smoke-grenade dischargers were installed on the rear of the turret to the right-hand side.

## Czech T-72 Main Battle Tank

Czechoslovakia did not build the T-62, but instead switched to the T-72 in the early 1980s. This was for both domestic use and for the export market. In excess of 1,000 were built.

## Czech/Polish OT-62 Personnel Carrier

This was a joint development by Czechoslovakia and Poland, and was essentially a copy of the Soviet BTR-50. It entered service with their armies in the mid-1960s. Export customers included Angola, India, Iraq and Israel.

## Polish T-54/55 Main Battle Tank

Initially the Polish tank plant at Bumar-Labedy went into production in 1951, also building the T-34/85 which ended three years later. This was followed by 2,855 T-54As from 1956 to 1964 and the T-55 from 1958 until 1979. In total, the Poles built 8,570 T-54/55s, many of which were issued to other Warsaw Pact armies and exported to the developing world. The Polish equivalent of the T-54B (Model 1957) was the T-54AM, a designation sometimes used for both Polish and Soviet models of this type.

Production of the D-10 tank gun was undertaken in former Czechoslovakia and Poland. It was probably built in former Yugoslavia as well. In Poland the 100mm D-10T2S was produced by Huta Stalowa Wola SA. The Czechoslovak and Polish T-55s that were capable of firing Bastion anti-tank missiles were known as the T-55AM2B and T-55AM2P respectively. The Czech version used the Kladivo laser range-finder rather than the standard Soviet KTD-2 mounted over the main armament. The Polish tanks utilized the Merida fire-control system with the laser range-finder integrated with the gunner's sight.

The Poles also produced a command or *dowodca* version of the T-54A designated the T-54D. To accommodate the extra communications equipment it had a modified turret with a slight extension at the rear. It was issued to regimental commanders and their chiefs-of-staff. A similar Polish T-55 version was also built.

Polish-built T-54/55 tanks are easily distinguishable from Soviet ones by the large rectangular stowage box on the left side of the turret. In addition, on the Polish and Czech models the cover fitting on the gunner's telescope opening to the left of the main armament was more oval than on its Soviet counterparts. Many Non-Soviet Warsaw Pact tanks were subsequently upgraded by their various operators with additional armour and computerized fire-control systems. Poland still had 1,758 T-55s in the early 1990s, Hungary over 1,100, Romania around 760 and Bulgaria 1,280.

## Polish T-72 Main Battle Tank

After building the T-54/55, Poland, like Czechoslovakia, then switched to producing the T-72 in the 1980s. By the early 1990s more than 1,600 had been built.

## Romanian TR-77 Main Battle Tank

The Romanians, like the Czechs and Poles, built a copy of the T-55, but they also went one step further and redesigned it, producing a somewhat modified version. Czechoslovakia and Poland both had a history of producing tanks that dated from before the Second World War. Romania did not, and the sharp learning curve was to cause problems.

Locally built Romanian T-55s were first seen in 1977 and were designated the TR-77 (or M1977 by the West). However, they may have been manufactured earlier. In light of Romania having no experience in tank manufacturing, these T-55s may have been supplied by Moscow as knockdown kits which the Romanians assembled. Subsequent Romanian-modified versions of the TR-77 included the TR-580, the TR-85 and the TM-800, though it is unclear if the latter went into series production.

## Romanian TR-580 Main Battle Tank

The TR-580 was powered by a 432.5kW/580hp engine, hence its designation, and entered service in 1982. It was armed with the standard 100mm gun with fume extractor, though it lacked a laser range-finder. The hull and chassis were similar to the T-55 but lengthened to allow for six unique spoked road wheels, with a gap between the first and second wheels on either side (the T-55 had five). To allow for this modification a single return roller was also installed. The T-54/55-type exhaust outlet was kept above the last two road wheel stations on the left-hand side and the rear engine decking remained similar to that on the standard T-55. The upper part of the front idler, road wheels and rear drive sprocket were covered by steel skirts which angled up at either end.

## Romanian TR85 Main Battle Tank

Romania then produced the TR-85, which entered service in 1987. This also had six road wheels, with distinct gaps between the first and second, second and third, and fifth and sixth wheels, again with the drive sprocket at the rear and idler at the front. It did not have the exhaust outlet on the left-hand side that was a standard feature of the T-54/55. This tank had a new German-built 641.3kW/860hp diesel engine that required modification of the rear hull compartment and decking. As a result, the engine compartment top differed from that of the T-54/55 series. This new engine gave it a top speed of 60kph and a range of 310 kilometres.

Like its predecessors, the TR-85 was armed with a 100mm gun, with a fume extractor near the muzzle and a thermal sleeve. A range-finder like that fitted to the Chinese Type 69 was mounted above the mantlet. Installed on the forward left side of the turret was a rectangular stowage box very similar to that on the Polish-built T-55. The commander, gunner and driver were provided with a full range of infra-red night-vision equipment. The TR-85 had a troubled production and proved to be mechanically unreliable, in part because it weighed almost 50 tons, more than 11 tons more than the TR-580. The Romanian leader Nicolae Ceauşescu was so alarmed at the poor quality that he almost cancelled the TR-85 programme. Some of these Romanian-built tanks were involved in the attempt to stop the rising that toppled Ceauşescu in 1989. In the early 1990s Romania still had more than 600 TR-85s and more than 400 TR-580s. A number of improved versions were developed, including the up-armoured TR-85M1 and TR-85N. A distinguishing feature of the M1 was that it had two return rollers.

*Appendix VI*

# Non-Warsaw Pact Cold War Tracked Armour

Yugoslavia was not a member of the Warsaw Pact but it received a lot of Soviet-built armour over the years. It also built its own tanks and armoured personnel carriers.

### Yugoslav M-84 Main Battle Tank

Yugoslavia produced the T-72 under licence in the mid-1980s, under the designation M-84. Prior to production, the Soviet Union supplied fifty T-72s for crew training. By early 1991 about 400 M-84s had been completed. The break-up of Yugoslavia then brought production to an end. Export customers included Kuwait, Libya and Syria.

### Yugoslav M-60 and M-80 Armoured Personnel Carriers

Yugoslavia also produced the indigenously designed M-60 armoured personnel carrier and the M-80 mechanized infantry combat vehicle in the 1960s and 1970s respectively. The M-80 featured a one-man turret armed with a 20mm cannon and 7.62mm machine gun. The turret also carried launch rails for two Sagger anti-tank missiles. All these armoured vehicles saw combat during the Croatian and Slovenian wars of independence.

# Soviet Cold War Anti-Tank Missiles

From the late 1960s wire-guided anti-tank missiles became a feature of the Soviet and Warsaw Pact armies. They were carried on a variety of platforms and were designed to give their tank and motor rifle divisions greater punch. In particular, Moscow wanted to ensure that in the event of a massive tank battle on the central German plain its infantry would have the capability to take on NATO's armour. The real threat posed by such weapons was highlighted by the AT-3 Sagger, which made its name by knocking out Israeli tanks during the 1973 Yom Kippur War.

## AT-1 Snapper

The AT-1, dubbed the Snapper by NATO, was the very first generation of Soviet anti-tank guided weapons (ATGW). The missile had a single-charge solid motor and four large cruciform wings, and carried a 5.25kg hollow-charge warhead. It had an effective range of 2,500 metres and could penetrate 380mm of normal steel, but it was wire-guided and had the disadvantage that the operator had to watch both the missile and the target throughout the missile flight. On firing, the missile flew like a fast model aircraft, playing out behind it the fine electrical wires that were attached to the operator's joystick.

Three Snappers were fitted to the turretless BRDM-1 amphibious scout car, mounted on launch rails over the rear of the hull (*see* Chapter 8). The Snapper saw service with the Arab armies during the 1967 Six Day War and many were captured intact by the Israelis.

## AT-2 Swatter

The radio-guided AT-2 Swatter appeared some years later. Again, it had four cruciform wings, but smaller than those on the AT-1. All the wings were fitted with elevons or control surfaces with two carrying tracking flares to assist with guidance during flight. A solid fuel motor with oblique nozzles between the wings fired the missile off a large launch rail. The warhead had a very blunt nose with two small fin-like projections. The Swatter had the same range as the Snapper but could penetrate 480mm of steel armour. The improved Swatter-C had an extended range of 3,500 metres and was converted from its original radio command to line-of-sight guidance and subsequently to semi-active infra-red guidance.

The AT-2 was installed on the BRDM-1 and BRDM-2 amphibious scout cars as well as on the Mi-24 helicopter gunship. On the BRDM it was in a four-missile ready-to-launch configuration (*see* Chapter 8). Like the AT-1, the AT-2 saw extensive combat during the Arab-Israeli wars. It was also used on Mi-24 Hind helicopter gunships in Angola and Afghanistan, and during the Iran-Iraq War and the 1982 Lebanon War. Both the Snapper and Swatter were rendered obsolescent by the much improved AT-3.

## AT-3 Sagger

The AT-3 Sagger called *Malyutka* ('Little One') by the Soviets was first detected in a Moscow parade in May 1965. A boost motor just behind the warhead, with four oblique nozzles, launched the missile. It had no aerodynamic controls but the small wings could fold in for transport. A tracking flare attached to the body enabled the operator to guide the missile, and it could be steered visually out to 1,000 metres and to three times that distance with a magnifying optical sight.

The Sagger was used to arm the BRDM with a six-round retractable launcher, the BMP and BMD with a single reloadable launcher above the main gun, and the Czech SKOT with a twin reloadable rear launcher. The Mi-24 Hind could also carry this missile on its four outboard launcher pylons. The BRDM-2, armed with the retractable six Sagger launcher, played a key anti-tank role with the Soviet Army. Each tank division had nine to support its BMP-equipped motorized infantry regiments. Likewise, each motorized rifle division had thirty-six BRDM-2s armed with ATGWs, nine in the anti-tank battalion, nine in the BMP-equipped motorized rifle regiment and nine in each of the two motorized rifle regiments equipped with the BTR. The missile could also be fired from a simple ground launcher and from helicopters.

The Sagger caused the Israeli Defence Forces a nasty shock in 1973 when two-man teams of Egyptians operated it from small, portable, carrying cases.

Each Egyptian infantry division included an anti-tank guided weapon battalion equipped with forty-eight Saggers and 314 RPG-7 anti-tank weapons. An individual soldier could carry the Sagger missile and the case converted into a launching platform that was connected to the joystick. The main problem in controlling the Sagger (and other wire-guided ATGWs) was in gathering it onto the line of the target after launching from a remote position. This took about a quarter of a mile, and once on target the operator needed nerve as much as skill to keep it on track.

## AT-4 Spigot

Codenamed Spigot by NATO, the AT-4 was a high-performance tube-launched missile similar to the European Milan missile that appeared in 1970. The design of the launcher ensured that the operator could remain under cover while firing the missile, as once launched only the launcher's black tracking head remained visible. The missiles were carried in their launch tubes, which were discarded after firing.

The system was widely deployed by the Soviet and other Warsaw Pact armies. In its man-portable configuration it weighed around 40kg. Control was by semi-automatic command line-of-sight (SACLOS) and guidance was by the standard means of wire. Range was assessed to be out to about 2,500 metres. In the late 1970s the AT-4 Spigot was supplemented by the AT-7 Saxhorn, which was lighter and easier to deploy.

## AT-5 Spandrel

The Spandrel AT-5 ATGW was a second-generation type SACLOS and was first seen during a Red Square Parade on 7 November 1977. A tube-launched system, it was mounted on the BRDM-2 with five ready-to-launch missiles. The tube was similar to the Milan and had a blowout cap at the front and a flared tail through which passed the efflux from the boost charge. This blasted out the missile before the ignition of its own flight motor. A further ten missiles were carried in the hull of the BRDM. The general similarity to the Milan was probably not a coincidence.

The HEAT warhead weighed around 7kg and could penetrate up to 600mm of armour. SACLOS guidance was via trailing wires, and the missile homed in on its target using an infra-red heat-seeking system. All the gunner had to do was keep the cross-hairs of his sight on the target to ensure a strike. A ground mount was always carried to allow Spandrels to be launched away from a vehicle. It had a maximum range of 4,000 metres.

By the late 1970s the Group of Soviet Forces in Germany significantly enhanced their anti-tank capability by replacing all their Swatter and Sagger missiles with the Spandrel.

Some BRDM-2s carried a mix of ATGWs. For example, some Iraqi Army BRDM-2s were armed with three AT-5 Spandrels on the right and two AT-4 Spigots on the left. This enabled the vehicle to carry a larger missile payload: rather than ten AT-5s, it could accommodate eight AT-4s and six AT-5s. Foreign-supplied BMP-2 vehicles were supplied with the 2,500-metre AT-4 Spigot ATGW in place of the Spandrel installed on Soviet BMP-2s. The Spigot version was distinguishable from the Spandrel by its shorter launch tube, which was parallel, while the Spandrel was about 200mm shorter, with a taper at the end.

## AT-6 Spiral

The Spiral was accepted into service in 1976 and was designed for use with the Mi-24 Hind helicopter gunship (*see* Chapter 11). It was subsequently installed on the MT-LB and there was also a shipborne version. Delays in the development of this missile initially meant that the Mi-24 had to be armed with an improved version of the AT-2. The AT-6 SACLOS missile had a small booster stage to launch it from the tube and then deployed a solid rocket sustainer. It had a radio command link which gave greater speed and range than the more traditional wire guidance. The launch range was 400 metres out to 5,000 metres and the HEAT warhead could cut through more than 550mm of armour. Understandably, this made it a missile to be greatly feared.

## AT-7 Saxhorn

The AT-7 Saxhorn (9K115 Metis or Mongrel) man-portable SACLOS wire-guided anti-tank missile went into service with the Soviet Army in 1979 to supplement the AT-4 Spigot. The Saxhorn was much lighter than the Spigot, with a lighter missile and simpler tripod launcher, but it only had half the range. This missile system, which included the 9P151 launching post, was issued to Soviet motor rifle companies. NATO dubbed the improved AT-7 which appeared in the 1980s the AT-13 Saxhorn-2.

## AT-8 Songster

When experiments with purely missile-armed tanks ended in failure, the Soviets looked to a hybrid system. The result was a SACLOS anti-tank missile that could be fired by the 125mm gun of the T-64 and T-80 tanks. Officially known as the 9K112 Kobra by the Soviets, it was first installed in the T-64B in 1976 and in the T-80B two years later. The T-64B, which was capable of carrying six AT-8s plus thirty-six tank rounds, could fire up to four Songsters a minute. The T-80B could only carry four missiles, but the T-80U was able to carry a similar number to the T-64.

The missile came as two separate sections and was stored in the autoloader in the same way as the conventional 125mm rounds. It was capable of engaging ATGW systems, tanks and even helicopters. The radio transmitter for the AT-8 was mounted in a steel box in front of the right commander's cupola, though the missile was guided to the target by the gunner. It was propelled out of the barrel by a boost motor; the main motor then cut in and powered it to the target. Songster had a muzzle velocity of 125m/s, increasing to 800m/s, and took just 10 seconds to cover 4,000 metres to penetrate 600mm of steel armour. It was assessed to be not very effective against ceramic and reactive armours.

# Bibliography

This work draws on a number of previous Pen & Sword books, all of which are listed below.

Arnold, James R., *The Illustrated History of the Vietnam War Volume 3: Armor* (New York: Bantam, 1987).

Barry, John, Chester, Lewis & Page, Bruce (eds), *Insight on the Middle East War* (London: André Deutsche, 1974).

Bearman, Sidney (ed.), *Strategic Survey 1987–1988* (London: International Institute for Strategic Studies, 1988).

Beckett, Ian (general ed.), *Communist Military Machine* (Twickenham: Hamlyn, 1985).

Bevin, Alexander, *Korea: The Lost War* (London: Arrow, 1989).

Bowen, Jeremy, *Six Days: How the 1967 War Shaped the Middle East* (London: Simon & Schuster, 2003).

Braithwaite, Rodric, *Afghantsy: The Russians in Afghanistan 1979–89* (London: Profile, 2011).

Bridgland, Fred, *Jonas Savimbi: A Key to Africa* (London: Coronet, 1988).

Brogan, Patrick, *World Conflicts: Why and Where they are Happening* (London: Bloomsbury, 1989).

Bron, Ben & Shukman, David, *All Necessary Means: Inside the Gulf War* (London: BBC, 1991).

Brown, Ashley & Grant, Reg, *The Military Yearbook 1987* (London: Oriole, 1987).

Bulloch, John & Morris, Harvey, *Saddam's War: The Origins of the Kuwait Conflict and the International Response* (London: Faber & Faber, 1991).

Buszynski, Leszek, *Soviet Foreign Policy and Southeast Asia* (Beckenham: Croom Helm, 1986).

Catchpole, Brian, *The Korean War* (London: Constable, 2000).

Cavendish, Marshall, *Tanks at War* (Leicester: Blitz Editions, 1996).

Cawthorne, Nigel, *Vietnam: A War Lost and Won* (London: Arcturus, 2003).

Chubin, Shahram & Tripp, Charles, *Iran and Iraq at War* (London: I.B. Tauris, 1988).

Clapham, Christopher, *Conflicts in Africa* (London: International Institute for Strategic Studies, 1972).

Cordingley, Major General Patrick, *In the Eye of the Storm: Commanding the Desert Rats in the Gulf War* (London: Hodder & Stoughton, 1996).

Crow, Duncan (ed.), *Modern Battle Tanks* (Windsor: Profile Publications, 1978).

Dayan, Yaël, *Israel Journal: June 1967* (New York: McGraw-Hill, 1967).

De La Billiere, General Sir Peter, *Storm Command: A Personal Account of the Gulf War* (London: HarperCollins, 1992).

Dunstan, Simon, *Armour of the Korean War 1950–53* (London: Osprey, 1982).

Dunstan, Simon, *Armour of the Vietnam Wars* (London: Osprey, 1985).

Dunstan, Simon, *The Yom Kippur War 1973(2): The Sinai* (Oxford: Osprey, 2003).

English, Adrian J., *Armed Forces of Latin America* (London: Jane's, 1984).

Finlan, Alastair, *The Gulf War 1991* (Oxford: Osprey, 2003).

Forty, George, *Tank Action: From the Great War to the Gulf* (Stroud: Sutton Publishing, 1995).

Frankel, Joseph, *International Politics: Conflict and Harmony* (Harmondsworth: Pelican, 1973).

Freedman, Lawrence & Karsh, Efraim, *The Gulf Conflict 1990–1991* (London: Faber & Faber, 1993).

Gavshon, Arthur, *Crisis in Africa: Battleground of East and West* (Harmondsworth: Penguin, 1981).

Halliday, Jon & Cumings, Bruce, *Korea: The Unknown War* (London: Viking, 1988).

Hanlon, Joseph, *Apartheid's Second Front: South Africa's War against Its Neighbours* (Harmondsworth: Penguin, 1986).

Hastings, Max, *The Korean War* (London: Michael Joseph, 1987).

Hawkes, Nigel (ed.), *Tearing Down the Curtain: The People's Revolution in Eastern Europe* (London: Hodder & Stoughton, 1990).

Heritage, Andrew, *The Cold War: An Illustrated History* (Sparkford: Haynes Publishing, 2010).

Hooper, Jim, *Bloodsong!* (London: HarperCollins, 2002).

Isby, David, *Russia's War in Afghanistan* (London: Osprey, 1986).

Jaster, Robert S., *South Africa and its Neighbours: The Dynamics of Regional Conflict* (London: International Institute for Strategic Studies, 1986).

Joffe, Ellis, *The Chinese Army After Mao* (London: Weidenfeld & Nicolson, 1987).

Johnson, Phyllis & Martin, David, *Frontline Southern Africa* (Peterborough: Ryan, 1989).

Karsh, Efraim, *The Iran-Iraq War 1980–1988* (Oxford: Osprey, 2002).

Katz, Samuel M., *Armies in the Lebanon 1982–84* (London: Osprey, 1985).

Kimche, David & Bawly, Dan, *The Sandstorm: The Arab-Israeli War of June 1967: Prelude and Aftermath* (London: Secker & Warburg, 1968).

Kinnock, Glenys & Matthews, Jenny, *Eritrea: Images of War and Peace* (London: Chatto & Windus, 1988).

Kyle, Keith, *Suez* (London: Weidenfeld & Nicolson, 1991).

Laffin, John, *Arab Armies of the Middle East Wars 1948–73* (London: Osprey, 1982).

Laffin, John, *The Israeli Army in the Middle East Wars 1948–73* (London: Osprey, 1982).

Laffin, John, *The War of Desperation: Lebanon 1982–85* (London: Osprey, 1985).

Langley, Michael, *Inchon: MacArthur's Last Triumph* (London: B.T. Batsford, 1979).

Lloyd, Selwyn, *Suez 1956: A Personal Account* (London: Jonathan Cape, 1978).

Looney, Robert E., *Third-World Military Expenditure and Arms Production* (Hounds-mills: Macmillan, 1988).

Loyd, William, *Challengers and Chargers: A History of the Life Guards 1945–1992* (London: Leo Cooper, 1992).

Luttwak, Edward, *A Dictionary of Modern War* (London: Penguin, 1971).

Martin, David & Johnson, Phyllis, *The Struggle for Zimbabwe: The Chimurenga War* (London: Faber & Faber, 1982).

Maxwell, Neville, *India's China War* (Harmondsworth: Pelican, 1972).

Messenger, Charles, *The Art of Blitzkrieg* (Shepperton: Ian Allan, 1991).

Micheletti, Eric & Debay, Yves, *War in the Balkans* (Poole: Histoire & Collections, 1993).

Milner, Laurie, *Royal Scots in the Gulf* (London: Leo Cooper, 1994).

Mollo, Boris, *The Indian Army* (Poole, Blandford Press, 1981).

Moynahan, Brian, *The Claws of the Bear: A History of the Soviet Armed Forces from 1917 to the Present* (London: Hutchinson, 1989).

Munro, Alan, *Arab Storm: Politics and Diplomacy behind the Gulf War* (London: I.B. Tauris, 2006).

Norman, Major Michael, *AFV Weapons 23: Soviet Mediums T44, T54, T55 & T62* (Windsor: Profile, no date).

O'Balance, Edgar, *The Wars in Vietnam* (Shepperton: Ian Allan, 1975).

Ovendale, Ritchie, *The Origins of the Arab-Israeli Wars* (Harlow: Longman, 1984).

Pivka, Otto von, *Armies of the Middle East* (Cambridge: Patrick Stephens, 1979).

Ridgway, General Matthew B., *The War in Korea* (London: Barrie & Rockliff, the Crescent Press, 1968).

Rottman, Gordon, *Armies of the Gulf War* (London: Osprey, 1993).

Schiff, Ze'ev, *A History of the Israeli Army: 1874 to the Present* (London: Sidgwick & Jackson, 1987).

Schiff, Ze'ev & Ya'ari, Ehud, *Israel's Lebanon War* (London: Unwin, 1986).

Sheehan, Michael & Wyllie, James, *The Economist Pocket Guide to Defence* (Oxford: Basil Blackwell, 1986).

Smith, Susanna, *Namibia: A Violation of Trust* (Oxford: Oxfam, 1986).

Spurr, Russell, *Enter the Dragon: China at War in Korea* (London: Sidgwick & Jackson, 1989).

Starry, General Donn A., *Armoured Combat in Vietnam* (Poole: Blandford Press, 1981).

Suvorov, Viktor, *Inside the Soviet Army* (London: Hamish Hamilton, 1984).

Teveth, Shabtai, *Moshe Dayan* (London: Weidenfeld & Nicolson, 1972).

Thomas, Nigel & Abbott, Peter, *The Korean War 1950–53* (London: Osprey, 1986).

Thomas, Dr N. & Mikulan, K., *The Yugoslav Wars (1): Slovenia & Croatia 1991–95* (Oxford: Osprey, 2006).

Thompson, Major General Julian (ed.), *The Imperial War Museum Book of Modern Warfare: British and Commonwealth Forces at War 1945–2000* (London: Sidgwick & Jackson, 2002).

Thompson, Sir Robert (consultant ed.), *War in Peace: An Analysis of Warfare Since 1945* (London: Orbis Publishing, 1981).

Tillotson, Geoffrey, *Modern Combat Vehicles 4: M48* (Shepperton: Ian Allan, 1981).

Timmerman, Kenneth R., *The Death Lobby: How the West Armed Iraq* (London: Bantam, 1992).

Tucker-Jones, Anthony, *Armoured Warfare in the Korean War* (Barnsley: Pen & Sword, 2012).

Tucker-Jones, Anthony, *The Soviet-Afghan War* (Barnsley: Pen & Sword, 2012).

Tucker-Jones, Anthony, *Armoured Warfare in the Arab-Israeli Conflicts* (Barnsley: Pen & Sword, 2013).

Tucker-Jones, Anthony, *The Gulf War: Operation Desert Storm 1990–1991* (Barnsley: Pen & Sword, 2014).

Tucker-Jones, Anthony, *The Vietnam War: The Tet Offensive 1968* (Barnsley: Pen & Sword, 2014).

Tucker-Jones, Anthony, *Soviet Cold War Weaponry: Tanks and Armoured Fighting Vehicles* (Barnsley: Pen & Sword, 2015).

Tucker-Jones, Anthony, *Dien Bien Phu: The First Indo-China War 1946–1954* (Barnsley: Pen & Sword, 2017).

Tucker-Jones, Anthony, *T-54/55: The Soviet Army's Cold War Main Battle Tank* (Barnsley: Pen & Sword, 2017).

Tucker-Jones, Anthony, *Iran-Iraq War: The Lion of Babylon, 1980–1988* (Barnsley: Pen & Sword, 2018).

Turner, Barry, *Suez 1956* (London: Hodder & Stoughton, 2006).

Urban, Mark, *Soviet Land Power* (London: Ian Allan, 1985).

Urban, Mark, *War in Afghanistan* (London: Macmillan, 1988).

Varble, Derek, *The Suez Crisis 1956* (Oxford: Osprey, 2003).

White, B.T., *Tanks and Other Tracked Vehicles in Service* (Poole: Blandford Press, 1978).

White, B.T., *Wheeled Armoured Fighting Vehicles in Service* (Poole: Blandford Press, 1983).

Yousaf, Mohammad & Adkin, Mark, *Afghanistan – The Bear Trap: The Defeat of a Superpower* (Barnsley: Leo Cooper, 2001).

Zaloga, Steven J., *Armour of the Middle East Wars 1948–78* (London: Osprey, 1981).

Zaloga, Steven J., *The M1 Abrams Battle Tank* (London: Osprey, 1985).

Zaloga, Steven J., *T-54 and T-55 Main Battle Tanks 1944–2004* (Oxford: Osprey, 2004).

# Index